WANT TO BE A
SECRETARY WITH CLOUT?

The CERTIFIED PROFESSIONAL SECRETARY® examination will give it to you—if you pass and earn your rating. Whether you're a business or community college student, a working secretary or administrative assistant, you can upgrade your present career status, earn a higher salary, and prove your professional capabilities by becoming a CPS®.

Here, in one information-packed volume, is the all-inclusive review that will prepare you for exam success—and help you achieve the high professional standard of excellence you seek.

- **All 6 test areas are completely discussed for greater depth of knowledge**
- **Detailed outlines of all subjects tested are provided for ease of preparation**
- **Actual CPS® exam questions and answers are included for test-taking practice**

TAKE CONTROL OF YOUR FUTURE!
BE A CPS®—THE ARCO WAY!

CPS®—
Certified Professional Secretary®
Examination

CPS®— Certified Professional Secretary® Examination

Sheryl L. Lindsell
and
Stanley L. Alpert

An Arco Book
Distributed by Prentice Hall Trade
New York, New York 10023

An Arco Book
Published by Prentice Hall Press
A Division of Simon & Schuster, Inc.
Gulf + Western Building
One Gulf + Western Plaza
New York, New York 10023

PRENTICE HALL PRESS is a trademark of Simon & Schuster, Inc.

Manufactured in the United States of America

1 2 3 4 5 6 7 8 9 10

Library of Congress Cataloging-in-Publication Data

Lindsell, Sheryl L.
    CPS—Certified Professional Secretary examination.

    ''An Arco book''
    Bibliography: p.
    1. Secretaries—Examinations, questions, etc.
2. Office practice—Examinations, questions, etc.
I. Alpert, Stanley L. II. Title.
HF5547.5.L554 1987   651.3'741'076   87-11381
ISBN 0-13-122805-6

CONTENTS

37752

IV. ACCOUNTING

V. OFFICE ADMINISTRATION AND COMMUNICATION

VI. OFFICE TECHNOLOGY

APPENDICES

Introduction

In a society that values credentials as much as ours does, the hallmarks of the professions are the letters that follow names (M.D., Ph.D., C.P.A., Esq., R.N., R.P.T., M.S.). Joining these prestigious ranks, Certified Professional Secretary® (CPS®) is now the capstone of the secretarial field, offering professional status to the secretary who wants to be identified as *outstanding*. It displays the measure of an individual who has attained a recognized level of knowledge, professional development, and performance.

- Those holding CPS certification earn approximately 15 percent more in salary than those who do not.
- Many colleges and universities are granting credit hours to CPS recipients who enroll in college programs.

Professional Secretaries International sponsors these examinations. A candidate **must** be either an experienced secretary, a student, or a business educator and **must** meet the criteria appropriate to his or her background.

EXPERIENCED SECRETARIES

The experienced secretary must fulfill one of the following:

- A high school diploma (or the equivalent) and a minimum of three years' secretarial experience—one of which must include continuous employment with one employer within the last five years, and the total experience within the last twenty-five years.
- Two years of education in a post–high school environment in addition to a minimum of two years' secretarial experience—one of which must include continuous employment with one employer within the last five years, and the total experience within the last twenty-five years.
- A degree from a four-year institution and a year's accumulated secretarial experience within the last five years.

STUDENTS

Students must fulfill one of the following two prerequisites:

- A certificate, diploma, or associate's degree earned at a two-year program at an accredited business school, two- or four-year college, or technical institute and two years' secretarial experience.
- A bachelor's and/or advanced degree and a year's secretarial experience.

BUSINESS EDUCATORS

Business educators must fulfill the following requirement:

- A minimum of a year's secretarial experience within the last ten years. (The degree is assumed.)

Please note that for the purpose of determining a candidate's experience: 1) no less than three months of continuous employment will be credited; 2) part-time employment must have constituted a minimum of twenty hours per week; and 3) volunteer experience must have constituted a minimum of twelve hours per week.

Candidates must pass a six-part examination administered over a period of two days. The subjects tested are:

> Behavioral Science in Business
> Business Law
> Economics and Management
> Accounting
> Office Administration and Communication
> Office Technology

For further information regarding fees, when and where the examination is given, and so on, contact:

> Professional Secretaries International
> 301 East Armour Boulevard (Suite 200)
> Kansas City, MO 64111
>
> (816) 531-7010

How to Use This Book Effectively

This book is formatted in accordance with the outline supplied by Professional Secretaries International that follows. "It should be understood that the outlines and the texts for the individual parts are not intended to prescribe exactly the content of the examination; they are intended to indicate areas in which secretaries possess knowledge, skill, understanding and judgment."*

For additional information in any subject area, refer to Appendix C for suggested readings.

We have supplied you with a key to your future—good luck in opening the door!

*Professional Secretaries International, *Outline and Bibliography*, Missouri: Kansas City, p. 1.

Certified Professional Secretary®
Examination Outline*

PART I—BEHAVIORAL SCIENCE IN BUSINESS

Items: 120   **Time: 105 Minutes**

This part of the examination tests the principles of human relations and organizational dynamics in the work place. It focuses on needs, motivation, nature of conflict, problem-solving techniques, essentials of supervision and communication, leadership styles, and understanding of the informal organization.

20%–25%   I.   Understanding the individual/self
    A.   Attitudes and values
    B.   Cognitive styles
    C.   Defense mechanisms
    D.   Heredity and environment
    E.   Motivation
    F.   Personality

10%–15%   II.   Groups
    A.   Characteristics of groups
    B.   Group identification and dynamics
    C.   Social pressure in groups
    D.   Type of groups

15%–20%   III.   Leadership dynamics
    A.   Characteristics of leaders
    B.   Different leadership styles
    C.   Leadership effectiveness
    D.   Leadership responsibilities
    E.   Leadership theory

10%–15%   IV.   Interpersonal communication
    A.   Active listening
    B.   Communications for understanding

*Reprinted by permission of Professional Secretaries International®

PART II—BUSINESS LAW

Items: 120   **Time: 105 Minutes**

(60% Theory, 40% Cases)

This part of the examination attempts to measure (1) the secretary's knowledge of the principles of business law and (2) knowledge of the effect of governmental controls of business.

A course in business law would be helpful in preparing for this portion of the examination.

Section I—Principles of Business Law

12%–14%   I. Contracts
          A. Elements
             1. Valid subject matter
             2. Mutuality of agreement
             3. Consideration
             4. Capacity of parties
             5. Form required by law
          B. Formation
             1. Offer
             2. Acceptance
          C. Types
             1. Quasi
             2. Bilateral and unilateral
             3. Express or implied
             4. Formal and simple
          D. Breach of contracts—remedies
          E. Statute of Limitations
          F. Statute of Frauds

2%   II. Bailments
          A. Creation and termination
          B. Relationship
          C. Types
          D. Obligations

4%–5%   III. Agency
          A. Creation
          B. Types of agencies and agents

Section II—Regulatory Legislation

PART III—ECONOMICS AND MANAGEMENT

Items: 120   **Time: 105 Minutes**

Items   This part consists of two major subject areas: (35%) economics and (65%) management. Emphasis is placed on understanding of the basic concepts underlying business operations. Key economic and management principles as well as the latest governmental regulations in business are covered in this part of the examination.

Courses in basic economics and management may be helpful in preparing for the examination.

35%   I.   Economics
        A.   Basic concepts of economics
            1.   Private property and the profit motive
            2.   Supply and demand—effect on cost and production
            3.   Markets—effect on prices and production
                a.   Competitive markets
                b.   Imperfectly competitive markets (monopoly, oligopoly, monopolistic competition)
                c.   Composition of output and allocation of resources
                d.   Distribution of income (wages, interest, profit)
        B.   National income and its determinants
            1.   National income measurement concepts
            2.   Determination of national income
            3.   Fluctuations in national income
            4.   Growth of national income
            5.   Current measures of economic performance (output, income, commodity prices, security prices, interest rates, yields, wages/hours, sales)
            6.   Public sources of economic information
        C.   The financial system
            1.   Monetary standards and money supply
            2.   Credit creation and credit instruments
                a.   Negotiable instruments
                b.   Letters of credit
            3.   Federal Reserve System and its role
            4.   Commercial banks

3. Authority, responsibility, accountability, and cross-functional relationships
4. Tools in organizing—charts and manuals

E. Leading
   1. Role of the supervisor
   2. Role of the subordinate

F. Controlling
   1. The control process
   2. Standards and standardization—quantity, quality, cost, and time standards
   3. Management by Exception

G. Communicating
   1. Policies and procedures
   2. Meetings
   3. Feedback

20% III. Fields of management

A. Human resources management
   1. Composition of labor force
   2. Job analysis, job description, job specifications, and job evaluation
   3. Recruitment and selection
   4. Training and development
   5. Employee performance appraisal
   6. Compensation administration (incentive and merit plans)
   7. Employee benefits (including statutory and nonstatutory plans, health, insurance, and pension plans)
   8. Employee suggestion systems
   9. Union-management relations

B. Production management
   1. Facilities
   2. Materials—procurements, processing, and control
   3. Methods and quality control
   4. Planning and scheduling

C. Marketing management
   1. Marketing policy
   2. Advertising
   3. Sales analysis and control
   4. Market analysis—consumer behavior—forecasting
   5. Transportation—traffic management functions (economical and efficient procurement and arrangement of all transportation services)

D. Public relations

PART IV—ACCOUNTING

Items: 100   **Time: 120 Minutes**

(80% Definition/Theory, 20% Computations)

Part IV attempts to measure (1) knowledge of the elements of the accounting cycle; (2) ability to analyze financial statement accounts; (3) ability to perform arithmetical operations associated with accounting, computing interest and discounts; and (4) ability to summarize and interpret financial data.

Preparation for Part IV should include a study of financial accounting and managerial accounting. Examinees should be aware of current regulations concerning income tax, payroll tax and unemployment compensation.

15%
  I. Principles and procedures
      A. Theory and classification of accounts
          1. Assets
          2. Liabilities
          3. Owners' and stockholders' equity
          4. Revenue, expense, and income
      B. Accounting cycle
          1. Analyzing transactions and recording
          2. Posting
          3. Trial balance
          4. Work sheet
          5. Financial statements
          6. Adjusting and closing entries
          7. Post-closing trial balance

55%
  II. Balance sheet accounts
      A. Accounting for cash receipts and disbursements
          1. Cash receipts
              a. Cash receipts
              b. Internal controls
          2. Cash disbursements
              a. Cash disbursements records
              b. Trade and cash discounts
              c. Imprest petty cash
                  (1) Establishing petty cash fund
                  (2) Replenishing petty cash fund
                  (3) Reconciling petty cash
              d. Types of checks and check registers
              e. Voucher system and the recording of accounts payable
              f. Internal controls

         (1)   Characteristics

         (2)   Recording the issue or retirement (par, no-par)

         (3)   Dividend payments

      b. Treasury stock

      c. Securities markets

         (1)   Stock exchanges

         (2)   Private placement

   3. Retained earnings

      a. Appropriated

      b. Unappropriated

7%   III. Income statement accounts

   A. Revenues

   B. Expenses

     1. Operating (payroll, payroll taxes, insurance)

     2. Federal individual income taxes

      a. Ordinary income/loss

      b. Capital gains/losses

      c. Deductions (business/personal)

10%   IV. Analysis and interpretation of financial statements

   A. Balance sheet

   B. Operating statements

   C. Retained earnings statement

   D. Statement of changes in financial position (funds flow)

   E. Cash flow statements

   F. Comparative statements

   G. Ratios, percentages, and turnovers

3%   V. Insurance (types)

   A. Property

   B. Casualty

   C. Life and health

   D. Fidelity and surety insurance bonds

   E. Co-insurance

   F. Insurance record maintenance

10%   VI. Managerial accounting

   A. Cost analysis

     1. Determining unit costs

     2. Variable and fixed costs

     3. Breakeven charts (cost-volume-profit analysis)

      a. Construction

      b. Use and interpretation

PART V—OFFICE ADMINISTRATION AND COMMUNICATION

Items: 120   **Time: 120 Minutes**

Part V measures the secretary's proficiency in office administration and communication. This part of the examination consists of 50% office administration covering subject matters unique to the secretary's position such as executive travel, office management, records management, and reprographics; and 50% written business communication, editing, abstracting, and preparing communications in final format.

50%
3%–8%

I. Office administration
   A. Executive travel
      1. Preparation of itinerary
         a. Source books
         b. Travel agencies and in-house travel departments
         c. Organization of materials for trip
      2. Type of travel
         a. Domestic
         b. International
         c. Ground transportation
      3. Documents and credentials
         a. Passport
         b. Visa
         c. Special requirements
      4. Travel reservations
         a. Transportation reservations
         b. Hotel reservations
         c. Reservations for special facilities
         d. Company policy on travel
         e. Executive's preferences
      5. Secretary's role in executive's absence
         a. Understanding limits of authority
         b. Communicating with executive
         c. Preparing materials to be handled on executive's return
      6. Follow-up activities
         a. Expense reports
         b. Special reports
         c. Correspondence

10%–15%

   B. Office management
      1. Planning

xxv

                a. Establishing priorities
                b. Managing time effectively
                c. Coordinating with other office personnel
            2. Organizing
                a. Organizing support personnel
                b. Organizing work
                c. Establishing work procedures
            3. Supervising
                a. Staffing
                b. Controlling
5%–10%   C. Work simplification
            1. Analyzing functions and processes
            2. Designing systems
            3. Implementing systems
10%–15%   D. Records management
            1. Analyzing records and record systems
                a. Classifying records
                b. Creating, using, retaining, and disposing of
                    records
            2. Designing and controlling records
                a. Forms development
                b. Forms management
            3. Filing procedures for manual systems
                a. Designing filing systems
                b. Organizing and maintaining filing systems
2%–4%   E. Reference materials
            1. Research facilities available
            2. Books and references available
3%–8%   F. Conferences and meetings
            1. Planning and organizing meetings
            2. Conducting meetings
                a. Using meeting time effectively
                b. Using proper parliamentary procedures
            3. Preparing and using audiovisual aids
            4. Preparing minutes
3%–8%   G. Reprographics management
            1. Determining reprographic needs
            2. Organizing reprographic systems
            3. Controlling reprographic systems
50%   II. Communication
20%–25%   A. Composing communications
            1. Fundamentals of writing
                a. Effective word selection
                    (1) Positive language
                    (2) Tone
                    (3) Familiar words
                    (4) Concrete language

xxvi

           (5)   Active words
           (6)   Contemporary words and expressions
           (7)   Sex-fair language

      b.   Effective sentence and paragraph construction
           (1)   Coherence
           (2)   Emphasis
           (3)   Unity
           (4)   Conciseness
           (5)   Variety
           (6)   Clarity
           (7)   Accuracy

     c.   Development of goodwill
           (1)   Considerateness
           (2)   Empathy
           (3)   Courtesy
           (4)   Sincerity
           (5)   Respect

2. Business letters
   a.   Positive letters—letters that say yes
   b.   Routine or neutral letters—letters that exchange information
   c.   Negative letters—letters that say no
   d.   Persuasive letters
   e.   Form letters
       (1)   Personalized repetitive letters
       (2)   Letters with variable information
       (3)   Letters from form paragraphs

3. Interoffice communications
   a.   Memoranda
   b.   Informal or short reports

4. Business reports
   a.   Planning and designing the report
   b.   Collecting data
   c.   Analyzing data
   d.   Reporting findings and drawing conclusions
   e.   Organizing the report
   f.   Writing the report

15%–20%   **B.**   Editing communications

1. Proofreading
   a.   Techniques
   b.   Use of proofreader's marks

2. Editing for technical correctness
   a.   Grammar and word usage
   b.   Punctuation
   c.   Capitalization
   d.   Format and appearance
   e.   Consistent style
   f.   Spelling and typing accuracy
   g.   Proper usage of numbers

3. Editing for application of writing fundamentals
   a. Effective word selection
   b. Effective sentence and paragraph construction
   c. Tone, goodwill, considerateness, and writing style
   d. Editing for organization
   e. Editing for completeness and content accuracy

2%–5%   C. Abstracting communications
   1. Techniques
      a. Photocopying and highlighting key points
      b. Preparing a summary of key points
   2. Effective abstracts
      a. Concise summary of all key points
      b. Relevant
      c. Reports all major conclusions
      d. Complete documentation
      e. Level of language consistent with original document
      f. Easy-to-read format

5%–10%   D. Preparing communications in final format
   1. Business letter format
      a. Letter style
         (1) Block
         (2) Modified block
         (3) Simplified
      b. Punctuation style
         (1) Open
         (2) Mixed
   2. Envelope style
      a. Conventional
      b. Computer style
      c. OCR requirements
   3. Memoranda format
   4. Business report format
      a. Physical layout
      b. Headings
      c. Pagination
      d. Documentation
      e. Graphics
   5. Statistical data format
      a. Tables within text
      b. Tables independent of text
   6. Other communications
      a. Minutes
      b. News release
      c. Itinerary
      d. Outline
      e. Speech

PART VI—OFFICE TECHNOLOGY

Items: 120   **Time: 105 Minutes**

This part covers the secretary's responsibilities created by data processing, communications media, advances in office management, technological applications, records management technology, and office systems.

10%–15%   I.   Ergonomics
                   A.   Rationale for ergonomics
                   B.   Office layout and design
                   C.   Work station design
                   D.   Office furniture and equipment procurement

25%–30%   II.   Word processing
                   A.   People/career paths
                   B.   Technology
                   C.   Procedures

20%–25%   III.   Data processing
                   A.   The data processing cycle
                   B.   Data processing technology
                        1.   Types of computer systems
                             a.   Mainframe
                             b.   Minicomputer
                             c.   Microcomputer
                        2.   Input/output devices
                        3.   Software for data processing systems
                        4.   Types of programming languages
                             a.   Machine
                             b.   Assembly
                             c.   Compiler
                                  (Knowledge of a programming language is not
                                  required.)
                   C.   Concepts and application
                        1.   Operation modes, e.g. real time, batch processing, etc.
                        2.   Integration with other office systems
                        3.   Networking

20%–25%   IV.   Communication technology
                   A.   Telephone communications
                        1.   Telephone services
                        2.   Switching systems
                        3.   Telephone equipment

B. Interoffice systems
1. Personal messenger systems
2. Automated systems
3. Intercom systems
C. Telecommunications
1. Voice transmission
2. Data transmission
3. Document transmission
D. Teleconferencing
1. Audio conferencing
2. Video conferencing
3. Computer conferencing
E. Electronic mail
1. Facsimile transmission
2. Computer-based message systems
3. Communicating word processing systems
4. Electronic computer-originated mail (E-COM)

5%–10%   V. Records management technology
A. Automated record systems
B. Micrographics
C. Equipment
D. Computer data banks

5%–10%   VI. Reprographics technology
A. Copying/duplicating systems
B. Phototypesetting and composition system
C. Imaging systems
D. Finishing processes

PART I

Behavioral Science In Business

CHAPTER 1

Understanding The Individual/Self

ATTITUDES AND VALUES

We are all composites of our experiences and backgrounds. Attitudes and values are learned during childhood from parents, peers, teachers, friends, and relatives. Additionally, innate characteristics can determine attitudes. People are inherently shy, aggressive, or high-strung, and so on. There is an ongoing dispute among psychologists regarding the degree of influence that heredity and environment have on our personalities, and there is no clear-cut determination as to how extensive a role each one plays.

As we mature, we tend to merge the attitudes and values of childhood into life's experiences. The result is autonomy—becoming a separate, unique individual. We must be aware of our value systems and evaluate and judge ourselves—not critically but objectively. The world around us is constantly changing and so are our lives.

- Have you ever taken time to evaluate your relationship with other people in your life?
- What elements make up your personality?
- Have you evaluated your professional goals?
- How did you get to where you are today?

COGNITIVE STYLES

Cognitive refers to the mental process that is intellectual rather than emotional; thoughts rather than feelings. Thinking, therefore, is a cognitive process.

Jean Piaget, a professor at the University at Geneva, was a leading psychologist in the study of the intellectual development of children. Piaget pinpointed the four basic stages of development.

- The *sensory-motor period* begins at birth and progresses through the first eighteen to twenty-four months. This is the time during which we learn to develop our bodily movements, to integrate impressions into perceptions, and to understand that objects exist as separate entities.

3

- The *pre-operational period* takes over until about age seven. At this point, we begin to respond to the environment, to develop language skills, to understand abstractions. During this time, we still perceive ourselves as the center of the universe.
- The *concrete operations period* extends to approximately age nine or ten. At this point, we have mastered the concepts of length, quantity (not weight), and numbers, and we begin the differentiate our inner selves from the outer world.
- The *formal operations period* continues until about age twelve. It is during this final stage of initial development that we learn to draw meaningful conclusions based on hypothetical data, to manipulate variables, and we learn that we must adjust to the world around us.

Sigmund Freud, often referred to as the father of psychoanalysis, systemized psychosexual development into the following stages:

- The *oral stage* lasts for about the first year of our lives. It is the period during which we learn to cope with minor frustrations through oral activities, e.g., chewing a pencil.
- The *anal stage* is the period associated with toilet training. It is the period during which awareness of genital pleasures emerges and predominates.
- The *phallic stage* begins during the third year. It is during this time that we become aware of our sexual differences and often develop sexual desires for the parent of the opposite sex. The Electra situation is the result of a father–daughter relationship; the Oedipal situation is the result of the mother–son relationship.
- The *latent stage* begins during the fifth and sixth years. It is during this period that we begin to place greater emphasis on relationships outside the home.
- The *genital stage* begins with puberty. It is during this period that we focus on sexual activities and realize that pleasure can be derived from same.

Freud also segregated the three parts of our personalities:

- The *id* is the Latin term for "it," and refers to the pleasure principle.
- The *ego* is the Greek term for "I" or "self," and refers to the reality principle that tries to keep the id under control.
- The *superego* refers to conscience, morality, and societal customs.

DEFENSE MECHANISMS

We all endeavor to avoid anxieties and stressful situations; the various steps for defending ourselves are defense mechanisms. These defenses are often unconsciously contrived and we are often unaware of them.

- *Repression,* also known as selective forgetting, is a defense that blocks out anxieties; for example, "I can't remember ever saying that."

- *Reaction formation* is a defense that represses a thought or feeling by projecting the opposite; for example, when one says, "I really love my [relative]," when just the opposite is true.
- *Projection* is a defense that attributes your thoughts to others; for example, "Nobody likes me."
- *Rationalization* is a defense that is the result of personal failures or disappointments; for example, "The teacher failed me because (s)he doesn't like women with curly hair."
- *Displacement* also known as scapegoating, is a defense that shifts a response from one person to another; for example, an employer takes out personal frustrations on an employee.

MOTIVATION

How well do you really know yourself? What motivates you? Motivation is a term that takes into consideration needs, satisfiers, and values. In 1954, Abraham H. Maslow developed a heirarchy of needs which explains that once you have reached satisfaction at a certain level, you will strive to reach satisfaction at a still higher level.

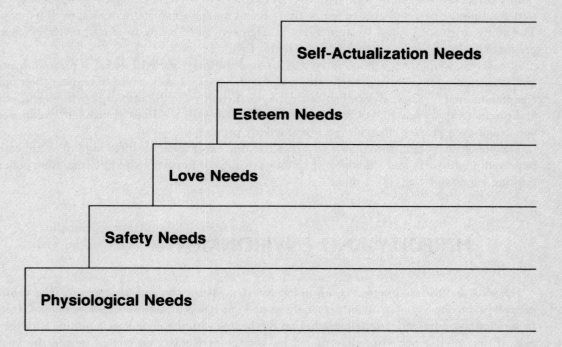

Self-Actualization Needs

Esteem Needs

Love Needs

Safety Needs

Physiological Needs

- *Physiological needs* reflect the most basic human need: survival (food, water, air, and shelter). They appear at the base because they must be satisfied before you can aspire to a higher level. Most people in the business world have achieved this level.
- *Safety needs* (the second human concern depicted in the diagram) reflect the need to feel free from danger and secure in our day-to-day activities,

including secure in our jobs. A worker who is not secure cannot perform effectively.

- *Love needs* reflect the need to socialize and belong to a group. The group can be a family, a club, an organization, or any other activity that offers the feeling of acceptance.
- *Esteem needs* reflect both self-esteem and the esteem of others. We all need to believe that we are worthy, capable, respected, and useful; and we must see that others view us as such.
- *Self-actualization needs* (displayed at the top of the diagram) reflect the need to reach one's potential. Only after all the aforementioned needs have been attained can you afford the luxury of self-actualization.

It is the keen manager who can determine the levels that have been satisfied and can motivate employees accordingly.

In a working environment we may be motivated by employee benefits such as insurance; pension contributions; bonuses; incentive plans; paid holidays, sick days, personal days, vacations; child-care facilities; credit unions; tuition reimbursement plans; a four-day work week; and so on.

The Hawthorne Effect

In 1927, a research study was conducted by the Western Electric Company in Hawthorne, Illinois, to determine the correlation between motivation and human relations in dealing with its employees. The study originated when Western Electric engineers were trying to elicit greater efficiency and productivity from employees by installing better lighting.

In essence, employees were granted a shortened workday, varied breaks, a piecework program, and other motivators. Through the entire program the workers were asked to register their opinions, complaints, and feelings. Regardless of any physical changes in the working environment, efficiency and productivity increased. As the motivators were removed, the lines of communication were kept open, and even greater efficiency and productivity prevailed.

The conclusions that were drawn as a result of this experiment are that employees are capable of improved productivity and efficiency when they are allowed to participate in formulating policies and working conditions that affect them.

HEREDITY AND ENVIRONMENT

Heredity and the environment work in concert to make us who and what we are. The contribution of each in the development of our personalities and our IQs is an issue still under debate. Hereditary factors influence human development in that life begins with the male sperm uniting with the female egg. If our intelligence is predetermined by hereditary factors, we cannot negate the fact that a heightened, stimulating environment does provide additional learning opportunities and experiences.

To shed light on this subject, many studies have been performed.

- *Family studies* have been found to be inconclusive. The more genes relatives share, the higher the correlation of IQs. It remains equally true, however, that close kinships imply shared environments.

- *Twin studies* have lead many psychologists to believe that heredity is the key determinant in the intellectual development of twins. This is based on studies of identical twins who share 100 percent common genes and fraternal twins who share 50 percent common genes. Twins reared apart show a strong correlation of IQs.
- *Adopted children studies* show split results. The correlation of intellectual levels is much stronger between biological parents and their offspring than between adoptive parents and their children. Conversely, adopted children have had higher IQs than biological parents—attributed to the influence of the adoptive parents; ergo, the environment.

PERSONALITY

What exactly is personality? It is a cornucopia of our behavior, values, motives, attitudes, emotional reactions, self-image, intelligence, and inner structure.

The term personality is derived from the Greek word *persona,* meaning "mask." It refers to ancient times when Greek actors wore masks in order to take on the personalities of the various characters they were portraying. We, too, wear masks to take on the personalities of the real life characters we portray. Our characters vary depending on our audiences. For example, we display assorted personality traits when relating to our families, our employers, our peers, our subordinates.

Every psychologst holds to his or her principle about human behavior and tries to explain why we do what we do. Whose theory is right and whose is wrong? Is there any right or wrong theory? Perhaps the answer is as simple as this: Each one in its proper perspective has made a contribution to the understanding of human behavior, but none are complete in and of themselves.

CHAPTER 2

Groups

GROUP DYNAMICS

A group can consist of two or more people, and the interaction between or among them is group dynamics. The dynamics increase as the group size increases.

Douglas McGregor, a professor of industrial management at the Massachusetts Institute of Technology (MIT) conducted a study of groups in a working environment. He theorized that people fall into two basic categories:

- *Theory X* people inherently dislike work, have little ambition, prefer to be directed, and have a strong desire for security.
- *Theory Y* people are deeply commited to objectives, exercise a high degree of initiative and creativity, and enjoy expending physical and mental energies in work-related activities.

SOCIAL PRESSURES

After our basic psychological and safety needs have been fulfilled, we can focus on our social needs. Security, love, and friendship offer a sense of meaning to our lives. Few of us can function as hermits. Therefore, in order to satisfy this need, people marry, enjoy friendships, join organizations, and so on.

On the business level, your professional success can hinge on your ability to function as an integral part of a group. If you are able to speak up in group situations and make a meaningful contribution, you can enhance your upward mobility. If you remain silent and do not contribute, you are limiting your chances of getting ahead.

Group Members

Although each group has its own unique blend of individuals, certain personality types seem to emerge:

- *Glory seekers* speak often but have little to say.
- *Silent ones* tend not to contribute for reasons of shyness, apathy, and so on.
- *Chronic complainers* have little to offer except criticism.
- *Fanatics* take issues to the extreme.
- *Workers* volunteer for everything.
- *Supportive members* are needed to add cohesiveness to any group.

TYPES OF GROUPS

Formal groups in the organizational setting are generally defined by organizational charts, which graphically portray the organizational (group) structure. Leaders and subordinates are predetermined and responsibilities are clearly outlined. Members of a formal group are drawn together, not necessarily by personal preference, but by necessity.

Informal groups generally satisfy the needs and desires of their members and emerge when people are frequently in contact with each other. In most informal groups, a leader assumes the reins of leadership by being chosen or by strength and personal recognition. A smart supervisor will make the effort to gain the respect and cooperation of group leaders inasmuch as they can determine how harmoniously the group will interact with members outside the group.

The supervisor should refrain from granting unwarranted favors to group leaders but should enlist their cooperation in a constructive and positive fashion.

CHAPTER 3

Leadership Dynamics

If you asked ten people to define leadership you would undoubtedly get ten different viewpoints. Leadership can simply be defined as the knack of getting people to willingly do the things you want them to do. Some people appear to be born leaders, others simply work hard to acquire that charismatic appeal. Leadership can certainly be learned, and many companies are offering leadership training programs for those employees who show potential leadership qualities.

PERSONALITIES AND CHARACTERISTICS OF LEADERS

Although a pleasing personality is a definite asset, it is no guarantee that you will be an effective leader. An employee will certainly respond more readily to a person with a warm smile who is friendly and outgoing; however, a strong leader cannot rely on personality alone. One must also do the following:

- Show a true interest in others.
- Make meaningful decisions.
- Demonstrate a sense of fair play.
- Develop shrewd judgment.
- Be sensitive to individual and group needs.
- Have good communication skills.
- Display confidence in oneself.

The personalities of your employees can be a major factor in the type of leadership you must exercise.

1. *Aggressive, hostile*—This person often requires an autocratic leader—one who firmly takes charge.
2. *Self-assertive, cooperative*—This person will probably perform best under a democratic or free-rein leader—one who will allow the individual to take a constructive path in the right direction.
3. *Insecure*—This person tends to be dependent on strong leadership and will perform best under an autocratic leader.
4. *Individualist*—Provided he or she is responsible and knows the job, this person will perform best under a democratic or free-rein leader.

FORMAL AND INFORMAL LEADERS

A *formal leader* is one who gains leadership through position and personal power (i.e., a top-level manager, a vice-president) and an *informal leader* is one who gains leadership because of the ability to control and manipulate (perhaps too strong a term) others.

EFFECTIVENESS OF LEADERS

In order to be an effective leader, you must possess certain qualities, including the following:

- A sense of purpose and belief in your ability to lead.
- The ability to endure the headaches of a job, often foregoing self-indulgences.
- A sense of honesty with yourself and with others.
- The competence to know the ramifications, problems, and rewards of the job you are supervising.
- The ability to recognize what is important and what is unimportant.
- Good health, good nerves, and a lot of patience—leadership is rarely a nine-to-five job.

The effective leader must understand the mechanics of human dynamics because he or she often influences levels of production, employee absenteeism, and turnover and accident rate.

Pointers

1. Be available when an employee has a problem.
2. Take care of complaints promptly.
3. Don't be critical of an employee for something that could not be helped.
4. Don't reprimand one employee in front of another.
5. If you make a promise, try to keep it.
6. Show an interest in employees and listen to their suggestions.
7. Openly discuss issues that affect your employees.
8. Be as quick to commend as you are to condemn.

In the final analysis, an effective leader must also be an effective follower. In any organizational chain of command, superiors have superiors.

CHAPTER 4

Interpersonal Communication

- *Encode*—translate an idea into a message

- *Decode*—convert a message into intelligible language

ACTIVE LISTENING

Listening is not "letting it go in one ear and out the other." It is an active process that involves perceiving and understanding what we hear and using idle brain time to its best advantage.

Most of us have spent endless hours learning the skills of reading and writing, but very few of us have engaged in learning the skill of listening. Failure to listen effectively can be costly in resultant errors and gross misunderstandings. Some suggestions follow:

- *Tune out unnecessary distractions.*
- *Listen for the total idea* and mentally sum up various points made by the speaker.
- *Listen to the tone* of the speaker for key words, pitch, and tone; be cognizant of body language, facial expressions, and other nonverbal communications.
- *Do not interrupt* with questions or comments (unless appropriate); instead make notes of anything you would like to discuss.
- *Keep in mind what is being said* and do not jump to conclusions. Weigh the facts being delivered.

INFORMAL AND FORMAL COMMUNICATIONS*

All communications is basically a three-directional process, as follows:

- *Downward communication* involves a supervisor giving assignments, instructions, evaluations, or any flow of information to lower-level employees.

*Formal communication is fully discussed in Chapter 31.

- *Upward communication* involves an employee communicating responsibilities, complaints, or any upward flow of information to supervisors.
- *Lateral (or horizontal) communication* involves employees at the same level communicating with each other regarding advice, business and/or personal problems, and so on.

Informal communication is commonly known as the "grapevine;" a term that dates back to the Civil War when intelligence telegraph lines, resembling grapevines, were strung between trees. Modern-day grapevines serve as a source of rumor, which seems to travel faster than the speed of lightning. The grapevine serves the positive purpose of bringing people together and exists in every organization, regardless of its size.

Managers must recognize the existence of grapevines and should respect their characteristics and influences. Managers must also keep the lines of communication open with employees because very often rumors begin because of a lack of information.

NONVERBAL COMMUNICATION

Nonverbal communication, often referred to as body language, is a branch of study known as kinesics. If you are slouching you are portraying disinterest; if you turn aside you are portraying disagreement; if you move toward the speaker you are portraying interest; if you raise your eyebrows you are portraying surprise, and so on.

Hidden messages are also perceived on the basis of vocal intonations and inflections. For example, "M-m-m" can communicate either doubt or enthusiasm depending on the tone.

Physical objects and space also communicate—generally status. For example, high-backed leather chairs and large offices generally indicate a high-ranking person. An invisible caste system will customarily dominate the lunchroom, parking lot, and other less formal areas.

It is important to be aware of nonverbal cues and what they mean; often what is not said is more significant than what is said.

CHAPTER 5

Managing Change

The one constant in our lives is change. Although we may pride ourselves on being flexible, modern, and up-to-date, many of us still maintain certain traditional ways of thinking. We may welcome a change to a newer or more expensive car yet feel threatened by a job change. Change often threatens the status quo, therefore threatening our security.

CONFLICT MANAGEMENT

As groups of people with diverse ideas, backgrounds, and talents amass, conflicts are inevitable. Conflicts can be a result of differences in group objectives; differences in perspective and views; competition over available resources, work arrangements; and so on. The successful manager must learn how to intervene and manage conflicts so that the objectives of the company are maintained.

All conflicts need not be all negative. Minor conflicts (disagreements) can lead to a healthy exchange of ideas that can be of enormous benefit to the company. There are three basic approaches to managing conflicts, as follows:

1. Discuss the points of conflict with the parties involved to see if the conflict can be settled internally.
2. You may have to resort to an externally imposed compromise, you may have to employ a majority rules approach, or you may have to appeal to a higher authority.
3. You may have to alter the situation in order to resolve the conflict.

NATURE AND PROCESS OF CHANGE

Change is a standard and ongoing aspect of most companies—the world around us is not standing still; therefore, no person or company can afford to. Change should be seen as an opportunity for growth, not as a threat to survival.

In order for change to be effective, many internal and external forces may need to be assessed, and—depending on the nature of your business—this may be an ongoing task.

1. Change is generally the direct result of pressures on top management. These changes may be internal, environmental, governmental, and so on.

14

Top management will often view these problems as temporary, the fault of unions or outside influences, and so on. Nevertheless, they must be addressed.

2. Once change has been indicated, a fact-finding group is generally engaged to diagnose the current problems and to pinpoint ways to forge ahead in a productive and meaningful manner. Many will elicit input from subordinates, realizing that the "people on the line" often have viable ideas.

3. Once the problem areas have been identified, a commitment to a new course of action must be ascertained. As previously mentioned in Chapter 1, the Hawthorne Effect indicates employees are more likely to endorse a program in which they have had input. For this reason, keep all employees abreast of any changes that will affect them, and listen to their input.

4. Changes are generally implemented on a small scale, when appropriate, for experimentation. Many pitfalls and shortcomings can be determined from experimentation.

5. Once the change has been deemed successful, you must elicit the support of all involved—from lower level personnel to top management.

RESISTING AND FACILITATING CHANGE

Resistance to change is a universal phenomenon inasmuch as most people are comfortable with the status quo. People inherently resist what they do not understand and often receive misinformation from uninformed sources. Many people have a low tolerance for change for fear of lowering their self-esteem or for fear of not being able to adapt to the new conditions. (A perfect example is the computer revolution.) It should be mentioned, however, that not all changes are perceived as threatening.

Overcoming opposition can be facilitated using a variety of approaches that may be applicable in different situations.

1. *Education and communication* can involve mass media, educational campaigns, one-to-one communications, group meetings, workshops, memos, news releases, reports, and so on. This helps to insure that the correct information is being disseminated and will show those involved that you are trying to "bring them into the fold." Be certain to communicate the whys—not only the whats and hows.

2. *Participation* takes into account that the more input those involved have, the more they will be willing to cooperate. This can have the advantage of unfreezing and reexamining fixed attitudes.

3. *Negotiation and bargaining* may mean making modifications to the original plan. Be careful not to be manipulated to the point that you deviate substantially from your objective. Listen to reasonable questions, suggestions, and modifications.

4. *Manipulation* is a quick method that can be employed in severe cases. You must be tactful and very careful *not* to make people feel manipulated.

5. *Coercion* may be necessary in cases where time is of the essence. Again great tact is called for inasmuch as this method can alienate people.

STRESS MANAGEMENT

The term *stress* is derived from Latin, and means "hardship, adversity, or affliction." Stress can present psychological, physical, and behavioral manifestations. The many stress factors intrinsic to a job may include time constraints and deadlines, excessive commuting, monetary pressures, too much or too little work, role ambiguity or conflict, relationships with superiors and subordinates. Outside factors such as family problems, relocation, and so on, will certainly bring on or complicate stressful situations. Although stress cannot be entirely eliminated, it can be managed.

- *Adaptive behavior* deals directly with the stressful situation by attempting to implement solutions.
- *Maladaptive behavior* does not deal directly with the problem but attempts to temporarily remove it.

A main question is how to switch from maladaptive to adaptive behavior, and whether and when intervention should take place. Of course, it is best when the initiative comes from the person under stress. Many suffer in silence, however, because they lack awareness or fear internal or external sanctions.

Eliminating Certain Job Stresses

- *Work overload* can be eliminated by not taking on more than you can handle. Learn to delegate, if possible.
- *Lack of autonomy* can be a consequence of working for a large company. Greater satisfaction can be derived from greater independence and direct participation.
- *Career development stress* is often the result of the disparity between expectations and achievements. Try to concentrate less on the monetary aspects of a promotion and try to focus on growing within your present position.

CHAPTER 6

Personnel Selection And Development

CAREER DEVELOPMENT

In order to develop a career strategy you must understand yourself. Many people do not think of pursuing careers but are content to routinely earn money to meet their objectives. Others have more directed goals. Either is fine provided that your decision does not lead to insecurity and dissatisfaction.

- Special aptitudes and natural talents may enable you to perform certain functions better than others.
- Know your special areas of interest and try to incorporate them into the working environment, when possible.
- Know your temperament and how it will fit into a particular career.
- Be aware of physical limitations that may limit your ability to perform a job at some level.

COACHING AND COUNSELING

There are many humanitarian and sociological reasons why we should be concerned with the problems of a co-worker. Problems are often characterized by tardiness, absences, changed behavior, and so on, and can affect the person's and company's productivity—to say nothing of the morale of fellow employees.

Often a supervisor or interested person can tactfully approach the person involved. If you find yourself in that situation, listen patiently, give your undivided attention, do not be critical, do not argue, and look beyond the mere words that are being spoken.

Often, a friendly ear will be a solution; other times the problem will need further attention. Should such attention be required, a manager or qualified medical person might be a good place to start.

Absenteeism and tardiness are almost epidemic and many companies are expending great efforts to curb these phenomena. Many are offering in-house counseling services, drug and alcohol rehabilitation programs.

EFFECTIVE INTERVIEWING

As the Interviewer

Recruiting should be from as broad an area as practicable since the wider your range of choices, the more the likelihood of finding capable personnel. *Internal recruiting* can offer the benefit of upgrading the morale of employees by providing them with performance incentives. You have the added benefit of hiring individuals who are already familiar with the company and its policies. You do, however, run the risk of in-breeding in that employees tend to demonstrate what they have learned in the organization rather than to introduce new ideas.

Conversely, *external recruiting* can afford you the benefit of acquiring employees with new, progressive ideas, but you will be negating some of the advantages described in the preceding. Sources for external recruiting are employment agencies (public and private), advertising, referrals, unsolicited applications, and colleges and universities.

When preparing to interview a candidate:

- Plan for the interview by reviewing the candidate's qualifications before he or she arrives.
- Provide comfortable surroundings.
- Put the candidate at ease by spending a few brief minutes in casual conversation about the weather, and so on.
- Allow ample time for both you and the candidate to share necessary information.
- State questions clearly and listen to the answers.
- Make notes as necessary but do not intimidate the candidate by spending most of your time writing.
- Conclude the interview tactfully and with a handshake.

As the Candidate

By the time you are granted the interview, you have already jumped over the first hurdle. You have been preliminarily screened and the company would now like the opportunity to meet you so that you and your prospective employer can determine whether this is a "match made in heaven."

When preparing for an interview:

- Know the time of your appointment and keep it. If you are going to be even slightly late, be certain to call.
- Let the interviewer make the first move.
- Know your previous employment history and be prepared to submit a résumé. (Even if one was previously submitted, have an extra on hand in case you are asked to present it.) If you are requested to fill out an application, use the résumé as a reference.
- Know enough about the position you are seeking and about the company to discuss them intelligently. Be prepared to demonstrate your ability to handle the job, as you may be asked to do so.

- Know your salary needs and don't sell yourself short. Remember, the dollars being discussed are yours. Salary requirements should be defended in terms of the contribution you can make to the company, *not* because you have excessive car payments or commutation expenses.
- Know how to respond to questions about previously held positions. Be honest but discreet, and refrain from disparaging a former employer.
- Know what to discuss and what not to discuss. Try to keep the interview on target and don't go off on tangents about the weather and sports.
- Know how to behave. Speak in a straightforward manner. A chuckle or smile is more appropriate than a hearty laugh at the interviewer's wit.
- Refrain from smoking, chewing gum, tapping your feet, or any other nervous habits you may have.
- Know and understand the use of body language as actions do speak louder than words.
- Know how to dress properly—first impressions are vital. A suit or dress is appropriate for a woman and a suit for a man.
- Show a genuine interest in the company. (Often the position will be offered to the qualified candidate who displays the most interest.)
- After the interview has been completed, a handshake and thank-you are in order. Additionally, a brief thank-you note will be remembered and further demonstrate your interest in the position.

Frequently Asked Interview Questions

- What are your future vocational plans?
- What do you know about our company?
- Why do you think you might enjoy working for our company?
- In what school activities did you participate?
- In school, what courses did you enjoy most?
- How did you rank in your graduating class?
- What qualifications do you have that you fell will make you successful in your field?
- What are your basic salary requirements?
- Do you prefer working alone or with others?
- Can you get recommendations from former employers?
- What is your greatest strength? Weakness?
- What do you do to stay in good physical condition?
- Would you be willing to relocate?
- What types of books (magazines) do you read regularly?
- What types of sports do you enjoy?
- Would you prefer to work for a large or small company? Explain.
- Do you like to travel?
- How do you enjoy spending your leisure time?
- How do you feel about working overtime?
- What do you anticipate doing ten years from now?

EVALUATION AND PERFORMANCE APPRAISAL

An appraisal need not be a means of criticism but rather a means of letting an employee know how to perform better and more efficiently. Appraisals consider two levels: Objective factors are measurable results such as attendance, quality, and quantity. Subjective factors cannot be easily measured but encompass attitudes, personality, and ability to adapt.

It is important to point out both strengths and weaknesses, recognize special abilities, and be unbiased.

Inasmuch as we are not all angels, we often allow a person's favorable or unfavorable salient characteristics to overshadow everything else. For example, an employer may be so impressed with the loyalty and perfect attendance record of an employee that other shortcomings are overlooked, or vice versa. This is known as the "halo" effect.

When rating an employee, therefore, be careful to rate each factor independently. Always provide the employee with an opportunity to discuss the evaluation.

ROLE-MODEL IMPLICATIONS

As young children, many of us tended to look up to an older brother or sister, a celebrity, a friend or relative. Many of these people influenced the way we acted, the way we dressed, and so on. We have all known or seen people who we wanted to emulate. Find a person or persons that you respect (possibly a person whose position you would like to elevate yourself to) and observe the way that person dresses, speaks, and interacts with others. Do not try to mimic that person, but use him or her as a guide.

CHAPTER 7

Training For Learning

CHARACTERISTICS OF THE TRAINING/LEARNING PROCESS

Training is the process of introducing people to new experiences in such a way that they will learn. Proper training can help an employee reach peak efficiency in a minimum amount of time. A collection of highly trained employees can greatly influence the success of a company.

Training is done for the following purposes:

- To orient new employees, providing them with the opportunity to adapt to their new environment and learn enough in the shortest amount of time to work efficiently.
- To provide probationary training to new employees (generally for a stated period of time). This initial training period may be supplemented by additional days, hours, or weeks, depending on the nature of the job.
- To offer promotional training to employees in preparation for new positions.
- To offer management training to subordinates who are being promoted into management positions.
- To retrain employees for new positions that have evolved as a result of a changing working environment.

LEARNING PROCESS

Learning is a process that continues throughout our lives as we constantly encounter varieties of experiences and people. Procedures must be established to hone the trainee's skills while overcoming natural learning barriers.

1. You must begin with effective and knowledgeable trainers. Effectiveness should be stressed because not all knowledgeable people can communicate effectively. Effective trainers can consist of office managers, personnel department specialists, or outside teachers. Said trainers must: (a) have knowledge of the job, training methods, and materials; (b) be able to

communicate effectively to trainees, and (c) must be able to motivate the trainees.

2. Be certain you have formulated a sound learning theory. The active learner will progress more quickly than the passive learner. Positive reinforcement should be incorporated into any training program, and feedback should be used. Allowances must be made for the fact that we all learn at different rates and by different methods. The trainee must be able to transfer the information that has been learned.

3. Effective training methods can include lectures, conferences, programmed instruction, audio-visual aids, computer instruction, sensitivity training, assertiveness training, transactional analysis, time management, role playing, and simulated experiences. It is best to incorporate a number of training methods, again on the premise that we all do not learn from the same methods.

4. Effective training materials can range from those prepared in-house to those prepared professionally. They can incorporate films, slide shows, textbooks, handbooks, and videotape cassettes.

TYPES OF TRAINING

- *Orientation (induction) programs* can help get a new employee off to a good start because first impressions are long lasting. These programs should cover all aspects of the new job and often introduce the new employee(s) to company benefits and policies, facilities, safety, and so on.
- *On-the-job training (OJT)* is learning by doing. OJT can consist of: 1) a buddy system in which a trained worker will be with the trainee during the breaking-in period; 2) an internship during which students have the opportunity to participate in the job market; and 3) job rotation whereby people work on a rotating basis learning various job skills.
- *Vestibule training* consists of skills learned away from the work area. This can incorporate in-house training, training seminars, planned sessions (group or individual).

Conditions Necessary for Learning

Training is most effective under the following conditions:

- Training simulates the job the trainee will encounter.
- One person is responsible for the trainee's progress.
- The trainee receives helpful, friendly, and practical instructions.

CHAPTER 8

===

Human Capabilities and Limitations

IMPACT OF TECHNOLOGY IN THE WORKPLACE

A few hundred years ago, reports filtered through from Paris that the quill penmen were rioting in the streets because they feared the advent of printing machinery.

As most people fear the unknown inherently, automation met with much resistance during its early years—and in many cases, still does. People look at the dehumanization factor of this giant leap forward and fear that they will be replaced by machines. In many cases, historically, these fears were not unfounded because machines are now used to perform routine functions that were once done by people. (The hardest hit population seems to be the unskilled workers.) Many jobs have been eliminated; many more have been created.

Think of the automobile industry as an example. Although the invention of the automobile eliminated jobs for buggy-whip makers, unprecedented doors opened. Aside from the obvious need for workers in the auto industry, think of the chauffeurs, mechanics, road workers, and the entire rippling effect of this giant industry. Technology is merely eliminating antiquated methods that have outlived their usefulness.

How will jobs be affected? Automation will not mean the end of manual labor as new jobs for unskilled workers are constantly being created: Many blue- and pink-collar workers are being retrained for white-collar positions, and their children are often pursuing white-collar professions. Some union leaders see technology as a threat to the status quo, and are fearful of their inability to provide job security for the rank and file. Other progressive union leaders are, however, jumping on the bandwagon by realizing that whenever major technological changes have taken place, the focus of the job market is altered. Major efforts are underway by large unions to implement employee-training programs. Union members are being encouraged to upgrade their skills to cope with new technologies to extend their working careers.

Automated equipment has crossed all industrial lines and is now handling many routine jobs such as filing, reprographics, assembly lines, generation of communications, accounting, telephone switching systems—all are being performed with a minimum amount of human effort.

For all you "doubting Thomases"—look around. Automated countries are more apt to have better standards of living. Where would the Western world be today without automation?

23

JOB DESIGN AND/OR REDESIGN

One of the axioms that has prevailed in United States business is that efficiency is increased by specialization. Many jobs have been segregated so that they are simple and repetitive and therefore, are done easily and rapidly. In the factory setting, piecework is done by individuals who then pass products (or parts) to the next individual. This is also prevalent in an office setting. Although the cost of training specialized workers is low, tedium prevails and the quality of the work can suffer. Employers are beginning to realize that the cost of more sophisticated equipment may be well spent.

A promising approach is job enlargement or enrichment—finding the balance between specialization and a broadening of skills, offering the worker a more challenging and responsible role. This is often a motivational tool which can lead to greater job satisfaction and therefore, greater productivity.

In order to pinpoint the most effective means of determining the amount of specialization needed, you must evaluate your environment and the nature and patterns of the jobs to be performed. The *serial* approach involves a segmentation of small work units. A project would progress from one unit to another until its completion. The *parallel* approach involves a division of two or more units operating as work teams, each one internally completing all phases of a given project.

TASK ANALYSIS

Task analysis involves: 1) organizing work activities into logical sequences, 2) scheduling your work, and 3) following up. For example, you may categorize your activities into: sorting and processing the mail, taking dictation, transcribing, taking incoming calls, making outgoing calls, scheduling meetings, greeting visitors, filing, and other duties. If you log the amount of time it takes you to perform each task, you may find that you have not had an accurate picture of how your day has been spent.

You can evaluate your heavy and light periods of work and schedule certain tasks around them. You know what they say, however, about "the best laid plans . . ." No matter how carefully you schedule your work, Murphy's Law can strike! A word to the wise: If possible, complete one task before proceeding to the next.

WORK TEAMS

There are many jobs that can be performed better by a team than by an individual. If one member of the team does not fit in or does not carry his or her share of the load, the entire team can be negatively affected. Congeniality and cohesiveness are key elements in providing a positive atmosphere that is conducive to effective teamwork.

Even if teams are not clearly defined, everyone in an organization is part of a team working towards a common goal. In effect, they are ad hoc committees. Supervisors should observe employees to be certain they get along and work well with the other staff members.

Developing a Cohesive Work Team

- Place friends together or let employees make the selection themselves. Although much personal chatting may take place, research supports the fact that when employees can select their teammates, productivity is higher. Be certain to tactfully integrate new or isolated employees.
- Within the group structure, rotate jobs. This will serve to strengthen each employee's identification with the team rather than with a particular task.
- Allow the groups to be self-managing and organize meetings to discuss major problems.
- Be aware of conflicts that may emerge among group members and be prepared to mediate and resolve issues, if necessary.

PART II

Business Law

CHAPTER 9

Contracts

In the course of our daily lives, we all enter into agreements, some of which are quite casual while others are more formal in nature. A contract is a legally enforceable agreement, binding between two or more competent adults (over the legal age governed by the state), based on consideration to do or refrain from doing something lawful and moral.

Once a contract has been validated, all concerned parties are legally bound to perform all the obligations therein. If there is a breach of said contract, the aggrieved party may seek compensatory damages in a court of law.

In order to fully comprehend the nature of contracts, one must understand its terminology.

Assignee	The person to whom a right or property is legally transferred
Assignor	The person making such transfer
Breach	To break or violate the contract
Consideration	The inducement to the contract (money, goods, services, and so on)
Discharge	Release from obligation
Duration	The period during which the contract is in force
Duress	Undue pressure or fear
Incompetent	A person who (for reasons of severe mental illness, drunkenness, drug addiction, and so on) is not aware of the consequences of his or her acts
Infant (minor)	One who has not reached the legal age of maturity (twenty-one in most states)
Injured party	The party who has been wronged
Mutual assent	Mutual agreement
Obligee	The person receiving performance of the contract
Obligor	The person bearing the obligation
Statute of Frauds	Requires the contracts sued upon to be in writing unless performance can be completed within one year (designed to eliminate injustices due to faulty memory or misrepresentation)
Statute of Limitations	Limits the length of time a suit for damages may be instituted
Tender	An unconditional offer of money, goods, or services to satisfy the obligation(s) of the contract
Valid	Having legal force and effect

Void   Discharge or nullify
Voidable   A contract that may be legally set aside for fraud,
                        mutual error, lack of capacity, a minor, or lack of free
                        will

TYPES OF CONTRACTS

- *Informal contract*—One that is loosely structured in format and language and one that is not necessarily under seal (signed). This may be written or oral.
- *Formal contract*—One that is written, signed, and delivered. The Plain Language Law, passed in many states, requires that contracts reflect language that is understandable to the average person, foregoing repetition, redundancy, flatulence, reiteration, and superfluity.
- *Executed contract*—One in which the terms have been performed by both or all contracting parties.
- *Executory contract*—One in which the terms (or some of them) are yet to be performed. A contract can be executed by one party and executory on the part of another.
- *Implied contract*—One in which the contract terms are understood without having been expressed in writing.
- *Express contract*—One in which the terms are expressed by written and/or moral obligation.
- *Bilateral contract*—One in which mutual promises are exchanged by all concerned parties.
- *Unilateral contract*—One in which one party promises to do something in exchange for an act to be performed by another.
- *Quasi contract*—One that is court-created; imposed in matters where it may be proven that the parties involved had never created a written, oral, or implied agreement.

CONTRACT ELEMENTS

1. Competent parties.
2. Legal and moral terms and conditions.
3. Sufficient consideration.
4. Absence of duress, fraud, or misrepresentation.

TERMINATION OF A CONTRACT

A contract is obviously considered terminated when all the obligations contained therein have been performed in accordance with the terms of said contract. Contracts, however, may be considered null and void under the following circumstances:

1. The death or insanity of any party in a contract for personal services.
2. Bankruptcy on the part of any party.
3. When tender is made and refused, the party submitting the tender is released from any further obligation; for example, a store delivering merchandise that is refused by the customer.
4. If duress, fraud, or misrepresentation is evident.
5. If the contract does not have a duration period, it will be terminated at the end of a "reasonable length of time."
6. The acceptance of a counteroffer.
7. The law assumes that youths are inexperienced; therefore, a minor can void a contract. An adult does not have the right to void a contract on the grounds that one of the contracting parties is a minor.

CHAPTER 10

Bailments

A bailment is an agreement by which possession of an article of personal property is surrendered by the owner with the understanding that said property will be returned at a later date.

- *Bailor*—The owner of the goods.
- *Bailee*—The one receiving possession of the goods.

REQUIREMENTS FOR BAILMENT

1. The bailor retains title to the goods.
2. The bailee receives possession and temporary control of the goods.
3. The bailor (or someone appointed by the bailor) will ultimately receive possession of the goods.

Kinds of Bailments

Bailment	*Example*
Those of benefit to bailor	Your friend leaves you responsible for the care of an item of property, and no provisions are made to compensate you.
Those of benefit to bailee	You borrow a friend's automobile for a week, and no compensation is awarded your friend.
Those of mutual benefit	You engage the services of a contractor for a repair to your house. The contractor receives a fee and you receive the benefit of said repair.

OBLIGATIONS

1. When the bailment exists for the benefit of the bailor, said bailee must exercise only slight care. (In the aforementioned case, you are not responsible for damages to your friend's item of property, provided slight

care has been rendered. After all, you were not receiving any compensation.)

2. When the bailment exists for the benefit of the bailee, said bailee must exercise extraordinary care. (You borrow the aforementioned car with the understanding that the car will be garaged during the one-week period. Instead, you leave the car on the street overnight and it is the target of vandalism. You have breached the terms of the bailment agreement and must assume full responsibility.)

3. When the bailment exists for mutual benefit, the bailee must exercise reasonable care. (Should a lawsuit ensue, the onus is on the bailee.)

Common Carriers

Common carriers perform a public service, are licensed by the Interstate Commerce Commission, maintain uniform rates, and must carry for all who request service within their area(s) of specialty. The care is based on that of mutual benefit with the exception of loss or damage resulting from:

- An act of God.
- Order of public authority.
- An act of an alien enemy.
- Inherent nature of the goods.
- Misconduct of the shipper.

CHAPTER 11

Agency

An agency is created when one person acts on behalf of and under the control of another in a representative capacity creating a fiduciary (trust) relationship. An employee acting on behalf of a company in the capacity of sales representative, purchasing agent, and so on, is serving as an agent of said company. Sports figures, actors and actresses, and writers often engage the services of agents to negotiate contracts on their behalf. Many people engage the services of a lawyer, bank officer, or other professional to act as an outside third party. A corporation, which is a legal entity, functions only through agents.

- *Agent*—The person or company who is authorized to enter into agreements on behalf of another person or company.
- *Subagent*—The person or company engaged by the agent with the express consent of the principal.
- *Principal*—The person or company for whom the agent acts.
- *Third party*—The person or company with whom the agent transacts business on behalf of the principal.

TYPES OF AGENTS

1. *Broker*—An agent who has the authority and power to secure customers to effectuate the sale of and/or exchange of property (such as a real estate agent). The broker does not have the authority to sell anything in his or her own name.
2. *Factor*—An agent who is in possession of and/or control of another's property. A factor does have the authority to sell property in his or her own name.
3. *General agent*—An agent who has very broad authority on an ongoing basis to transact all the business of the principal.
4. *Special agent*—An agent who has limited, clearly defined authority to perform a single transaction or a series of transactions.

RIGHTS AND RESPONSIBILITIES

The agent has a basic responsibility to work for the benefit and general well-being of the principal and to explicitly follow the principal's instructions. The agent cannot allow personal interests to

34

become antagonistic to those of the principal. The principal, on the other hand, is obliged to compensate the agent for the performance of his or her duties.

Agents

Generally, the agent is not liable for the acts of a disclosed principal regarding contracts. Inasmuch as the agent is merely following instructions, responsibility rests with the principal. There are, of course, exceptions:

- If the agent enters into a contract and neglects to execute it in the principal's name and/or fails to display his or her representative capacity, said agent assumes personal liability.
- The third party may request that the agent be bound to the contract. This is done in cases where there may be lack of confidence in the principal.
- If the agent fails to or is unable to disclose the identity of the principal, said agent assumes personal liability.

Principals

Inasmuch as a principal may wish to maintain an undisclosed identity, contracts with undisclosed principals may be entered into on the strength and reputation of the agent. Therefore:

- The agent absorbs contractual responsibilities until such time as the third party may choose to hold the principal.
- The principal is ultimately responsible for all the acts of an assigned agent and may be listed as a defendant in any impending lawsuit.

Third Parties

Third parties maintain their own liability:

- Principals are generally entitled to performance and fulfillment of contractual obligations by third parties.
- Agents, having no interest in the cause of action other than that created for the principal, generally have no right to institute a lawsuit for lack of performance. However, the agent of an undisclosed principal or a factor having direct vested interest may institute a lawsuit against a third party.

The principal–agent relationship is parallel to that of the employer–employee relationship and is, therefore, subject to the same commitments outlined in Chapter 18.

Know Your Terminology

Terminology	*Definition*
Disclosed principal	Identity of principal is made known
Estop	To prohibit
Estoppel	The inability of the principal to deny that authority was granted

Express authority	Authority that is explicitly outlined by the parties involved
Implied authority	Authority that arises from ordinary business customs
Independent contractor	A person who performs a service for another
Ostensible authority	Also known as apparent authority; authority a principal knowingly permits the agent to hold
Power of attorney	A formal instrument transferring authority to an agent
Tort	A civil offense not arising out of a contractual problem (trespassing, copyright infringement, and so on)
Undisclosed principal	Identity of principal remains anonymous

CHAPTER 12

Sales

Sales transactions are conducted constantly, and the nature of these transactions is as varied as the goods and services that are available. In a previous chapter we have extensively discussed contractual obligations which are often the forerunners to and/or the aftermath of a sale.

TRANSFER OF TITLE

This nebulous term is often associated with ownership. (The methods under which title for real and personal property can be transferred are clearly described in Chapter 13.

WARRANTIES

Warranties basically refer to the obligation of the seller regarding the goods or services that have been sold and offer legal assurance that said goods or services meet certain characteristics. Historically, the rule of thumb was *caveat emptor* ('let the buyer beware') imposing the responsibility for defective products on the buyer. In recent times, however, as the nature of sales has changed, so has the philosophy. *Caveat venditor* ("let the seller beware") has become a more recognized premise. Warranties fall into two main categories:

- An *express warranty* is one in which the buyer and seller have bargained for certain specifics and the seller verifies that the goods or services be of a certain type and quality.
- An *implied warranty* is one that is a matter of law with or without any bargaining. Implied warranties may include such provisions as: the buyer receives ownership of property that the seller has the authority to sell and that the goods or services are what they are represented to be.

PRODUCT LIABILITY

Product liability was imposed to protect buyers against defects in design and manufacturing. Under the impetus of the Consumer Protection Safety Act, the onus is on the manufacturer when a consumer suffers injuries as a result of using a product. Product liability suits can be brought against the

37

manufacturer, the seller, or anyone involved in the chain of the sale. Damages can be sought for 1) negligence, 2) breach of warranty, 3) express or implied warranty misrepresentation, or 4) strict liability.

RIGHTS AND REMEDIES

The law understands that parties to contracts assume certain rights and responsibilities thereto.

The Buyer

- The buyer assumes the right to inspect merchandise (or services) prior to making payment and can reject said merchandise if it does not conform to the terms of the contract.
- If the delivery is made C.O.D., it must be paid for prior to inspection. All expenses may be recovered, however, should an inspection reveal that the merchandise does not conform to the terms of the contract.
- The right to reject nonconforming goods is subject to the buyer's taking action within a "reasonable time" of delivery. If not, the buyer could forfeit his or her right to reject them.
- The aggrieved buyer assumes the right to 1) terminate the contract, 2) collect damages, 3) enforce the contract and demand acceptable goods or services, or 4) acquire the goods or services from another source—if the seller fails to conform to the terms of the contract.

The Seller

- The seller assumes the right to correct a defect if said defect is minor and is performed within a "reasonable time."
- The seller assumes the right to hold merchandise if it is discovered that the buyer is insolvent.
- The seller assumes the right to reclaim goods if the goods were wrongfully rejected or if the buyer fails to make payment.
- The seller assumes the right to resell the goods if the preceding conditions prevail. The seller can also institute a claim for damages for the difference between the original price and the resale price, if lower.
- The seller assumes the right to sue for the contract price in the event that the buyer accepted the goods or the goods were damaged *after* the buyer accepted delivery.

NOTE: None of the above actions regarding the rights of the buyer or seller can preclude the possibility of litigation.

Additional Terminology

Terminology	*Definition*
Chattel	Items of personal property
C.I.F.	Cost, insurance, and freight; the price includes these
Cover	To acquire goods and services from another source

Cure	To correct a defect in merchandise
F.O.B.	Free on board; the seller is obliged to have the goods delivered to the buyer via a carrier, and the risk of loss remains the seller's until delivery is made
Goods	Things that can be moved
Tender	An unconditional offer of money or services

CHAPTER 13

Real And Personal Property

REAL PROPERTY

Real property can be identified as land or anything affixed to or growing from the land (houses, furnaces, central air conditioning, trees, and so on). In addition to surface land, real property accounts for land below and above the surface, known as *mineral rights* and *air rights*, respectively.

TRANSFER OF REAL PROPERTY

1. *Deed*—A formal document that is executed and notarized.
    a. A *warranty deed* is one in which the grantor (seller) warrants or guarantees to the grantee (purchaser) that: 1) the property is free of encumbrances; 2) he or she has clear title to the property; 3) heirs will have peaceful enjoyment of the property; and 4) the grantor will defend title to the property should said title be questioned.
    b. A *quitclaim deed* is executed when the grantor does not wish to make the aforementioned guarantees.
2. *Judicial sale*—The court may order a competent party to sell the property in order to secure money to pay a judgment against the owner.
3. *Adverse possession*—A person who enters and remains on a piece of land for a time specified in the statute of limitations will acquire legal title to the land at the end of the statutory period.
4. *Accretion*—New land created by the deposit of soil by rivers and lakes.
5. *Will or intestate succession*—Transferral of ownership upon owner's death.

Mortgages

A mortgage is an interest in real property created for the purpose of securing a debt. The owner of the property is referred to as the *mortgagor* and the bank or lender is referred to as the *mortgagee*. The mortgagor is responsible for repayment of the mortgage debt. If payment is not forthcoming as contracted, the mortgagee can begin foreclosure proceedings. The results of such proceedings could mean that the mortgagee gains possession of said property via sale of all the land at public auction. An extensive definition follows:

- *Conventional mortgage*—One that bears a fixed rate of interest over the term of the loan and one that has no backing by the government in the way of insurance or guarantee.
- *Variable-rate mortgage*—One that bears a rate of interest that fluctuates with the prime rate.
- *Graduated-payment mortgage*—One that bears a fixed rate of interest; however, the monthly payments increase over the term of the loan. (This has an advantage for young people insofar as it is expected that their earning power will increase during later years.)
- *Balloon-payment mortgage*—One that bears a relatively low fixed rate of interest and a large final payment. This is generally written for a short period of time—perhaps five years—and the mortgagor (borrower) must secure new financing at the end of the designated period.
- *FHA and VA mortgages*—Ones that are backed by federal agencies. The Federal Housing Administration and Veterans Administration will reimburse the mortgagee (lender) in the event of a default and will foreclose on the property in question.
- *Second mortgage*—One that is secured over and above a first mortgage. This can be acquired to gain additional equity, for home improvements, for investment purposes, and so on.

Additional Terms

Easement	Land granted by the grantor to the grantee for a stated purpose
Encumbrance	A claim against property (mortgage, lien, and so on)
Escrow	Money held by a third party for a stated purpose
Fixture	An article of personal property that has become annexed to the property (furnace, shrubbery)
Intestate	One who dies having left no valid will
Lien	A legal claim against property
Mechanic's lien	A lien by a contractor or subcontractor for nonpayment of a service performed
Metes and bounds description	Establishes boundary lines by roads, fences, streams, and so on
Title report	A letter in which a title company verifies that the grantor is in fact the true and lawful owner of the property in question.

LANDLORD AND TENANT RELATIONSHIPS

Parties to the landlord–tenant relationship are referred to by a variety of interchangeable terms:
- The landlord may be termed *lessor, owner,* or *party of the first part.*
- The tenant may be termed *lessee, renter,* or *party of the second part.*

Types of Leases

1. *Tenancy for a stated period*—The duration of said lease may be six months, a year, two years, or any stated period of time, depending on the negotiated terms thereof. Said lease terminates without notice at the end of the indicated tenancy period. It may, however, be renewed by mutual consent.

2. *Tenancy from period to period*—A lease may be negotiated to run from December 1, 1987, to November 30, 1988, and would continue from year to year thereafter until sufficient termination notice has been rendered by either party. Most states require thirty days' notice when a lease is on a month-to-month basis and ninety days' notice on a year-to-year basis.

3. *Tenancy at will*—There is no predetermined termination period and the tenancy period will remain in force until such time as either party gives the required statutory notice.

4. *Tenancy at sufferance*—This occurs when the tenant does not vacate the premises at the time of termination. In such case, the landlord may elect to allow said tenant to remain in occupancy of said premises or may elect to evict said tenant.

Contents of a Lease

- Date of signing.
- Names and addresses of involved parties.
- Location of the unit(s) to be leased.
- Term of the lease.
- Provisions for termination.
- Amount of rent and date due.
- Any additional expenses that may be incurred (utilities, parking, recreational facilities, and so on).
- Amount of security deposit, if applicable.
- Provisions for subletting, if applicable.
- Regulations for pets.
- List of items supplied, if furnished.
- Military or transfer clause, if applicable.

PERSONAL PROPERTY

Personal property falls into two categories:

- *Tangible*—Includes goods such as clothing, automobiles, jewelry or anything can be physically held.
- *Intangible*—Includes such things as accounts receivables, trademarks, goodwill, or anything of value that is transferrable but cannot necessarily be physically held.

Transfer of Personal Property

1. *Sale, gift, last will and testament, or operation of law* (judicial sale, mortgage foreclosure, intestate succession).
2. *Accession*—The acquisition of title when personal property is incorporated into other property. For example, if you bring your auto in for repair and parts are installed without your authorization, you are entitled to be the gratis beneficiary of the new parts unless the original parts can be replaced without damage.
3. *Confusion*—One unit may not be distinguished from another. This is commonly referred to as *fungible property* and is sold by weight or measure (grain, logs, wine, hay, and so on). For example, grain which is stored in a public warehouse by many individuals with each owner possessing interest in the mass. Should the supply of grain be destroyed, the loss would be divided proportionately.

CHAPTER 14

Insurable Interest

Insurable interest is the monetary interest the holder of an insurance policy has in the person or property that is insured. Inasmuch as the act of living involves risks, people try to protect themselves against losses.

LIFE INSURANCE

A person who insures another's life must have an interest in the insured insofar as suffering a financial loss upon the insured's death. For example, an insurable interest could result from the death of a partner or spouse. There are various types of policies available, and the best one for you is totally dependent upon individual circumstances.

- *Whole-life insurance*—A standard policy whereby equal payments are made periodically from the date of purchase until the death of the insured. This is also known as straight life.
- *Endowment life insurance*—A policy that stresses savings possibilities in that the cash surrender value increases rapidly. This is paid over a period of "X" years and premiums are higher than a whole-life policy.
- *Term life insurance*—A policy that does not accrue a cash surrender value. This provides for payment if the insured dies within a specified period of time.
- *Specialized life insurance*—A policy that provides life insurance for particular needs. For example, business partners may maintain policies on each other naming the surviving partner(s) as beneficiary.

PROPERTY INSURANCE

Real property, automobiles, and other goods can be covered by property insurance.

- *Fire and theft coverage*—This insurance pays for losses from these causes. Additionally, windstorm, vandalism, and water damage can be covered under comprehensive coverage. In order to collect a fire claim, the insured must have had an insurable interest in the property at the time of the fire.

- *Liability and bodily injury coverage*—This insurance pays for losses resulting from an automobile injury to people or property.
- *No-fault coverage*—The driver collects damages from his or her insurance company regardless of who is at fault in the accident.

Know Your Terminology

Terminology	*Definition*
Beneficiary	The person to whom compensation is or will be provided
Binder	Interim agreement issued between the time an application for insurance is made and approved or rejected
Grace period	A period of (generally) thirty days within which the policy may be paid and remain in force
Lapse	When the insured fails to pay the required premiums, the policy terminates
Premium	Amount paid to the insurer accepting your risk
Subrogation	The right of the insurer to claim damages from a third party through whose fault the insurer was required to pay a claim
Warranty	The insured's guarantee of facts and statements contained in the application

CHAPTER 15

Negotiable Instruments

Negotiable instruments (also referred to as commercial papers) are legal, written documents which substitute for currency in business transactions. Said instruments must circulate like cash, must be properly endorsed, must contain an unconditional promise to pay, and must freely move through the financial community.

TYPES OF NEGOTIABLE INSTRUMENTS

Negotiable instruments fall into two basic categories: *notes*, the promise to pay money, and *drafts*, directions to someone else to pay money.

1. *Draft*—An order to pay money to another person.
2. *Check*—A draft drawn on a bank.
    a. *Certified check*—The drawee bank will place a stamp on the check certifying that the necessary funds are available.
    b. *Cashier's check*—A check the bank draws upon itself.
    c. *Traveler's check*—Issued by banks and become negotiable when completed by identifying signature (Often used by vacationers to substitute for cash).
3. *Certificate of deposit*—A savings account where money is left on deposit for a specified period of time at a specified rate of interest. (There is a penalty for early withdrawal.)
4. *Promissory note*—A document in which the borrower agrees to repay a debt with all the repayment details clearly stated.

NEGOTIABILITY

Negotiability or transferability is subject to certain terms and conditions. Such instruments must:

- Be signed by the maker (drawer).
- Contain an unconditional promise to pay (a note) or an order to pay (a draft).
- Be payable at a certain point in time (either a specific date or on demand).
- Be payable to someone's order (or to bearer).
- Not show any signs of tampering.

CHAPTER 16

Court Procedures

Your automobile is struck from behind . . .
A contractor performs substandard work . . .
You fall in an icy parking lot and are injured . . .
Your spouse wants a divorce . . .
A store refuses to refund your money for damaged merchandise . . .

"I'm going to sue!" How many times have we heard that expression? Many people, however, offer more than just lip service and commence legal proceedings.

Attorneys have long enjoyed the wisdom of the old adage, "The result of a trial is usually determined by what has preceded it." Summonses, complaints, pleadings, witnesses, examinations of the parties—all under the umbrella of the rules of procedures and practice known as *adjective law*, the methods by which the individual's rights are protected. This is in contrast to *substantive law*, those procedures that the courts administer.

Know Your Terminology

Affidavit	A sworn statement of facts
Affidavit of service	An affidavit certifying that service of a document has taken place
Allegation	A statement of what someone undertakes to prove
Answer	A legal document in which a defendant can admit or deny each allegation in the complaint
Appeal	Take a case to a higher court
Caption	The portion of a legal document that lists the jurisdiction, venue, case title, and document title
Cause of action	The action(s) upon which the lawsuit is based
Civil suit	A lawsuit to protect someone from a wrongdoing other than breach of contract (business relationships, property ownership, and so on)
Complaint	A court document in which the plaintiff's grievances are enumerated (often served with the summons)
Counterclaim	A claim by a defendant intended to counter the claim of the plaintiff
Criminal action	When the "people" bring action against a company, an agency, or an individual (The title might read:

47

	THE PEOPLE OF THE STATE OF CALIFORNIA, Plaintiff . . ."
Defendant	The person being sued
Deposition	Also known as examination before trial; testimony given under oath prior to court proceedings where each attorney has the opportunity to examine (question) the opposing party
Docket	Book containing records of court actions
Filing	Depositing the document with the court clerk's office and placing same in the law office files
Filing fee	Fee paid to the court clerk's office for each filing
Judgment	The outcome of the lawsuit
Motion	An application made to the court to obtain a ruling or decision
Notary public	Person authorized by the state to authenticate signatures on documents
Petition	The legal document addressed to a particular court wherein the petitioner (person instituting action) seeks relief
Plaintiff	The person initiating the suit
Probate court	The arm of the court primarily concerned with administering estates and dealing with matters relating to guardianships, conservatorships, and so on
Service	Certain legal papers must be personally served (delivered)
Statute of limitations	The period of time during which a lawsuit may be instituted
Subpoena	A legal document commanding a person to appear in court (must be served)
Subpoena duces tecum	Legal document commanding a person to appear in court and produce certain documents
Summons	Issued by or on behalf of the plaintiff, advising the defendant that an action has been commenced and when he and she must appear in court (must be served)
Venue	The geographic location where the legal action arises

COMMENCEMENT OF AN ACTION

Legal procedures are established by law and can vary slightly from one state to another and from one court to another. Actions are commenced to redress or prevent a wrong and are initiated by the service of a summons (often accompanied by the complaint).

- The *summons* is prepared by the plaintiff or plaintiff's counsel and must personally be served upon each defendant. If the defendant fails to answer the summons within the prescribed period of time (generally twenty to thirty days) he or she may lose the lawsuit by default.

- The *complaint* is a sworn statement prepared by the plaintiff or plaintiff's counsel enumerating all the plaintiff's grievances. It is concluded with a *prayer for relief* in which the plaintiff summarizes the relief requested. (Initial pleadings may also be called *declarations, petitions, bills or narrations*—determined by local jurisdiction.)

- The *answer* to the complaint gives the defendant the opportunity to rebut the alleged grievances. The answer is often the defendant's only pleading before the court. It must be prepared by the defendant or defendant's counsel within the statutory period of time. Failure to do so can result in judgment for the plaintiff by default.

- If a *cross-complaint* is filed by the defendant, the plaintiff must file his or her answer within the statutory period of time.

- Many other interim steps take place (depending on the nature of the lawsuit) including depositions, motions, and so on, prior to the time the trial actually occurs. Very often the case is settled before it actually goes to court.

COURT ORDERS

Court orders are the judgments or conclusions of a court granting or denying a certain motion or proceeding.

Cease and desist	A command which mandates a certain practice to be stopped; for example, National Labor Relations Board (NLRB) restraining an employer from certain unfair labor practices
Interlocutory order	An intermediate or temporary order prior to final disposition of a controversy
Order to show cause	A court order instructing one to give reason why he or she is unable to perform a specific act
Restraining order	An order of the court stopping someone from doing something specific
Writ	A process or order to perform a specific act
Writ of attachment	Issued at the beginning of a lawsuit—intended to seize and hold property of a named party subject to the outcome of a claim
Writ of execution	A command of the court to the sheriff ordering the sheriff to carry out the mandate
Writ of habeas corpus	A command to offer immediate relief from confinement
Writ of mandamus	A command to perform a specific duty
Writ of mesne	An order in landlord–tenant situations

BANKRUPTCY

Bankruptcy is the legal condition in which one becomes insolvent and liabilities exceed assets. Such cases are federal matters and are heard in a United States District Court. The court will appoint a referee to liquidate (sell) the assets, and said assets will be divided among the creditors (people or organizations owed money).

- *Involuntary bankruptcy*—When a person or company is unable to pay debts, and creditors file a petition seeking payment and asking that the debtor be declared bankrupt.
- *Voluntary bankruptcy*—When a person or company is unable to pay debts and declares himself or itself bankrupt. This is commonly referred to as Chapter 11.

Procedures for Corporate Bankruptcy

- The bankrupt files a debtor's petition with the clerk of the United States District Court.
- The Court refers the petition to the office of the referee.
- Creditors are sent notices of a meeting at which time they are asked to submit statements of amounts owed.
- A receiver is appointed to take charge of the property and a trustee is appointed to administer the assets.
- Assets are generally liquidated at sale or auction and proceeds are divided among the creditors.
- A discharge is filed and the bankrupt is relieved of all debts.

In some cases, businesses will be awarded temporary protection from creditors giving them an opportunity to reorganize and earn enough money to pay their creditors.

CHAPTER 17

Business

Nearly all businesses in the United States are owned by private citizens, either individually or in groups.

TYPES OF BUSINESS ENTITIES

Which is best? That totally depends on individual circumstances and includes factors such as available capital, management ability, skills, down time (illness), tax basis, and so on. In making such a decision, it might be best to consult an attorney and/or accountant.

Sole Proprietorship

Sole proprietorship, one-person operation, is the simplest form of business ownership in which the sole proprietor accumulates enough capital (from personal resources and/or personal credit) to start the business. No legal papers are necessary and the business can be terminated at the owner's discretion.

Advantages	Disadvantages
1. Reap all profits	1. Unlimited liability*
2. Low start-up costs	2. Difficult to raise capital
3. Lowest tax rate	3. Long-term illness could cause
4. Minimum regulations	loss of business
5. Direct control	

*Personally liable for all claims, debts or legal actions that may arise.

Partnership

A partnership is the voluntary merger of two or more parties.

- *General partner*—One who contributes to the management of the partnership and is known to the general public.

51

- *Limited partner*—One who does not contribute to the management of the partnership, but rather contributes money or other property; has limited liability.
- *Secret partner*—One taking an active role in the partnership but is not known to those outside the partnership.
- *Silent partner*—One who has no active role in the partnership.
- *Dormant partner*—One who does not take an active role in the partnership and is unknown to the public.
- *Nominal partner*—One who is not actually a partner but takes an active role in the partnership.

Advantages	Disadvantages
1. Diversity of talents	1. Unlimited liability
2. Low tax rate	2. Lack of suitability of partners
3. Easy to form	3. Division of authority
4. Minimum regulations	4. Difficult to raise capital
5. Shared start-up costs	

If you are forming a partnership, it is imperative to prepare a partnership agreement so that each partner fully understands his or her rights and obligations. Said agreement should include:

- Date.
- Names of partners.
- Nature of the business.
- Name and location of business.
- Duration of partnership.
- Investment of each partner.
- Sharing of profits and losses.
- Record keeping agreements.
- Salaries.
- Duties and responsibilities.
- Restraints.
- Termination agreement.

Franchise

A franchise is a licensing agreement that allows an independent company or person to pay a parent company (e.g., Burger King, Holiday Inn, Midas-International Corp., Singer Co.) for the right to sell or market its product or service. In return for the use of its trademark, trade name, or copyright licenses, the parent company receives a royalty from part of the profits. Franchising accounts for more than a half-million businesses in the United States and is rapidly growing.

Advantages	Disadvantages
1. Gives parent company control over its network 2. Limited liability 3. Limited investment requirements 4. Fast growth due to availability of established name and massive advertising campaigns	1. Additional buying power does not necessarily assure profits 2. Parent control can stifle initiative at local level 3. Financial rewards are shared with parent company

Corporations

This is the most common form of business ownership in the United States accounting for more than eighty percent of all business ventures. A corporation is an association of people who own shares of stock in a company, with each share representing a percentage of ownership. Large corporations must be approved by the Securities and Exchange Commission and are regulated by certain rules and regulations. Corporate liabilities are independent of its owners.

- *Domestic corporation*—One designated to carry on business in the state in which it is chartered.
- *Foreign corporation*—One designated to carry on business in and out of the state in which it is chartered. Many states have imposed licensing and taxation measures on foreign corporations.
- *Alien corporation*—One that is formed in another country and trades in the United States.
- *Close corporation*—One that does not offer stock for sale to the general public. Usually has a limited number of owners who are directly involved in the management of the corporation.
- *Open corporation*—Also known as public corporations; one that offers stock for sale to the general public.

The formation of a corporation requires a charter (or articles of incorporation)—a legal document recognizing the existence of the corporation to be filed with the appropriate state(s). At its first directors' meeting, bylaws (rules and regulations) are prepared governing the time and place of shareholders' and directors' meetings, the required quorum, qualifications and responsibilities of directors, and rules and regulations that govern the day-to-day running of the corporation. If the corporation is issuing stock (an open corporation) it must file a prospectus with the Securities and Exchange Commission.

When a corporation wishes to dissolve, it must file a certificate of dissolution with the appropriate state(s).

Advantages	Disadvantages
1. Limited liability 2. Specialized management 3. Easy to raise capital 4. Investment easily withdrawn	1. Complex to start 2. Highest tax rate 3. Double taxation 4. Restricted by charter 5. Extensive recordkeeping 6. Lack of motivation of employees

REGULATION OF INDUSTRY

Antitrust Legislation

- *Sherman Act*—Established in 1890 to regulate interstate commerce in two basic areas: contracts and monopolies. Price fixing is the offense that most commonly violates this act.
- *Clayton Act*—Enacted in 1914 and designed to make the Sherman Act more specific in areas having an adverse effect on competition. For instance, a person cannot be a member of a board of directors of two or more corporations simultaneously where a conflict of interests could exist.
- *Federal Trade Commission Act*—Enacted in 1914 to prevent unfair competition in commerce; for example, advertisers may be called upon to substantiate the truthfulness of advertisements.
- *Robinson–Patman Act*—Enacted in 1936 and designed to amend Section 2 of the Clayton Act. Its main purpose was to promote equality in treatment to buyers and sellers where a monopoly might otherwise be created. This enables a small businessman to purchase merchandise at prices comparable to those of the large businessman, thus protecting the small businessman from being driven out of business.
- *Celler–Kefauver Act*—Enacted in 1950 to amend Section 7 of the Clayton Act regulating the acquisition of stocks or assets of corporations.

Uniform Commercial Code

The Code is basically a body of commercial laws that covers statutes on sales, negotiable instruments, contracts, banking practices, warehousing, agricultural items, bills of lading, investment securities, and general business contracts.

The Code was introduced in 1957 to provide guidelines for consistency in state laws regarding interstate commerce. Although most laws regarding interstate commerce are federal, individual states have the authority to pass laws controlling their own business practices. The Code has no legal force, but it has somewhat simplified business's job of dealing with the legal sales environment.

PUBLIC UTILITIES AND TRANSPORTATION

Public utilities are private companies that are inherently monopolistic. By their very nature, they are protected from free competition so that they can best serve the public. For example, if several companies set up telephone lines, you would not be able to communicate with the customers on another line. By the same token, it does not benefit the public to have several bus companies competing for the same well-traveled route. In this case, it is also likely that *no* company will cover less-traveled routes; the public in these areas is deprived of what is considered a basic need. This encompasses such industries as:

- Gas.
- Electric.
- Water (in some areas).
- Telephone lines (AT&T was recently demonopolized).
- Mass transportation.

Due to the monopolistic nature of public utilities, they are closely monitored and regulated by local, state, and federal governments. States have created public service commissions to regulate rates and services of utilities. The Federal Energy Regulation Commission (FERC) controls rates for interstate electric power, and in conjunction with the Interstate Commerce Commission (ICC) maintains authority over interstate pipelines. The Civil Aeronautics Board (CAB) and Federal Aviation Administration (FAA) regulate air transportation, and the Federal Communications Commission (FCC) regulates rates and services for interstate telephone and telegraph transmissions.

CONSUMER PROTECTION LEGISLATION

- *Consumer Product Safety Act of 1972* established the Consumer Product Safety Commission (CPSC) to protect consumers from injuries and risks due to the manufacture of hazardous products.
- *Federal Trade Commission* (FTC) deals with deceptive or misleading trade practices in commerce. It further 1) mandates a cooling-off period giving purchasers three days to rescind the purchase of door-to-door materials costing more than $25; 2) requires mail-order houses to ship goods within a reasonable period of time; 3) prohibits bait-and-switch schemes in which advertised merchandise lures customers into a store only to have the customers pressured into purchasing higher priced items.
- *Food and Drug Act* (FDA) has been amended several times. It gives the government regulatory control over food and drugs.
- *Fair Packaging and Labeling Act* of 1966 gave the FDA power to require the uniform and accurate labeling of all foods, drugs, and cosmetics.
- *Truth-in-Lending Act* of 1968 authorized the Federal Reserve Board to require full disclosure of all credit terms before a consumer credit account is opened, spell out how finance charges are determined, spell out methods

of computing interest on open-end credit transactions, disclose annual percentage rates, and set statutory limits of credit cardholder liability.

- *Fair Credit Billing Act* gave customers a fair and equitable means of correcting billing errors and provided protection for a customer who charges damages or faulty merchandise.
- *Fair Credit Reporting Act* provides customers with access to their personal files maintained by credit bureaus and enables them to delete any information which proves to be inaccurate.
- *Equal Credit Opportunity Act* prohibits credit discrimination on the basis of race, sex, origin, age, or marital status.

ENVIRONMENTAL PROTECTION LEGISLATION

- *National Environmental Policy Act* of 1969 established a national policy to produce harmony between the individual and his or her environment.
- *Water Quality Improvement Act* of 1970 established liability for oil spills and increased restrictions on pollution from nuclear power plants.
- *Clean Air Act Amendments* of 1970 and 1977 set deadlines for automobile emission standards and gave the public the right to institute lawsuits against those polluting the environment.
- *Federal Environmental Pesticide Control Act* of 1972 mandated the registration of pesticides and gave the EPA the authority to ban the use of hazardous pesticides.
- *Federal Water Pollution Control Act* amendments of 1972 established controls for the construction of sewage plants and municipal pollutant discharge permit programs.
- *Noise Control Act* of 1972 set national noise standards for commercial products, airports, and aircraft.
- *Safe Drinking Water Act* of 1974 regulates allowable standards for pollutants and chemicals in drinking water.
- *Toxic Substances Control Act* of 1976 banned the manufacture and use of PCB's and mandated the testing of chemical substances considered detrimental to the environment.
- *Toxic Waste Clean-Up Act* of 1980 established funding to clean up toxic waste and gave the EPA the authority to institute legal action against those responsible for toxic spills.

FREEDOM OF INFORMATION ACT (FOIA)

The Freedom of Information Act (FOIA) was passed in 1974 to protect individuals against misuse of information that is on file. All your private records (medical, legal, employment, financial) must be made available to you by the organization maintaining those records.

The Privacy Act, also passed in 1974, goes one step further in that it restricts the dissemination of said files without your permission.

SECURITIES AND EXCHANGE COMMISSION (SEC)

The SEC has quasijudicial powers and serves as the watchdog of the investment market. It was created to prevent the public from investing money in fraudulent securities; and it regulates the trading and issuing of stocks, bonds, and other securities. It further disseminates financial information on companies to potential investors. (The term *security* connotes any investment in which money or property is turned over to another with the intention of making a profit.)

CHAPTER 18

Regulation of Employment

Most laws regarding employer–employee relations have developed on the basis of decided cases. Additionally, the Fair Labor Standards Act regulates minimum wages that must be paid, hours that may be worked, and records that must be maintained by the employer. Each state regulates child labor, safety, worker's (workmen's) compensation, unemployment compensation, and fair employment practices.

EMPLOYER RESPONSIBILITIES

Employers are responsible for enforcing all the rules and regulations contained in this chapter.

EMPLOYEE RESPONSIBILITIES

Employees are responsible for doing the following:

- *Maintain loyalty*—Shall not undertake a business venture in direct competition with employer and shall not divulge any information that is of a confidential nature.
- *Obey reasonable instructions*—Shall obey reasonable instructions that do not impose an unfair burden and are not illegal or immoral.
- *Not be negligent*—Shall act in good faith and perform responsibilities diligently.
- *Be accountable*—Shall keep receipts and accurate records and shall not mingle company funds with personal funds.
- *Give proper notice*—Shall fully inform employer of all acts and facts that affect said employer or place of employment.

UNEMPLOYMENT BENEFITS

Unemployment benefits fall under the mandate of each state; therefore, they differ slightly from state to state. Unemployment benefits are paid to the state by your employer as a form of insurance to compensate you during a time when you may be out of work through no fault of your own. In order to be eligible you must:

- Have worked long enough to have earned enough to qualify.
- Be ready, willing, and able to accept employment.

If you believe you are entitled to benefits, you simply report to the Unemployment Office nearest you and bring in your social security number, your employment records for the last fifty-two weeks, and pertinent information regarding all employers within that period of time (name, address, and so on). At the time you register, you will be apprised of the qualifications and will be issued a booklet explaining all the information for claimants.

EQUAL EMPLOYMENT OPPORTUNITY

It is illegal to discriminate against any employee or prospective employee in the areas of: hiring, promotion, salary, or layoffs on the basis of: race, color, creed, sex, national origin, or age. Also, the testing of employees or prospective employees is prohibited unless it is *directly related* to job performance.

Employee Protection

- The *Equal Employment Opportunity Commission* (EEOC) has the primary responsibility of enforcing equal employment opportunity. EEOC regulations forbid an employer from classifying or advertising job requirements based on gender, unless being male or female can be *proven* to be a valid condition. Additionally, the EEOC has the power to file a civil suit and to represent a person charging the violation of this act.
- *The Equal Pay Act* requires an employer to pay equivalent salaries to men and women for equivalent work.
- *The Fair Labor Standards Act (FSLA)* is commonly referred to as the Wage and Hour Act and regulates minimum wages, overtime compensation, exemptions, and child labor.
- *The Civil Rights Act* was enacted to assure equality in employment in the areas of hiring and firing.
- *The Age Discrimination in Employment Act* forbids discrimination in local, state, and federal government; public and private educational institutions; public and private employment agencies; and labor unions.
- *The Rehabilitation Act* requires government contractors to take affirmative action to promote employment for qualified handicapped workers.
- *The Federal Employers' Liability Act* covers certain employees for disease or injury arising in the course of employment.
- *The Social Security Act* provides retirement and disability benefits based on employee contributions matched by the employer.
- *The Employee Retirement Income Security Act (ERISA)* regulates pension plans and established a branch which insures benefits from private pension plans.
- *Worker's (Workman's) Compensation* mandates that employers have certain responsibilities to employees. Among them are 1) warning them of any hazards involved in their employment, 2) properly supervising their activities, and 3) furnishing a reasonably safe work environment.

All states, therefore, require businesses to carry compensation insurance for death or injuries suffered on the job, and each state mandates its own compensation laws. Worker's compensation covers medical expenses, a portion of worker's salary during the time she or he is unable to work, and payments to a worker's family should death result.

- *The Occupational Safety and Health Act (OSHA)* was enacted to administer health and safety regulations that all employers must adhere to. Although the law's purpose is to provide a safe working environment for all workers, it is especially aimed at industries who traditionally have a high rate of injuries (e.g., manufacturing, construction). OSHA has the power to levy fines on those businesses that do not comply with the law.

CHAPTER 19

Government Regulatory Agencies

Although a free enterprise system prevails, the government has taken an active role in the regulation of many business practices in an effort to protect the rights and general welfare of its citizens. As a result, many regulatory agencies have been established monitoring consumer interests, property rights, fair competition, and so on.

INTERSTATE COMMERCE COMMISSION (ICC)

The ICC has emerged as one of the most significant of the federal regulatory agencies. Its powers include regulating the rates and services of companies that provide land and/or water transportation of passengers and freight. This includes rates, schedules, mergers, services, safety features, and other decisions governing interstate commerce.

NOTE: *Interstate* relates to regulations between states while *intrastate* relates to regulations within state borders. State laws generally govern intrastate transportation.

FEDERAL ENERGY REGULATORY COMMISSION (FERC)

The FERC was created by the Department of Energy Organization (DOE) in 1977. Its responsibilities include regulating the transportation of natural gas and electricity for interstate commerce and regulating the prices of same. It reviews decisions made by the DOE relating to petroleum allocation and prices and assists the Environmental Protection Agency (EPA) with enforcing clean air and water pollution control acts.

FEDERAL COMMUNICATIONS COMMISSION (FCC)

The FCC maintains control of communication networks such as telegraph, telephone, and cable companies. It further allocates and oversees radio frequencies and radio and television stations.

ENVIRONMENTAL PROTECTION AGENCY (EPA)

The EPA is responsible for setting and enforcing standards in all antipollution programs including pesticides, air, noise, water, solid, and toxic wastes.

CONSUMER PRODUCT SAFETY ACT

Under this act, the federal government has placed the burden of legal responsibility on the manufacturer (or seller) regarding compensatory claims for injuries sustained while using a product.

STATE PUBLIC UTILITIES COMMISSIONS

Each state maintains control over its utility companies and provides an arena for the airing of disputes between consumers and utility companies. The state commissions also govern rates and related issues.

CHAPTER 20

Copyrights, Patents and Trademarks

A *copyright* is the exclusive right granted by law to an author, musical composer, playwright, publisher, photographer, painter, and so on, that prevents his or her creative work from being stolen or copied. Copyrights run for a period of twenty-eight years with a renewable option for an additional twenty-eight year period.

Foreign originals are eligible for copyright registration in the United States, and American originals are eligible for copyright registration in foreign countries (provided the United States and the particular country have reciprocal copyright relations).

Further information can be ascertained by contacting the Register of Copyrights, Library of Congress, Washington, DC 20540.

Patent Law, 35 U.S.C. 31; R.S. 4886 applies to any person or company who has ". . . invented or discovered any new and useful art, machine, manufacture, or composition of matter, or any new and useful improvement thereof . . ." After a patent has been granted to the inventor, it may be sold or leased, and said inventor may be paid a royalty for its use. A patent expires after seventeen years and can be renewed only by an act of Congress.

Said invention becomes public property after the expiration date. An American patent protects the invention in United States territories and possessions. One year after the patent has been filed in the United States, it may be applied for in another country.

Further information can be ascertained by contacting the Commissioner of Patents, Washington, DC 20231.

A *trademark* is any coined name, symbol, emblem, device, monogram (initials) autograph, or picture by which a product is identified, distinguishing it from other products. After a trademark has been registered, it should bear one of the following markings:

Registered U.S. Patent Office
Reg. U.S. Pat. Off.
®

Further information can be ascertained by contacting the Commissioner of Patents, Washington, DC 20231.

PART III

Economics And Management

CHAPTER 21

Economics

BASIC CONCEPTS

Private Property and the Profit Motive

The basis for the United States economic system is the concept of private enterprise. Regardless of their size, companies are free to operate in a competitive environment with their success based on *sales*, *profits*, and *ability*. Though most corporations exist in this manner, the government provides certain services and goods to its citizens.

All the objects that a person owns or has exclusive rights to are *private property* and all objects possessed by local, state, or federal governments are *public property*. Businesses and corporations have the same rights of ownership. The following tables provide examples.

Private Property	*Public Property*	*Company Property*
Bicycles	National Parks	Computers
Houses	Street Lights	Delivery Trucks
Furniture	City Hospitals	Copiers

All private property has a worth or market value and its owners are free, within certain defined guidelines, to sell, lease, or give away any of its holdings. The desire to gather and possess private property leads to economic growth. A general marketplace or economic system is created for goods and services with freedom of selection as a major factor to motivate profit making. The entrepreneur is the basis for the capitalistic type of economy.

Supply and Demand

The price of every item and service is based on the factors of supply and demand.

Supply—Quantity of goods available for sale at a given time and place.
Demand—Readiness and capability to buy goods at a given time and place.
Law of Supply and Demand—The price of goods fluctuates directly with demand and inversely with supply.

Society has created a great need for a variety of goods and services, and the economic system must maintain a balance between the goods and services available and the demand for them. Stable prices are the result of balanced supply and demand. Many factors come into play in trying to maintain this balance:

- Economic conditions.
- The amount of resources available.
- Weather conditions.
- Seasonal limitations.
- Location.

The ripple effect has a great influence on the number of employees hired, the materials ordered, and so on.

For example, let's look at the sale of ski equipment. The supply and demand will reach the high point during the months of December through February, and during that time manufacturers will see a potential for high profits. After the season has peaked, however, the demand will start to drop. Lower prices towards the end of the season will encourage the sale of ski equipment thereby creating greater demand. Other factors such as competition and costs of production and merchandising also influence price.

Markets

A place where buyers and sellers can interact with one another is called a *market*. Markets can range in size from worldwide exchanges to the corner store. Their transactions vary from billions of dollars to several cents. Regardless, all fall within the definition of a market.

A *monopoly* exists when one supplier or producer controls the entire marketplace such as in the case of utility companies.

Composition of Output

The goods and services manufactured or produced by a company are generally measured by their total value. The more a company can produce, the greater the value of its output.

Allocation of Resources

The designation of a country's resources to manufacture or supply the goods and services that it requires to function is called the allocation of resources. This includes land, capital, and labor. All resources are limited and must be carefully controlled.

Distribution of Income

The payment that is earned or received from production, sales, or services is called the distribution of income. Income is generally distributed unequally among the individuals of a particular country. Factors that can influence income are: education, ownership of property, natural talents and innate qualities, control of a marketplace, and so on.

Additional Terms

Wages—Money received for labor or services.

Interest—Money received for use of capital.

Profit—Share of earnings after all the expenses have been met.

NATIONAL INCOME AND ITS DETERMINANTS

National Income Measurement Concepts

Countries, like individuals, must keep track of their finances. The amount of income of a nation during a set period of time (usually a year) is called its national income. National income is not calculated as a fruitless exercise; these figures provide us with much useful information. Policies and decisions are established by utilizing this data. The measurements also give us an objective view of the nation's production, distribution, and output; and show relationships among government, business, and foreign economic groups. Another way of defining national income is the total amount of production and resources required for goods and services.

In 1934, the idea for determining the Gross National Product (GNP) was conceived, and in 1942 the numbers were first published. It is perhaps the most well-known measurement used and is defined as the total market value of a country's goods and services produced within a set period of time (generally one year). The GNP is determined quarterly and annually. It is an excellent guide for comparing the standard of living of our country against those of others.

The federal government utilizes other statistics, measurements, and terminology in recording of the nation's economic condition. Listed below are a few of the most common:

Final sales—The items that are purchased by the ultimate buyer and are part of the GNP. (When buying a new automobile, the price of the car is included in the GNP for that particular year.)

GNP deflator—The average level of costs for goods and services in the GNP in comparison to their level in a base year.

Consumer Price Index (CPI)—A comparison of the prices of goods used by consumers from one year to a base year. Over 400 items are considered in this index, and it is used in determining the adjustments in Social Security benefits.

Wholesale Price Index (WPI)—Similar to the CPI except that it compares wholesale prices paid by retailers. It measures alterations in the prices of many industrial and agricultural items.

Real GNP—A true measure of the GNP with adjustments made for inflation.

Inflation—An increase of prices for goods and services. Sometimes computed in terms of changes in the various indexes.

Net National Product (NNP)—The subtraction of depreciation (wearing out) of machines and other items from the GNP. It is the net value of goods and services during a given year.

Personal Income (PI)—The disposable personal income before subtracting personal taxes.

Disposable Personal Income (DI)—The total amount of moneys paid to consumers after items such as personal and corporate taxes have been removed and other items, such as interest payments, have been added to the national income.

Implicit Price Deflator (IPD)—An index that enables one to compare the prices of the GNP of one year to a base year.

Determination Of National Income*

In order for the United States government to determine its national income, three areas must be considered: government, commerce and business, and private individuals.

Though extremely complicated, the calculations use many of the topics discussed previously in this section. The following components are some of the items used in formulating the final numbers:

- *Payment to employees*—Includes salaries of individuals in private industry, government and military personnel, as well as supplements to wages.
- *Proprietor's income*—Includes farm and nonfarm.
- *Rental income*—From individuals.
- *Corporation profits*—With inventory valuation and capital consumption adjustments.
- *Net interest*

*Source: Bureau of Economic Analysis

Fluctuations In National Income

National income and the other measurements can provide both private and public economists with a clear picture of economic conditions. It can be a useful tool in analyzing our status and assists government in establishing fiscal policy.

The measurements give us an index of a country's well-being. Many economists attempt to forecast (predict the future) our growth by using econometrics (measuring the economy with mathematics including models, statistics, and computers).

Because of the tremendously complex interactions among the economic factors involved in the makeup of the national income, fluctuations can occur. A few of the items that can influence the national income are:

- Shortages of essential goods.
- Bankruptcies.
- Government spending.
- Depressions.
- Recessions.

At different periods of time, nations experience varied spurts of growth or declines in economic activity. These trends are observed through the various indexes and measurements, which assist both business and government to respond accordingly.

Growth Of National Income

The table below provides you with some idea of the growth of the United States national income. All numbers are in the billions of dollars.

Year	National Income*
1929	$ 86.8
1933	40.3
1941	104.2
1950	241.1
1970	800.5
1975	1239.4
1980	2116.6
1984	2959.9

The growth of the United States GNP has also changed over the years. All numbers are in billions of dollars.

Year	GNP*
1929	$ 103.1
1933	55.6
1941	124.5
1950	284.8
1970	977.1
1975	1549.2
1980	2631.7
1984	3662.8

*Source: Bureau of Economic Analysis

CURRENT MEASURES OF ECONOMIC PERFORMANCE

In order for a society to evaluate its economic performance, established measuring devices or indicators must be utilized. We have previously discussed the large-scale indicators such as the GNP.

Listed below are other indicators that are used by economists and the business world in comparing and evaluating our economy:

1. Average weekly hours reimbursed to workers (production or non-administration) in manufacturing.

2. Average claims for unemployment insurance per week.
3. 500 common stock price index.
4. Monthly estimate of new businesses formed.
5. New housing starts (index).
6. New order of goods and materials for consumers.
7. Money supply.
8. Changes in credit for consumers and businesses.
9. Changes in twenty-eight materials prices (index).
10. New plant and equipment orders and contracts.
11. Change in inventory on hand or on order from manufacturing and trade.

Output

One method of measuring performance is the amount of output produced. It is calculated on the value of what is manufactured. It should be observed that there is a relationship between output and income; producers earn income from output. Output can be that of an individual, company, or entire nation.

Income

Income, either personal, business, or national, is a measurement of performance. It includes the moneys made from professionals, farmers, corporations, and laborers. It includes interest and rental payments and other sources of moneys. In today's society a person's success is often measured or evaluated by his or her income.

Commodity Prices

Commodities include not only agricultural crops but also cattle, metal, and financial items. The Dow Jones Future and Spot Commodity and other indexes are published each business day to provide a measure of commodity prices and performance.

Businesses can hedge their risk or assign them to someone else through a commodities market. At these locations, futures contracts are bought and sold. Prices are based on supply and demand with daily fluctuations observed. Weather conditions, wars, shortages, and overproduction can all influence the price of a particular item.

Listed below are several of the Futures and Options Exchanges:

Chicago Board of Trade
141 West Jackson Blvd.
Chicago, IL 60604

Commodity Exchange
4 World Trade Center
New York, NY 10048

Chicago Board of Options Exchange
400 South LaSalle
Chicago, IL 60605

Commodities trading is regulated by the Commodity Futures Trading Commission. It keeps a close eye on not only the actual trading of contracts and prices but on the commodity exchange members.

Some of the commodities traded through these exchanges are: gold, silver, copper, wheat, corn, oats, soybeans, sugar, orange juice, cotton, potatoes, T-Notes.

Security Prices

Individuals and institutions buy and sell securities through security markets. Securities prices fluctuate based on supply and demand. Some of the factors that can affect the price of stocks or bonds are:

> *Earning per share*—Net income per share after taxes.
>
> *Dividends*—Part of a company's earnings given to its shareholders (given per share).
>
> *P/E ratio*—Ratio between the closing price of the stock and the company's twelve-months' earnings.
>
> *Hot tips*—Supposedly factual inside information concerning an equity.
>
> *Book value*—The value of a company per share based on its liabilities subtracted from its assets.
>
> *Market value*—The price of a stock at a given time.
>
> *Par value*—The value stated on stock certificates.

There are many securities exchanges around the world. In the United States the following are a few of those present:

- New York Stock Exchange (NYSE) "Big Board."
- American Stock Exchange (AMEX).
- Over-The-Counter Market (OTC).

A common share of stock is ownership in a company. Shareholders have the right to vote on issues and to elect the directors of the company. A preferred share, on the other hand, is sometimes issued by a company. The holders of these stocks are given preference in dividend payments and in some cases, their voting rights are restricted.

Bonds are loans to the company. Bondholders do not own the corporation but rather loan it money. Bonds are generally backed by the assets of the company. If the company fails, the bondholders are paid back before the common shareholders. Debentures, convertible bonds, serial bonds, and sinking-fund bonds are several of the many varieties of bonds located in the financial marketplace.

In order to purchase a stock or bond, one generally deals with an account executive. Account executives can be found at many brokerage houses, including Merrill Lynch, Prudential-Bache, and Charles Schwab and in other financial institutions such as large commercial banks. It must be remembered that the broker is merely a middle person between the buyer and seller of an equity. You will be charged a commission for this transaction.

The Dow-Jones Average and the Standard & Poors Index are two of the many indicators of the securities market. Many others exist and monitor specific segments of the marketplace.

For those lacking expertise or time, another method of purchasing equities is through a mutual fund; a company that raises money to invest in other companies. Mutual funds are extremely diverse and numerous. Listed below are a few of the types of mutual funds available:

Money Market Mutual Funds
OTC Mutual Funds
Growth Oriented Mutual Funds
Income Mutual Funds
Government Securities Funds
Tax-Free Mutual Funds
High-Yield Funds
Ginnie Mae Funds

In order to follow a stock's performance, many of the major exchanges are listed in the newspapers. Often the full name is not used but rather a symbol or shortened version, such as IBM for International Business Machine is listed. Also quoted is the high the stock has sold for during the current calendar year, the low for the year, the current selling price, and other information.

Like many other marketplaces, the securities exchanges are regulated by the government. The Securities and Exchange Commission (SEC) keeps a close eye on the industry for any irregularities.

Interest Rates

There are many different types of interest rates, and a market for each. Some are mortgage rates, bond rates, and United States treasury bill rates. The commonly heard term *prime rate* is defined as the rate given to the best of borrowers. It is one of the lowest rates available at that time. It should be noted that the prime rate can and does fluctuate according to economic conditions.

Corporate bond rates provide a company an opportunity to borrow moneys from investors; however, like any other loan, interest payments must be included. This type of bond is generally considered a long-term rate or investment.

Short-term interest rates or money market rates are generally related to ninety-day treasury bills, short-term commercial paper, and bank certificates (short term). Usually these mature in less than one year. Long-term rates or capital market rates (treasury bonds, industrial, or municipal bonds) mature in periods of longer than one year. The nominal interest rate is the return before adjusting for inflation.

The purchase of EE Savings Bonds from the United States Government for a gift will give the owner varied interest rates during the lifetime of that bond. The interest rate of series EE Bonds may rise, with the market, to any level, but are protected against falling below a set level. This protects the investment during periods of fluctuating interest rates.

During economic periods when the interest rates are high, companies and individuals must pay more to borrow money. This may inhibit economic growth; people tend to think twice before buying a luxury car or home that will entail more expensive borrowing.

Yields

The return of one's money obtained from an equity is the *yield*. Many investors during the evaluation of a security will consider the percentage return on their initial capital. If you take the yearly dividend and divide it by the selling price, the yield is obtained.

For example:

Big Milky Inc.	Current price	$10.00
	Yearly Dividend	.50
	Yield	5%

If the price of the equity rises and the dividend remains the same, then the yield will decrease. For those investors whose goal is income, the yield is an important aspect of a company's financial data.

Wages Per Hours

The wage that a person receives from a company is based on the hours worked. The rate can be preset to a certain monetary value or be determined on productivity (paid per segment).

Several factors that can influence the hourly rates paid to an employee are:

- Legal minimum wage rates.
- Union scales.
- General financial status of the company.
- Overall economic state of the industry and country.
- Skill and value of the employee to his or her employer.

If a company is doing extremely well, employees are generally well compensated. During difficult periods, it is not uncommon for employers to reduce hourly rates and other employee benefits.

Sales

The amount of sales and profits is extremely important to a corporation for they generally determine its success or failure. The higher the sales figures, barring any abnormal circumstances, the better the company is doing.

Publicly held stocks seem to rise in value when their sales and profits improve. Conversely, they can decrease if the sales and profits are lower.

Salespersons strive for increased sales. This will produce more revenue for their company and, if they work on a percentage or incentive plan, more money for them personally.

In order to obtain more sales, departments in larger corporations are established solely with this objective in mind. National or international sales forces are commonplace in huge companies. Smaller organizations with limited funds may have sales representatives or only one salesperson. Regardless of their size, all companies must sell their products in order to survive.

PUBLIC SOURCES OF ECONOMIC INFORMATION

In order to utilize economic data in business decisions, one must be able to first find it. There are many ways to accomplish this feat. Information can be obtained directly from the United States Government or from peripheral sources.

The Bureau of Economic Analysis (BEA) is continually monitoring the nation's economic picture. Its role is to provide data to the government itself, the general public, businesses, economists, and to other interested parties. Below is a sampling of the work it performs:

- National, regional, and international analyses.
- Economic growth and inflation observations.
- Objective observations of production, distribution, and output.
- Analyses of personal income and profits and of the national economy.
- Perspectives on future economic problems.
- Information to government to help influence decision- and policy-making.

Materials from this bureau are available to the public. To obtain information about the BEA's publications and programs simply write to:

> Bureau of Economic Analysis
> United States Department of Commerce BE-53
> Washington, DC 20230
>
> (202) 523-0777

Economic information is also available from many other sources. Listed below are a few of these:

> Periodicals: *Wall Street Journal*
> *Barron's*
> *New York Times*
>
> Data on public companies: *Moody's Investor Services*
> *Standard & Poors Corporation*
> *Million Dollar Directory*

Indexing and other data can be obtained from the following:

> Superintendent of Documents
> Government Printing Office
> Washington, DC 20402
>
> Federal Information Centers (FICs)
> 18th and F Streets NW
> Washington, DC 20405

These sources represent only a small group of those available. They did not include any of the newsletters or economic advisory services that are quite widespread or the numerous government bureaus or agencies that can provide this information.

THE FINANCIAL SYSTEM

Monetary Standards and Money Supply

Money is anything which can be utilized as a medium of exchange. Man has used rocks, shells, and other objects for this purpose. Instead of exchanging goods and services directly (bartering) money is a unit of account. Through it all products and transactions have a common basis.

Money also has a value of "store." Wealth can be held until the owner is ready to purchase another item. An important aspect of money is that it is liquid. Other characteristics that make certain forms of money acceptable are that it can be:

- Divided into different units (nickels, dimes, quarters).
- Transported easily.
- Used as a base with a fairly steady value.

Any change in today's currency would require tremendous alterations in many industries and businesses.

The Federal Reserve System determines our money supply several ways. The results are given out in terms of M 1, M 2, and M 3.*

M 1—The total of traveler's checks, currency, demand deposits, and other checkable deposits.

M 2—It is the total of M1 and also the overnight purchase agreements and Eurodollars, money market deposits accounts, non-institutional money market funds, and savings and small time deposits.

M 3—It consists of M2 plus large time deposits, term repurchase agreements, and institutional money market funds.

*Source: Public Information Department, Federal Reserve Bank of San Francisco.

CREDIT INSTRUMENTS

Negotiable Instruments

In the daily business, it is not uncommon for individuals and companies to utilize various kinds of commercial paper. They can be any of the following:

- Checks
- Drafts
- Notes
- C.D.s (certificates of deposits)

Letters Of Credit

Many companies require a line of credit from their banks in order to function fully. The bank agrees to provide credit to the corporation that is secured. They are generally for a short term and allow the borrower to determine the amount and duration. It is not uncommon for financial institutions to charge a percentage for this service. The borrower is usually screened before this type of credit is established.

Many credit cards offer a personal line of credit. You are permitted to purchase items and use the card up to a specific amount. If this amount is paid back within a certain period of time, no interest is charged. Many financial institutions allow their credit cardholders to withdraw money either from a banking machine or directly from the bank.

Federal Reserve System And Its Role

In 1913, President Woodrow Wilson signed the Federal Reserve Act that established the Federal Reserve System. It created twelve regional banks that controlled the scope of banking in the United States. In Washington, DC a board of governors (seven members) supervises the system. Twenty-five other reserve banks are located throughout the United States. Each reserve bank has its own board of nine directors and each branch of a reserve bank has a board of five or seven members.

The Federal Reserve System
LEGEND
— **Boundaries of Federal Reserve Districts**
— **Boundaries of Federal Reserve Branch territories**
● **Board of Governors of the Federal Reserve System**

⊙ **Federal Reserve Bank cities**
● **Federal Reserve Branch cities**
▪ **Federal Reserve Bank facility**

Source: Federal Reserve System

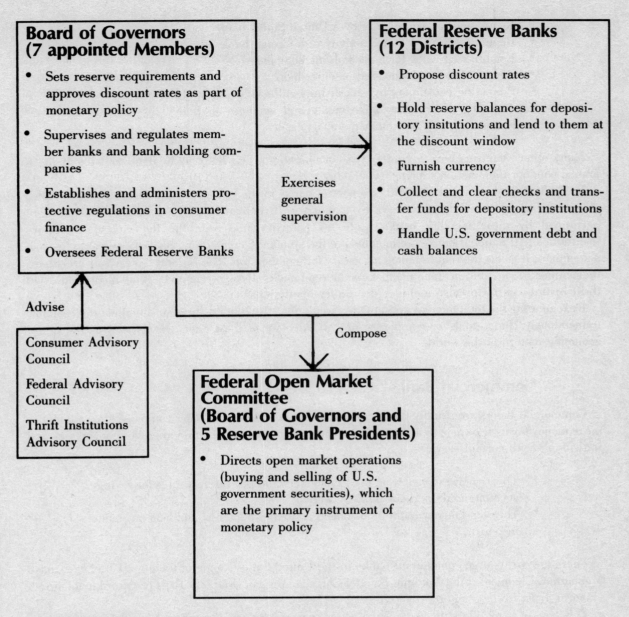

**Board of Governors
(7 appointed Members)**

- Sets reserve requirements and approves discount rates as part of monetary policy

- Supervises and regulates member banks and bank holding companies

- Establishes and administers protective regulations in consumer finance

- Oversees Federal Reserve Banks

**Federal Reserve Banks
(12 Districts)**

- Propose discount rates

- Hold reserve balances for depository insitutions and lend to them at the discount window

- Furnish currency

- Collect and clear checks and transfer funds for depository institutions

- Handle U.S. government debt and cash balances

Exercises general supervision

Advise

Consumer Advisory Council

Federal Advisory Council

Thrift Institutions Advisory Council

Compose

**Federal Open Market Committee
(Board of Governors and 5 Reserve Bank Presidents)**

- Directs open market operations (buying and selling of U.S. government securities), which are the primary instrument of monetary policy

Organization of the Federal Reserve System

Source: Federal Reserve System

By influencing money and credit, the Federal Reserve System attempts to reach the nation's economic and financial goals. The Federal Reserve regulates the amount of money in circulation. Other functions and powers of the Federal Reserve are:

- Altering reserve requirements of member banks.
- Dictating the discount rate.
- Altering the open-market operations.

- Regulating foreign activity by a United States bank.
- Regulating United States activity of a foreign bank.
- Establishing rules for bank holding companies.
- Supervising state-chartered member banks.
- Protecting consumers by establishing rules for credit and borrowing.
- Assisting government departments and agencies in policy discussions, economic goals, and other monetary issues.

Many other countries have a similar type of operation. The Bank of England and the Bank of France conduct their nation's monetary strategy.

In 1983, there were nearly 15,000 commercial banks in the United States. Almost 5,700 of these were members of the Federal Reserve System. Over 70 percent of all commercial deposits were performed by these member banks while 40 percent came from the deposits of depository institutions. All national banks are members of the system. A commercial bank may elect to become a member if it meets the requirements necessary for membership. The Federal Reserve also regulates the nonmember institutions (nonmember commercial banks, foreign-related banking institutions, and thrift institutions.) This also includes depository institutions.

By regulating the total moneys available in circulation, the Federal Reserve can affect the economy tremendously. Individuals or companies are all affected by their decisions as well as the entire economic pattern of the world.

Commercial Banks

Commercial banks are usually profit-making businesses. Like any other company, they attempt to make money for their owners or shareholders. They accomplish this by providing both businesses and individuals with certain services.

- They receive money from their customers and pay interest rates for savings accounts and open checking accounts.
- They lend money to their customers and receive interest and loan payments in return.

There are many large commercial banks in the United States. Some of them are Citibank, Chase Manhattan, Chemical, First National Bank of Chicago, Morgan Guaranty Trust & Co., Manufacturers Hanover Trust Co.

This type of bank offers its customers a wide range of services. A variety of checking and savings accounts as well as other specialized departments (mortgage, trust) are commonplace. These banks also offer advice to businesses through their expert specialized personnel. Many large institutions will assist specific segments of commerce via banking experts most familiar with that field. Many are insured by the FDIC.

SAVINGS AND OTHER FINANCIAL INSTITUTIONS

Besides the commercial bank, there exist other places where the customer can save and receive financial services. Each has its advantages and disadvantages.

Savings Banks

Most savings and loan (S&L) associations offer a line of savings accounts as well as provide mortgage funds to their customers. They can be owned in various ways: depositors, officers of the company, public shareholders, or state and federal government. It is not uncommon to find several branches of S&L located in the same large city or county.

Some of the largest S&L associations in the United States are American Savings, Home Savings of America FA, Great Western Savings FSA, Glendale Savings, First Federal of Detroit, City Federal.

The S&L institutions have been experiencing some difficulties lately. Both the interest rate deregulation and the fall of interest rates have caused a number of associations to fail. The Federal Savings and Loan Insurance Corporation (FSLIC) will protect customers up to $100,000.00.

Investment Banks

In the financial community, the investment bank markets securities for companies. It can be in the form of stocks, bonds, or notes. Many large commercial banks perform this service through a specific division. For this service, the investment banker generally charges a commission.

Insurance Companies

The selection of an insurance company is an extremely important decision. The two general types of companies are:

- *Stock insurance company*—By selling policies, it raises money for its shareholders.
- *Mutual insurance company*—Since the company is owned by its policyholders, the profits are divided as insurance premiums.

Insurance is usually sold through agents. They can work for one specific company or, in the case of independent insurance agents, they can represent several at one time. It must be remembered that since agents often work on a commission basis, you must be very careful before making any purchases.

You should compare prices and the insurance company itself. Find out the company's rating in *Best's Life Reports* and *Best's Insurance Reports* (located at many libraries). The ratings go from A+ to C. The A and A+ signify strength and a quality company.

Insurance companies offer its customers a wide range of policies and plans. Tax-sheltered annuities as well as insurance are available by many companies. Before investing any money (either corporate or personal), a careful analysis should be performed.

Credit Unions

Credit unions are not-for-profit cooperatives. They are owned and operated by their members, and their depositors are usually protected up to $100,000.00 by state or government agencies.

Credit unions offer the following services to their members: savings accounts, payroll deduction, share drafts, direct deposit, loans, education and counseling, credit/debit cards, automatic bill paying, money orders, traveler's checks, and home mortgage loans.

The credit union offers members rights and responsibilities of ownership. They can vote for the credit union directors and committee members. It is not uncommon to find a credit union formed by the employees of a large corporation. There are many in the United States. Credit unions usually charge a loan interest rate lower than that of commercial banks.

Federal Loan Insurance Agencies

Federal Housing Authority (FHA)—This is an agency of the United States Government that regulates the sections of the National Housing Act. It promotes the purchasing and renovation of homes, rental housing, cooperatives, and condominiums. It accomplishes this by providing loans (government-backed) to these owners. Under the United States Department of Housing and Urban Development, it insures loans and mortgages given by institutions.

Federal Deposit Insurance Corporation (FDIC)—It was created under the Banking Act of 1933. Though amended, it currently guarantees deposits in many commercial banks and mutual savings institutions up to $100,000.00 for each account. All the national and state banks (members of the Federal Reserve System) must be part of FDIC. It can also assist member banks which are in trouble by either arranging a merger or assisting them to remain open. It also can regulate insured non-member banks.

Small Business Administration (SBA)—This is a government agency that was established in 1953. It was created to help small businesses by providing advice, loans, loan guarantees, and assistance. Through federal programs, it assists small businesses that have been hurt by riots, natural disasters, and damage. It tries to assist these companies in competing against larger corporations. The Minority Business Enterprise Development Agency was established to assist minority groups as owners of small businesses.

Federal Home Loan Bank Board—It was established in 1932 for thrift institutions. In 1934, it took control of the Federal Savings and Loan Insurance Corporation (FSLIC). It guarantees up to $100,000.00 for each account in a federal and state S&L.

Banking Services

Today's banking services are a far cry from those of years ago. With the complexity of the economic environment, the financial institutions have been forced to open their vistas (within permitted regulations) and offer a great many things to the business community.

Listed below are just some of the services offered by banks: This list is far from complete.

- Checking plans
- Business lines of credit
- Personal loans
- Personal lines of credit
- N.O.W. accounts
- Business loans

- Money market accounts
- Holiday clubs
- Statement savings
- Passbook savings
- Rent security deposit accounts
- Student loans
- Auto loans
- Home improvement loans
- Mortgages
- Free senior citizen services
- Keogh and other pension accounts
- IRA accounts
- Certificates of deposit
- U.S. savings bonds
- Charge cards
- Traveler's checks
- Night depository
- Safety deposit boxes
- Home equity loans
- Life insurance
- Certified checks
- Foreign currency
- Trust services
- Automatic billpaying
- Money orders
- Direct deposits
- Automatic teller machines
- Bond buying
- Brokerage services
- Cashier's checks
- Financial services to businesses
- Payroll deductions
- Home and business computer hookups
- Signature guarantee

NATIONAL MONETARY AND FISCAL POLICY

The Federal Reserve can change the overall money supply by altering the sums of reserves (supply of reserves). Monetary policy can be controlled by utilizing the open market operation (purchasing and selling government securities in an open marketplace); changing the discount rate (rate paid by depository institutions when dealing with the Federal Reserve Banks); and by altering reserve requirements.

Though the Federal Reserve is an independent agency, it still is responsible to the Congress. The Federal Open Market Committee (FOMC) makes decisions concerning the open market operations. The Board of Directors of the Reserve Banks suggests modifications in the discount rate and the Board of Governors has the final word regarding reserve requirements.

The ultimate goals of the monetary policy cannot fully be controlled by the Federal Reserve. Only an intermediate target strategy (targeting the economic variables that the Fed can actually control) can be utilized.

The objectives of the United States monetary policy are:

- High employment.
- No inflation.
- Uniform growth in productive capacity.
- Steady exchange (foreign) equivalency for the dollar.

Through the actions of the Federal Reserve, the average citizen's overall spending ability is controlled. By limiting increases in bank reserves and in the money supply, the Feds can attempt to stabilize inflation. Conversely, during recessionary periods, the Federal Reserve will increase bank reserves to stimulate borrowing. Overall, the Federal Reserve plays an important role in regulating our economy. Often it is indirect and somewhat limited but none the less most significant.

BUSINESS INVOLVEMENT IN CURRENT SOCIAL AND ECONOMIC PROBLEMS

Regardless of a company's size, location, or product line, social responsibility is a must in the overall management decisions and goals. Business ethics and social involvement generally play an important role in a company's basic philosophy and policy. Should a company fail to address considerations, often the government steps in. Business is faced with two problems in this regard:

1. Carrying out of these objectives.
2. Making sure that they are working as desired and planned.

At the same time, business must produce profits and answer to its shareholders. In order to handle this dilemma, many large corporations have established Public Affairs Departments.

These departments handle:

1. Public relations.
2. Lobbying.
3. Company contributions.

Personnel departments, also known as human resources departments, now play an important role in many companies.

They must deal with:

1. Constantly changing regulations in Equal Opportunity Programs.
2. Occupational Safety and Health Administration (OSHA) and other employee health and safety regulations.
3. Assisting employees with personal problems or job related situations.

Pollution Control

The Environmental Protection Agency (EPA) attempts to keep our environment free of the various types of pollution: water, air, hazardous wastes, and so on. Through legal means, it can either fine or close companies that harm or threaten our surroundings. Many energy-saving and antipollution devices are in use. Several methods of curbing pollution are:

1. Emission devices on automobiles.
2. Recycling bottles and cans.
3. Cleaning waterways.

Consumerism

There has been a recent movement among consumers to take a firm stand against unfair business practices. The most popular consumer advocate is Ralph Nader. As a result of his and other similar efforts, many consumer protection laws have been legislated. In order to handle this situation, many large companies have set up consumer affairs departments and hot lines.

The old saying "let the buyer beware" is outdated. The government, through the Federal Trade Commission (FTC), has the power to investigate and react to corporate abuses.

Examples of consumerism are:

1. Unit pricing in supermarkets.
2. Access to credit ratings.
3. Recalling of defective products such as cars.

Conservation of Natural Resources

All natural resources are limited in quantity. The oil embargo in the 1970s was one of the most recent reminders of this. Companies and nations alike must learn to conserve all natural resources before they are depleted completely. Alternate methods will have to be developed and the Federal Department of Energy has established many plans to assist corporations.

Examples of resource conservation are:

1. Reduced highway speed limits.
2. Tax incentives for energy conservation.
3. Developing energy-saving devices.

Equal Employment Opportunity

In 1964, the Civil Rights Act mandated that discrimination was illegal, including discrimination in employment and job-related activities. The Equal Opportunity Commission (EEOC) was established to control this act. Further legislation has only reenforced this concept.

Areas covered by this act are:

1. Increased employment for women and minorities.
2. An end to job discrimination on the basis of race, religion, sex, or country of origin.

The EEOC helps employers in setting up Affirmative Action Programs. Examples of equal employment opportunities are:

1. Promotion of females and minorities.
2. Purchasing of supplies from minority-owned companies.

International Trade

The importing and exporting of products and services among the nations of the world is international trade. World trade exists among almost every country including China and the Soviet Union. It would be very difficult for any nation to be 100 percent independent of all goods and services.

The advantages of international trade are that it:

- Promotes harmony.
- Lowers prices through specialization.
- Enables you to purchase items not readily accessible.
- Eliminates the need to grow or manufacture everything.

The disadvantages of international trade are that it:

- Creates a vulnerability and defensiveness.
- Opens the doors to boycotts.
- Fails to protect American workers and their wages.
- Makes it difficult for newer companies to compete.

Terminology used in international trade:

Imports—Bringing and purchasing foreign goods into a country.
Exports—Selling of goods to another country.
Tariffs—Taxes on items from abroad.
Revenue tariffs—Obtain money for a government.
Protective tariffs—Increase the retail price of foreign items.
Embargo—Ban on items.
Import quotas—Limits number of items to be imported.

Common Markets

An agreement among several nations to formalize trade rules is called a Common Market. Examples of Common Markets are as follows:

LAFTA—(Latin American Free Trade Association) Argentina, Bolivia, Brazil, Chile, Mexico, Paraguay, Peru, Uruguay, Columbia, Ecuador, and Venezuela

EFTA—(European Free Trade Association) Austria, Iceland, Norway, Portugal, Sweden, and Switzerland. (Finland is an associate member.)

EEC—(European Economic Community) Spain, Portugal, France, West Germany, Italy, Belgium, Luxembourg, Netherlands, Denmark, United Kingdom, Ireland, and Greece.

Balance of Payments

The association between the movement of money in and out of a nation is called the balance of payments. Ideally, it is best to have a greater amount of money coming into a country than leaving it. Areas included in determining the balance of payments are: trade, tourism, financial assistance to foreign nations, military expenses, American investments abroad, and the tremendous imports of oil and other products.

Balance of Trade

The association between a nation's imports and exports is termed the balance of trade. It is better to export more goods and services than you import. This situation is called a favorable balance of trade. Conversely, if the exports are less than the imports, you have an unfavorable balance of trade.

International Finance

Each working day, the ratio of worldwide moneys changes in relation to each other and to gold. This is called the exchange rate. Though intended for large financial transactions, it can affect many aspects of our lives; for example, traveling to foreign countries and purchasing items from abroad. The rates are crucial for international trading and can cause the success or disaster of a company.

Examples of currencies on the foreign exchanges are:

Argentina—Austral
Austria—Schilling
Canada—Dollar
Denmark—Krone
France—Franc
Italy—Lira
India—Rupee
Japan—Yen
Mexico—Peso
Saudi Arabia—Riyal
Spain—Peseta
West Germany—Mark

Supply and demand can influence these ratios daily.

The International Money Fund (IMF) was established to assist nations economically. It issues SDRs (a world currency) that can be utilized among governments. The IMF also assists countries in foreign exchanges.

Many large corporations have specific personnel that monitor the exchange rates and assist in policy making regarding international trade and business. Some will buy and sell various currencies to protect their investments against any large rate differences.

Large international banks and other financial institutions can help smaller businesses by following the exchange rates. Most also will provide advice if requested by these companies.

Multinternational Business Operations

A corporation that does business on an international basis or scope is considered a multinternational business. Many companies function in several countries; for example, in some countries for production and in other countries for sales and management. It is not uncommon recently to find many foreign multinternationals setting up business in the United States. An example is Japanese automobile manufacturers.

These companies can invest directly or indirectly in a foreign country. They can establish divisions abroad or purchase stock positions in corporations.

Several multinternationals outside the United States are as follows:

- Royal Dutch/Shell Group
- Renault
- Siemens
- Fiat

Several United States multinternational companies are as follows:

- Exxon
- Colgate-Palmolive
- Johnson & Johnson
- Coca-Cola
- Ford Motor

There are many reasons for a company to go international. Some of the advantages are: to locate the best economic and geographical conditions for the company, to be able to purchase raw materials and goods cheaper, and to sell at a high profit elsewhere.

Nothing is perfect and the multinational corporations have their disadvantages. Several are: may influence local politics, there is a fear of losing the company through nationalization, there are language differences, exchange rates fluctuate, and foreign laws and customs vary.

The elaborate and complex intertwining of today's multinternational business are unparalleled. This type of operation continues to grow accordingly.

CHAPTER 22

The Nature and Functions of Management

FORMS OF BUSINESS ORGANIZATION

There are many ways in which a business can be formed. A lot of thought must be given to the appropriate format as all have advantages and disadvantages. Using a good attorney and accountant before actually structuring the business configuration and design may save the owner(s) a great deal of money and aggravation. One is no better than another, overall; each should be utilized when indicated.

Individual Proprietorship

An individual proprietorship is defined as an entity that is owned by one person. Business size is generally small. This type of operation usually has a limited life and is dependent upon the owner for existence. It is the easiest and least expensive to run. This entity has no separate tax structure; it is based solely on those of the proprietor. Advantages are as follows:

- Simplicity—The owner and employees (if any) are the organization: The owner keeps all the profits; the owner makes all the decisions; the owner can sign any contract for the business.
- Less costly to operate.
- Fewer regulations and reporting requirements.
- Credit is based on the owner and not limited to the strength of the business.
- No double taxation.

Disadvantages are as follows:

- If the owner dies or becomes disabled, the business could terminate.
- All liability falls on the owner.
- The strength of business depends solely on the owner's abilities and skills.
- Unless sold, the business has a limited life.

89

Partnership

A partnership consists of two or more individuals who organize (unincorporated) to form a business or to achieve a common goal. Each shares both the profits and losses. The size of the partnership can range from two to a huge international group (CPA firms). More legal regulations exist because of the greater number of owners. It is a voluntary association.

Often in business dealings and tax shelters, we see the terms *limited* and *general partners*. A general partner actually runs the operation while the limited partner is generally the investor and has no say in the actual running of the organization. The general partner can be held liable for all the obligations of the partnership while the limited partner is only liable to the amount of his or her investment. Since each partnership is different, each must file a separate tax return (in addition to those of the individual partners).

When a partnership is first formed, the individuals involved must agree to a partnership agreement. Though an oral agreement is acceptable, a written agreement is preferred. A lawyer should be utilized and the agreement should include such items as capital requirements, types of partners, salaries, liquidation procedures, and many other pertinent topics. A poorly written agreement can cost each partner a great deal of money, time, and distress.

It should be noted that this form of business endures only as long as the partners themselves. Each partner within the group can act as an agent for the remainder of the partners with the normal business activities. Therefore, great care and thought should be given before signing a partnership agreement with another individual(s). All assets are jointly owned by all the partners within the partnership.

Advantages are as follows:

- Easy to form and less regulated than corporations.
- Shared responsibilities among partners.
- Greater resources than a sole proprietorship.
- Not subject to a federal income tax.
- Capital borrowing is based on all the partners rather than one individual.
- Liabilities are shared among the partners.
- Partners can act freely; they do not have to answer to shareholders.

Disadvantages are as follows:

- Must share profits.
- Partnership has limited life.
- Each partner is liable for others in the partnership.
- May be costly and difficult to end a partnership.
- Any partner can act as an agent for the partnership.

Corporations

A corporation is an entity that is approved by a government upon an application of a group of persons. These individuals are called incorporators. The owners can also be called shareholders or stockholders, but they are not the corporation. The corporation is an artificial person and separate from its owners.

Once approved, a corporate charter is prepared. It will define the rights and obligations of the corporation. Bylaws are also prepared to establish details of the corporation (shareholders' meetings, officers, directors, and so on.)

Though not involved with the daily running of the corporation, the real owners are the shareholders. They have the power to elect the board of directors and can raise issues at the shareholders' meetings.

Advantages of the corporation are as follows:

- Separate entity from its owners (shareholders).
- Unlimited life.
- Shareholders are not liable for actions of the corporation.
- Shares of ownership can easily be given to another person.
- Allows companies to raise capital easily.
- A shareholder cannot bind the corporation into a contract.

Disadvantages of corporations are as follows:

- *Extra taxation*—corporations are subject to federal and in many cases state and local taxes. Shareholders are also taxed on any dividends received (double taxation).
- *Tremendous government rules and regulations*—Publicly traded companies are also regulated by the Securities and Exchange Commission (SEC).

S Corporation

An S corporation permits its owners to be taxed as if they were a partnership rather than subjected to the double taxation that exists for a standard corporation. This generally applies to certain kinds of small domestic corporations and the level of taxation depends on the shareholder's tax bracket. Many of the benefits of a regular corporation exists for the S corporation.

Professional Corporations

When ever you see the letters PC, PA, or whatever, on your accountant's, lawyer's, or physician's stationery or sign, realize that they do not stand for a professional degree but rather that he or she is functioning as a professional corporation. Though recent legislation has caused many professionals to not utilize this type of corporation, some continue to operate in this mode. A good lawyer and accountant can advise as to the pros and cons. The professional corporation is costly to set up and maintain, limited as to pension and deductions, not available to every person, and generally under close watch by the IRS. Certain tax advantages still make this attractive to many professionals and include medical and dental expense reimbursement plans, life and health insurance plans.

Conglomerates

In order to enlarge a corporation, the management often elects to merge with other companies. A conglomerate is created when a grouping of separate companies (all producing or manufacturing different items) are merged via their corporate stock. By using this method, the management hopes to achieve vigorous expansion and augment their earnings. Because this growth has occurred in assorted areas, antitrust backlash has been minimal.

Three examples of conglomerates are: Gulf & Western Industries, Litton Industries, and LTV.

Holding Companies

Any corporation that has stock of another corporation is considered a holding company. By acquiring this stock, the company attempts to gain control and the second company becomes a subsidiary of the holding company. Control is obtained by establishing the policies and selecting the officers of the subsidiary. Government agencies, such as the SEC, keep a close eye on potential mergers and purchases of stock to prevent a monopoly from developing.

Foundations

A foundation is a nonprofit organization with funds. It is not government affiliated and usually obtains its moneys from a person, family, or company. The foundation is governed by trustees who establish grants for charitable, educational, social, or religious purposes. The IRS identifies different types of foundations and sets very strict rules and regulations on how they can handle moneys, how they give it away, and who shall receive it.

Four common types of foundations are:

1. *Company-sponsored foundation*—Funds are provided by a profit-making company but the foundation is run by a separate board of trustees.
2. *Operating foundations*—These are private foundations whose purpose is research or social welfare.
3. *Independent foundations*—These make grants and are generally sponsored by a family or person.
4. *Community foundations*—Funds come from many donors.

Syndicate or Joint Venture

The joint venture type of business relationship is common in real estate situations. It comprises two or more individuals joined for a restricted function and it differs from a partnership in that it lacks the formal relationships and responsibilities. For example, several people buy land together and hope to sell it at a future date.

When a group of security firms function together to sell a security (on a temporary basis), the situation is called an underwriting syndicate. A syndicate exists when a transitory firm or company is established to fulfill a specific reason or goal. Once it is achieved, the syndicate is ended.

Cooperative

A cooperative is a form of incorporation that is common in agriculture and retailing. The co-op or cooperative is not designed to make money but rather to benefit its members in other ways, for instance, by buying and selling goods to members at low costs. They differ greatly from corporations and have very specific regulations and laws. Consumer co-ops have been established in many areas to enable their members to purchase foods at near wholesale costs.

DECISION-MAKING PROCESSES

Logical Reasoning

In order for any businessperson to make a good decision, he or she must evaluate several methods or approaches. Making the correct choice is not performed randomly by the business professional but is the result of careful analysis and research. Rationally looking at and studying each course for the desired goal(s) is the method utilized by experienced personnel. The following paradigm illustrates the process.

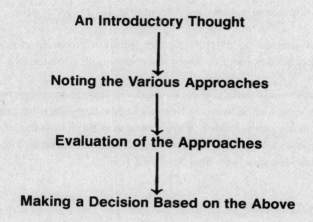

An Introductory Thought

Noting the Various Approaches

Evaluation of the Approaches

Making a Decision Based on the Above

In order to rationally make a decision, you must be aware of the available data. Once you have collected this information, then and only then, can you logically and rationally make a wise decision. In reality, today's businesspeople must sometimes act quickly and often under pressure, but a good businessperson will weigh as many choices as possible and then attempt to come up with a good logical and rational answer.

Quantitative Analysis Techniques

In the decision-making process, there comes a point when the individual is faced with several choices or paths of selection. One of the critical steps is to evaluate each of these and to choose the one best suited for the desired goal. Besides utilizing experience, analysis and research, and experimentation, the manager can utilize three quantitative analysis techniques to accomplish this feat. These are discussed below.

> *Use of statistics*—The use of statistics and computers is widespread in business. Common areas of usage are: identifying cycles and movements, analysis, and formulas and models. Two drawbacks are the initial costs of staffing and equipment and the inability to be one hundred percent correct all the time.
>
> *Operations research*—The use of scientific applications to evaluate the choices in decision-making. It does not give the exact answer but provides the businessperson with enough quantitative information so that decisions can be determined rationally and with some basis.

Important parts of operations research are:

- Constructing the problem area.
- Making up a model (mathematical).
- Obtaining an answer from the model.
- Analyzing the model.
- Setting restrictions on the model and selections.
- Making the model operational.

When utilizing a distribution logistics model, you can evaluate the entire flow of goods throughout a business. Some of the other applications used in operations research are:

- Linear programming (establishes the optimum grouping of resources).
- Probability theory (occurs based on change and probability).

Decision tables—By using this method, a businessperson is capable of determining all the avenues that his or her decision might take. Because of the many complexities, a computer may be necessary in constructing this type of table. The table(s) provide major available alternatives and gives an idea of where decisions can lead.

Brainstorming

This is a technique used by business to assist problem-solving by locating new and unusual ideas. It is a group approach in which all members participate freely. All thoughts are considered and each is carefully scrutinized. Far-reaching ideas are encouraged and each group member builds to improve any good idea that the group develops.

CONTROLLING

Controlling is the managerial function of evaluating, changing, and/or directing employees toward certain goals and objectives. It further involves determining whether or not the objectives are being met, whether or not progress is being made, and correcting shortcomings that stand in the way of meeting the objectives.

The Control Process

Whether controlling money, employees, products, or whatever, the same principles should be considered. One must first develop standards. After this plan has been devised, one can then utilize these standards to gauge and evaluate whatever is being observed or appraised. Finally, once deviations are observed, corrections and changes must be performed. Often a deviation may be positive in nature and can actually enhance the existing situation. Controlling should be influenced by past, present, and future performances of a company.

In order for controls to really work, they must be:

- Specifically fitted to plans and jobs.
- Specifically fitted to individual supervisors.
- Objective, but not completely rigid.
- Cost-effective, accessible, and remedial.
- Comfortably situated within the company.

Standards and Standardization

In a small situation, a supervisor might be able to personally watch everything, but in a large company this is impossible. Therefore, a supervisor must select certain critical sites to observe. By doing this, the manager can ascertain overall performance easily and effectively.

Every operational procedure and business function has standards (or they can be established) to which performance can be compared. Listed below are some of the more common standards:

Physical—Generally observed at an actual operating situation. Noted in degrees of quantity (numbers produced by a particular group), quality (cloth durability), and time (units per day by a particular machine).

Cost—Put monetary measures at an operating situation (labor costs per hour).

Capital—Applying costs and monetary measures to real items (ratios of assets to liabilities).

It is generally safe to say that once good standards are established and objectively practiced, the standardization process is accepted by all those concerned.

Management by Exception

There is an management principle that states: the greater the supervisor's concern and constraining of exceptions, the greater the control will be. This is known as management by exception. Once standardization has been developed, the supervisor must be constantly alert for any exception to the established norm.

COMMUNICATING

Communications is the transmitting of data from one individual to another. The individual receiving the information must comprehend the intended message.

Communications is vital to any company. It connects and combines individuals within the association into one entity. Through communications, alterations can be easily performed throughout an entire group or corporation. It must be both internal and external in nature to be most fully effective.

Everyone working for a company is accountable and each utilizes communications to some degree. The correspondence can be either downward (from the upper echelon of the company to the staff below), upward (from staff to the upper echelon), or lateral (staff from same levels or different levels).

Three forms of communication commonly used:

1. *Oral*—Word of mouth.
2. *Written*—Memos and letters.
3. *Nonverbal*—Body or facial movements.

As companies increase in magnitude, their network of correspondence also grows. Many have specific personnel who handle the external flow of communications and internal controls, such as restricted information. Good communications are vital to the company's growth and overall success.

Policies and Procedures

Like any other aspect of corporate life, set policies and procedures should be established for communications. This can protect the company from a multitude of situations including, but not limited to, lawsuits, poorly directed public announcements, misunderstandings.

By developing a set procedure of communications, the organization can allow all employees to channel their concerns or thoughts to the appropriate source. In this manner, the corporation will be strengthened, by serving the desires and needs of its workers.

Formal communications concerning practices, and procedures must also have written guidelines. Job descriptions, procedure manuals, handbooks, and media communications should all be formally written and controlled by corporate policies and procedures.

Meetings

While many organizations complain that there are too many meetings and that they take up a lot of time, they do provide an opportunity to exchange opinions, share experiences, and often develop solutions to problems. Communicating at a meeting can be accomplished at several levels.

- *Upward*—Communicating with people in higher positions of authority.
- *Downward*—Communicating with people in lower positions of authority.
- *Lateral*—Communicating with people in equal levels of authority.

Feedback

One of the essentials of good management and communications is feedback. To ensure that the information received is correct, feedback is important. In an ideal situation, the receiver should be able to respond, but often supervisors tend not to listen or become indifferent to the responses given. Many companies offer courses to their managers and other personnel on effective listening and communication skills.

CHAPTER 23

Fields of Management

HUMAN RESOURCES MANAGEMENT

Composition of Labor Force

In order to fully comprehend the American labor force, you must use classifications such as sex, race, education. The chart below will give some idea of the changes that have occurred within recent years to the work force in America.

Civilian Labor Force By Race, Sex, and Age

Race, Sex, and Age	Civilian Labor Force (millions)						
	1970	1975	1980	1982	1983	1990	1995
Total*	82.6	93.8	106.9	110.2	111.5	125.0	131.4
White	73.6	82.8	93.6	96.1	97.0	107.7	112.4
Male	46.0	50.3	54.5	55.1	55.5	59.2	60.8
Female	27.5	32.5	39.1	41.0	41.5	48.5	51.6
Black†	9.2	9.3	10.9	11.3	11.6	13.67	14.8
Male	5.2	5.0	5.6	5.8	6.0	6.7	7.3
Female	4.0	4.2	5.3	5.5	5.7	6.9	7.6
Male	51.2	56.3	61.5	62.5	63.0	67.7	70.0
16-19 years	4.0	4.8	5.0	4.5	4.3	4.1	4.0
16 and 17 years	1.8	2.1	2.1	1.6	1.6	1.7	1.8
18 and 19 years	2.2	2.7	2.9	2.7	2.7	2.5	2.3
20-24 years	5.7	7.6	8.6	6.6	8.6	7.2	6.5
25-34 years	11.3	14.2	17.0	17.6	18.0	19.6	18.1
35-44 years	10.5	10.4	11.8	12.8	13.4	17.5	19.4

Civilian Labor Force By Race, Sex, and Age

Race, Sex, and Age	Civilian Labor Force (millions)						
	1970	1975	1980	1982	1983	1990	1995
Male (continued)							
45-54 years	10.4	10.4	9.9	9.8	9.7	11.1	13.8
55-64 years	7.1	7.0	7.2	7.2	7.1	6.4	6.3
65 years and over	2.2	1.9	1.9	1.6	1.8	1.8	1.7
Female	31.5	37.5	45.5	47.8	48.5	57.3	61.4
16-19 years	3.2	4.1	4.4	4.1	3.9	3.8	3.8
16 and 17 years	1.3	1.7	1.8	1.6	1.5	1.5	1.6
18 and 19 years	1.9	2.4	2.6	2.5	2.4	2.3	2.2
20-24 years	4.9	6.2	7.3	7.5	7.5	7.0	6.8
25-34 years	5.7	8.7	12.3	13.4	13.8	16.8	16.3
35-44 years	6.0	6.5	8.6	9.7	10.2	15.0	17.4
45-54 years	6.5	6.7	7.0	7.1	7.1	8.7	11.1
55-64 years	4.2	4.3	4.7	4.9	4.9	4.6	4.7
65 years and over	1.1	1.0	1.2	1.2	1.2	1.3	1.3

*Beginning 1975, includes other races not shown separately. †For 1970, Black and other.
Source: U.S. Bureau of Labor Statistics, *Employment and Earnings,* monthly and *Monthly Labor Review,* November 1984.

Sex—The number of women in the labor force is increasing. Despite recent advances, women doing jobs similar to the jobs of male counterparts are often paid lower salaries. It is hoped that parity will occur in years to come so that both males and females will be treated equally by employers, businesses, and professional societies and organizations.

Education—High school diplomas or equivalency degrees are more commonplace in the adult labor force. It is almost a prerequisite for obtaining respectable employment. In many cases, a college degree or even post-graduate work, such as M.S., M.B.A., Ph.D., is required to obtain management or white collar positions. Generally, salaries are greater for individuals having more education than those without a diploma or degree.

Age—It is not unexpected to find that the majority of our labor force is between twenty-five and forty-four years of age. During the earlier years, many drop out to attend colleges or women leave to establish families. In the later years, many workers retire from active employment. The average worker's median age is increasing steadily, causing stiff competition among members of this group.

Job Analysis

The means of establishing the specifications and provisions of a job and the requirements of an employee for that job is called job analysis. Aspects such as developing other skills and methods of evaluation should also be considered in this process.

Job Description

The job description is a declaration of the job to be performed. It should include the responsibilities and functions of employment, which often are listed in the order of their importance. The job description will assist in the following ways:

- Provides job facts and data during interviews
- Reminds employees of their responsibilities
- Introduces new employees to their positions
- Provides data if grievances occur
- Appraises employee accomplishments during employment

Job Specifications

The requirements that a person must have in order to fill a job description are called job specifications or "job specs." Job specifications can vary widely but some of the more common areas included are: education, previous experience, and abilities needed.

In larger businesses where there are many specialized positions, job specifications will assist the job placement interviewer screen potential employees. Care must be taken by all employers not to discriminate when establishing their job specifications.

Job Evaluation

In order to properly evaluate a position, one must either run a correlation between jobs in the same company or observe a correlation between the job and measuring system. This procedure assists in developing a relationship between wage and salary rates. Several of the more common methods of job evaluation are as follows:

1. *Point system*—A manual is usually established that lists standards for each position. Various factors and degrees are developed that, in turn, break down to points. Job specifications are next standardized with each one rated as to a factor and point worth. Once the points are totaled, the job is put into a position based on the evaluated total number of points and the wage rate is given to the position.
2. *Factor comparison system*—It is similar to point system but differs because the factors of job specifications are compared to key position specifications within the company. Instead of an established point scale, a factor comparison should be part of the job evaluation.
3. *Grade system*—Jobs are categorized and placed into preset grades or classes of wages. It is quite simple to implement but less exact than the

point and factor comparison systems (civil service classifications are an example of this method).

4. *Job ranking system*—Jobs are put in order from the highest to the lowest. The rankings are evaluated by job descriptions and placed in the sequence of hierarchy and then are grouped into classes. Every job within each class will be paid at a rate previously determined. This system is used basically for very small businesses.

Recruitment and Selection

Once a company's manpower requirements are known, the next function is recruitment. Recruitment will fill both immediate needs and also find potential employees for future vacancies. Many circumstances can influence recruitment success. Some of these are: salary offered, benefits, quality of present personnel, and the extent to which the company is growth-oriented.

Affirmative action has altered the way today's businesses conduct themselves. All potential employees must and should be considered regardless of race, age, or sex. The Equal Employment Opportunities Commission's (EEOC) guidelines should be followed at all times.

The recruitee will look objectively at the employment package available. Since most interviews are for a short duration, it is imperative that the recruiter make the best presentation of the company during this time, and lastly, realize that selections are often based on judgment, "gut" feelings, and preconceived ideas.

Methods of recruiting personnel or filling vacancies are as follow:

- Advertising (Newspapers, magazines, trade and professional journals).
- Searching within the company itself.
- Referrals from current or present employees.
- Agencies.
- School and college recruiting.
- Union hiring halls.

The expense of hiring and training personnel in a company is very high. In order to minimize this, careful selection is essential. During this process, the individual responsible must make a judgment or decision as to which candidate he or she believes will succeed best in the vacancy. The purpose is to locate an individual best-suited for a particular job.

There are many methods of selecting the applicant. Some are listed below:

- *Job application*—Essential information is provided along with the applicant's skills in writing, organization, and thoughts.
- *Interviews*—The interviewer has a chance to evaluate the candidate in person.
- *Testing*—Many types of tests are used (performance, intelligence, aptitude). All tests should be valid and the examiner should fully understand the procedures and limitations of every test. If the testing is not directly job-related, it may be illegal.
- *Physical exam*—Anyone unable to meet the physical requirements of the position should be screened out.

- *Credential and qualification investigating*—Checks should be made with former employers and references. (This could include educational background.)

Some larger corporations utilize assessment centers in evaluating and selecting managers and executives. The centers place the candidates in realistic situations and observe how the applicants react to stress and other businesslike simulations.

Training and Development

The success and ability of a business is often contingent upon the training its employees receive. This is true of both new and established workers since positions are becoming more complex with changes often occurring quite rapidly. Some other reasons for training individuals are:

- Preparing for advancement.
- Stimulating working potential.
- Keeping up with new developments.
- Developing employee—employer relationships.
- Enhancing morale.

Training personnel takes place not only formally but with almost every incident that the employee faces. The educational process is generally present from many avenues within the organization and it is up to the management to attempt to filter out anything negative and try to educate the employee along accepted guidelines and objectives. Much care should be taken when determining how employees are taught. In larger companies, special departments are assigned to this task. Computers, programmed instruction, and simulators can also be utilized to train employees.

Training can occur both on the job or in classrooms, in lectures, seminars, and other off-the-job activities. Some of the areas that are generally covered are:

- Newer ideas and methods.
- Remedial education and reeducation.
- Advancement assistance and education.
- Assisting of displaced and disadvantaged individuals.
- Apprenticeship education.

In order for any training and development program to be successful, all involved must have a clear understanding of the educational and learning process. They, themselves, must be familiar with methods of motivation, behavior modification, interference, and other principles of the psychology of learning. They should also be aware the special needs of minorities and female employees.

Periodically, the training and developmental program should be evaluated. Several of the methods available are: responses of teachers and employees and doing pre- and post-performance testing.

The development of an executive or manager is somewhat more difficult at times. Programs should be used not only for education but also for motivation. The development can be performed by the mentor system (coaching), position and responsibility rotation, committee assignments, and a series of projects and experiences. Off-the-job education can take the form of lecture courses and conferences, company institutes, professional associations, and further management schools.

Employee Performance Appraisal

It is not uncommon for a formal employee performance appraisal to be conducted on a regular basis. With the advent of the EEOC, employers find that they should have complete and precise records of an employee's performance.

In many cases, the company's personnel department develops the performance program. Other members of the business should assist during this process and in the actual evaluation with the employee. Several reasons for the evaluation are to give the employee an idea of his or her job performance and to give supervisors information for future positions.

The phases of evaluation are:

1. Develop criteria for standards and tell employees (criteria must be appropriate, objective to the position, and reliable).
2. Apply standards to employee's actual work.
3. Perform a comparison between actual work and the criteria.
4. Do a performance appraisal with the employee and make corrections where necessary.

Managers are usually best-suited to administer the appraisal because they usually see the employee on the job and have a working knowledge of the tasks. Often peer review, self-evaluations, and subordinate appraisals are used to judge an employee's performance. Any manager or supervisor who is responsible for evaluations must be properly educated in performing the task.

Some of the modes of performance evaluation are the following:

- *Rating scale*—Each criteria is rated by the evaluator to the extent that he or she believes is indicative of the employee's performance.
- *Essay*—Statements are written about the performance.
- *Checklist*—Statements are checked regarding the performance.
- *Ranking*—Employees are ranked as to performance.
- *Critical-incident*—This records critical facts.

Purely objective performance evaluations are often difficult. Some factors that can deter this goal are: a too lenient evaluator, restrictions of rating systems, and evaluator subjectivity. Businesses can improve appraisals by using several properly trained raters and by allowing raters to evaluate areas with which they are most familiar.

Request for employee transfer, promotion, demotion, or layoff are some of the possible actions resulting from the employee performance appraisal. Each must be handled carefully and within accepted guidelines in order to avoid any future difficulties.

One popular method for performance evaluations is called management by objectives (MBO). A manager and subordinate, together, describe goals and objectives and then clarify what each is expected to do (plan of action). Once this is performed, individual appraisal is instituted. Regular reviews are common and revised when indicated.

Compensation Administration

Compensation is of enormous interest to both an employee and an employer. Since the moneys paid to employees represent a considerable portion of a company's expenses, care must be taken to delegate these funds effectively to insure both profits and the ability to exist. If well-paid, the employee's incentive to produce will probably be greater. Both parties' requirements must be considered and carefully researched for both to survive. Compensation policies are essential to help supervisors develop critical decisions.

Rates can be paid in a variety of ways. Wages are usually paid on an hourly or daily basis whereas salaries can be distributed weekly, biweekly, or monthly. An employee's salary is governed by many factors. Some are: supply and demand of work force, comparable salaries or wages, difficulty of position, bargaining agreements, and inflation.

Incentive Plans

There are many reasons why an employer uses an incentive plan. Each company may function differently in the actual plan (stock, money) but in reality the method is designed to keep employees on the job and to increase productivity.

Plans can vary according to positions. Incentives for the laborer can be based on piecework while a salesperson's plan may be commissions and/or salary and bonus. Executives usually receive stock or cash incentives. Many corporations possess profit sharing, and employee stock investment plans.

Merit Plans

Many corporations utilize merit ratings to compensate employees above their established salaries and wages. As with incentive plans, merit plans are designed to promote productivity and enhance employee moral.

Merit reviews, special merit rating forms, and a merit interview are usually common. Supervisors must grant raises on an employee's performance and not subjectively. If not handled properly, this type of plan can do a great deal of harm to employee morale and to the company's overall employer–employee relationship.

Employee Benefits

Compensation given to an employee by an employer besides salary or wages is called benefits (often called fringes or fringe benefits). Benefits now account for over thirty percent of the payroll expenditures and this figure could increase in the future. Most benefits are for the protection of the employee in some way covering many possible negative circumstances. Since all employees are usually covered by these benefits, their sole purpose is not strictly motivation. Performance is not a criteria for coverage.

Reasons why benefits have increased include requests by unions and employees, owners' moral responsibility.

Types of benefits possible but not given to everyone:

- *Money for time not actually worked*—Vacations, holidays, jury duty, unemployment benefits, bonuses instead of vacation, paid sick days, military leave, money for time off for personal reasons or death in the family, lunch periods, and rest periods.
- *Insurance*—Disability insurance, life insurance, accident insurance, medical and dental insurance (including prescription and optical care), membership in health maintenance organization (HMO), workmen's com-

pensation, social security (survivors and disability), and automobile insurance.

- *Health*—Employee health services (on the job), wellness education and equipment, counseling for alcohol, drug abuse, nutrition, health club membership or discounts, and yearly physicals.
- *Retirement*—Pensions, preretirement programs, profit sharing and stock ownership programs, and annuities.
- *Required benefits by law*—Social security, old age, survivors, and disability benefits, unemployment compensation, and worker's compensation.
- *Additional benefits*—Financial services, legal and accounting services, recreational and social activities, tuition refunding, credit unions, housing, purchasing discounts, day care centers, paid meals, subsidized loans, corporation automobiles, country club membership, credit cards, free transportation, and moving expenses.

It is not uncommon in large corporations to have a separate department that deals exclusively with benefits. Those in charge not only supervise and administer programs but also keep up with new legislation and regulations in this area.

Employee Suggestion Systems

The use of employee suggestion systems is commonplace in American industry. Once started and fully accepted by management, the system can provide a twofold benefit. First, the company can profit from their employee's knowledge and experience. It can add many new ideas or correct existing methods. Second, it will increase employee motivation and provide him or her with a company spirit.

The use of a suggestion box is most prevalent. The employee will utilize a special form and drop it into the box. All suggestions are considered and evaluated by either a committee or manager. In many cases, a financial reward is given to any suggestion that is employed.

Union–Management Relations

Two major areas where union and management must work together are contracts and methods of handling complaints. The labor agreement or contract is a formal pact that establishes the terms of employment by union members. These contracts can run for one or more years in length and require much skillful negotiation by both the union and management personnel. Often a mediator is called in when a deadlock is reached. In some cases, the government may intercede in a deadlock by sending in a fact-finding board. The agreement may cover one small company or include all the workers of a particular trade, e.g., United Federation of Teachers, AFL-CIO.

Coalition bargaining occurs when one company bargains with several unions at the same time. The final contract is usually quite long and covers many aspects of employment (wages, benefits, layoffs).

The company makes decisions regarding personnel; however, the union can file a grievance if it believes the terms of the contract have been negated. If both union and management cannot come to terms, then a arbitrator will be called in to make a decision—which is final.

Many companies oppose unionization for the following reasons:

- Decisions affecting personnel are carefully screened and examined.
- Both are bidding for the employee's allegiance.

- Contracts establish strict guidelines for union members.
- Company must deal with non-employees in negotiations.

The management must develop a good working relationship with not only employees but also with the union. In order to function, this association must be professionally handled from both sides if the company itself is to survive. Unions have used strikes, picketing, or boycotts while companies employed lockouts.

Starting in the 1930s, the government became drawn into the topic of labor–management relationships. The Norris–LaGuardia Act, Wagner Act, Taft–Hartley Act, Landrum–Griffin Act, and others established regulations concerning this area. The civil rights and women's movements have been instrumental in the passage of additional laws forcing adjustments in policies and procedures of the union and management.

With foreign competition and other topics clouding the future of both labor and corporations, the trend has been toward more cooperation between the two forces. In order to continue and be successful, both must understand the other's needs and work together to compete in a new and different world.

PRODUCTION MANAGEMENT

The terms *manufacturing* and *operations management* are often used synonymously with production management. The production manager must be aware of his or her employees as well as the techniques that will improve production efficiency.

The production manager must become involved with the company's planning, organizational development, and controlling procedures and policies if the corporation is to operate maximally. Using models and systems, he or she can make both decisions and develop alternate choices to achieve the goals and strategies of the company.

Utilizing management skills, the production manager can evaluate growth patterns and economic shifts and adjust production and operations accordingly. As the technology changes, the operations or production manager must assimilate these changes and alter the company's operations. Cost, inventory, and quality control are all functions of the production manager.

Facilities

The location of a new facility is extremely important to any company. The site must be properly situated if the goals and objectives are to be achieved. Aspects such as cost and revenue must be carefully examined and studied before any decision is made. The production manager should gather data from many sources and utilize models to evaluate each and every possible site. Factors such as transportation, sources of employees, economic considerations, and transforming newer technology should be considered in establishing a final decision.

The management of international corporations entails many of the factors already discussed as well as others. Social or cultural differences and the lack of natural resources may have to be taken into consideration. The transition to an international scope is a difficult and involved task for the production manager and requires a great deal of skill and ability.

Materials

Procurements

Procurements, the buying of equipment as well as materials for the company is the responsibility of the production manager. Creating a smooth and efficient system is a difficult task. Not only is the initial buy important but subsequent purchases must insure a steady inflow of materials to the company. Any loss of momentum could result in tremendous hardship in the manufacturing process.

Since procuring materials requires capital, the production manager should aim to buy correctly. Aspects to be considered are quality, service, and price.

In larger companies, purchasing agents perform this task. They must be fully aware of the company's needs and activities in order to purchase correctly. An incorrect decision can reduce profit and even cause financial ruin to the corporation itself. Regardless of the business size, a definite plan for procuring items, equipment, and materials must be clearly established. Lists should be prepared and reevaluated on a regular basis showing vendors, essential or priority items, costs.

Buying the correct amount of materials is extremely important. Purchasing too great a quantity can lead to an inventory buildup that ties up the company's capital. Systems must be established to ensure a continuous flow of materials into the company.

Purchases can be made by contracts with suppliers. This can insure a steady supply of goods and price stabilization. Competitive bidding is essential and should be utilized.

Purchasing agents should attempt to buy honestly and intelligently. Only the quantities actually required should be procured and inventories should be maintained at a working level.

Processing

The production manager receives the materials and must then decide which process is to be used by the company. Processing is critical and must be carefully selected.

The process best suited for a particular company requires knowledge, management skills, and constant observation. Labor costs should not be the main consideration for any process but rather many factors must be considered.

Aspects to be studied when evaluating a process are:

- Different available techniques.
- Equipment available.
- Specifications to be accomplished.
- Methodology available to employees.
- Controls available.

In order to fully evaluate a process, thought must be given to the company's goals and objectives. Considerations for future technological alterations must be also developed. Modernization is essential when indicated and it is the responsibility of the production manager to lead in this function.

Control

The production manager must orchestrate the entire process of control. In order to accomplish this feat, he or she must have control over every situation. Each small segment must be directed in order for the entire system to function efficiently.

Organized controls over the quality of materials ordered and the frequency of ordering are essential. Control is essential over the following:

- Scheduling of orders.
- Transmitting of orders.
- Checking up on orders.

Methods and Quality Control

One of the chief jobs of the production manager is to organize work. He or she must possess the ability to depict jobs, establish criteria, and to measure work performance.

Many methods of establishing jobs or positions are available. Flow and activity charts are utilized for this function. Other considerations are human anatomy and physiology and environmental status. It is essential that the production manager use accepted and up-to-date concepts in developing these methods. Standards should be given the same thought and planning.

Quality control is interwoven with other functions of production management. Product quality is the ratio of the final product to the original specifications. If the quantities are numerically close (and the ratio is small), then a high degree of quality exists. Quality of a product should also be observed and determined along the entire stage(s) of development. Maximum quality controls can be established at all levels of production with nothing left to chance. The entire process must be clearly established and implemented with set criteria previously determined. Many companies will place quality considerations during the actual designing stage and will continue this control even if a redesign or modification is executed.

Product reliability and quality assurance are aspects of the manager's concern and are included in the control process. Many larger corporations have specific personnel whose sole job is to monitor and check the quality of the company's materials and products.

Methods of quality control include the following:

- Inspection (raw materials, during actual development, or final product).
- Random sampling.
- Control charting.

It is imperative that the quality control manager try to instill motivation in employees as a method to maintain and improve quality within the company. Today's consumers are quality-oriented and an organization must consider this important aspect in order to compete successfully against other companies.

Planning and Scheduling

An organized plan for operations must be developed. It should cover the entire scope of the business—from basic resource(s) determinations to the final product. Every aspect must be carefully planned out and considered.

Planning examined by the production manager:

- Complete study of the working process.
- Create uniformity of the working process (policies, procedures).

- Development goals to conform with the company's objectives.
- Study possible present and future needs and events.

The manager must plan both the physical facility as well as the actual process itself. At all times workers' limitations and requirements (present and future) are to be considered. The use of models can assist the manager in developing and evaluating his or her plan.

Planning also encompasses a business's capacity. This must include: evaluating the present physical plant and forecasting any future requirements and studying all possible alternatives or substitutes. Thought must be given to economic conditions and present and future technology.

Decisions concerning layout must be meticulously planned. Their design affects the actual running of the entire operation. Each step along the way must be very carefully developed and evaluated. All layouts should be designed to meet predetermined objectives and goals. The use of models can assist the manager in his or her final decision concerning layout.

Once a plan has been established, scheduling must be determined. At all times, the goals of the company must be kept in mind. The number of employees, stock and inventory, use of employees and independent laborers, and other aspects must be considered. The manager must attempt to utilize the correct number of employees as needed and balance the amount of stock according to demand. Service companies may find that scheduling varies season to season, e.g., lawn service must schedule more personnel in the summer than in the winter.

MARKETING MANAGEMENT

Marketing Policy

Crucial to any company is the functioning of its marketing management. Products can be created or manufactured, but in order for the company to survive these items must be sold (to create capital). All marketing systems must be carefully thought out through the process of planning, carrying out, and evaluating.

The planning stage involves several aspects. Management must develop specific goals and objectives. They must determine what is to be achieved and why. To avoid any problems, these must be completely written out. The objectives should be realistic and not too vague. A good objective might be: To increase our yearly sales from $50,000.00 to $100,000.00 next year. It is specific in time frame and easily mathematically measured.

The next step is to create a plan of action in order to accomplish the objectives and goals previously set. Both tactics and strategies are utilized. Tactics are short-term operations that assist the overall strategy.

Policies should be established to prevent deviations from plan of action developed previously. It serves as a guide to management.

Strategic planning usually occurs with top management and then filters to the marketing department. Important aspects of strategic planning are the following:

- It is an entire company concept.
- Strategic business units (SBU) are used in very large companies. Each division or unit will act as a separate operation and each must be responsible for profits, production, and marketing.

- Strategic market planning contains an examination of the corporation's present status, establishing goals and objectives for marketing, determining the target market, and the development of a strategic marketing mix (product, price, promotion, and distribution or place).

Advertising

Any paid type of communication (written or oral) about a product or idea by an identified sponsor is called an advertisement. They are nonpersonal and are distributed through the media. Advertising can be for a specific product and idea or be cooperative in nature. They can be for: a new item or service, comparing those already in the marketplace, or reminding the consumer or purchaser of an established product or service.

Marketing management directs the following advertising policies:

- Determines the target or audience for advertising.
- Establishes goals and objectives.
- Determines capital expenditures available.
- Develops ads and chooses media.
- Analyzes advertising.

Advertising can be performed from either the company's own department or from an outside agency. Often, in larger corporations, the two will work together to formulate ideas and concepts.

Sales Analysis and Control

Sales analysis and data will assist the marketing manager in the evaluation of overall performance and objective accomplishments. Using information obtained from the sales force, a manager can evaluate the strategy and procedures currently being utilized. Such data can also assist the sales force through recommendations and other decisions.

Sales performance can be based on amount of sales, number of orders, and number of accounts.

Once planning has been achieved and the company's salespersons are working on achieving set goals and objectives, a manager must evaluate the personnel and control their actions. Supervision is often difficult because of the very nature of their working relationship; however, close communications must be developed between the manager and his or her staff. Other methods commonly used are reports and meetings.

Market Analysis

Consumer Behavior

Once a target market has been chosen and goals selected, the marketing manager must determine the general approach to take. One possibility is market aggregation (one mass market), and the other is market segmentation (small, homogeneous parts). In deciding which avenue to pursue, subjects such as sales potential and financing must be considered.

The consumer or industrial purchasers must be evaluated. Both are extremely different and must be marketed individually.

Divisions of consumer markets can be determined along the following lines:

- Arrangement of population (regionally).
- Age and sex.
- Population breakdown (urban, rural, suburban).
- Race, education, occupation, and religion.
- Income distribution.
- Social and psychological factors.

Divisions of industrial markets can be determined according to:

- Type of market (government, agriculture).
- Total marketplace or size of industrial buyers.
- Regional placement of buyers.
- Amount spent by users.
- Methods of purchasing.

In order to fully comprehend the marketplace, the marketing manager must understand his or her ultimate buyer. Consumer motivation (including physiological and psychological aspects), perception, and cultural changes (roles of women, alterations in today's family, changes in work and free time, and methods of purchasing) must be considered.

The marketing manager must be aware that this country and other countries are melting pots of many subcultures. Other areas of concern are social classes, and special interest groups.

All these factors and others must be studied carefully before any final decision is made by the market manager or staff. The ultimate success of a product, service, or the corporation itself may depend on it.

Forecasting

The ability to predict the outcome or success of a product or service is essential for the marketing manager. He or she attempts to determine the impact of the company's product and to estimate the potential sales volume. Strategy and planning must be developed before forecasting can be accomplished. Forecasting usually is performed on an annual basis. The use of computers has made this process quicker and less costly. Several methods of forecasting are the following:

- *Sales force composite*—Gathering data from the company's salespersons.
- *Executive judgments*—Opinions from executives.
- *Testing of markets*—Exposure of a product to a small limited area.
- *Survey of purchasers*—Sampling potential customers.
- *Analysis of previous sales*—Based on the history of past sales.
- *Correlation methodology*—Use of mathematical formulas.
- *Product replacement*—Replacement of an older product with a newer one.

Transportation

The function of a traffic manager is to ensure that his or her company utilizes the fastest and cheapest forms of transportation. The manager must be able to analyze all modes of transportation and objectively select the best. The ability to check freight billing and to negotiate the best prices is essential. The traffic manager must be fully aware of local, state, federal, and international rules and regulations governing the company's products and transportation of such items. Common methods of transportation are railroads, trucks and motor carriers, airplanes, and ships and other water vehicles.

PUBLIC RELATIONS

The public relations (PR) department is the connecting arm between the company and the public. The public relations manager and staff utilize mass media to contact the public. A skill in communications is essential for all members of the PR staff. Functions of public relations departments include:

- Improving communications between the public and the company.
- Providing company information to the public.
- Dealing with government agencies, stockholders, and consumer activists.
- Assisting in lobbying.
- Alerting executives concerning community changes and other relationships affecting the company.

The public relations department can be set up in-house or an independent firm can be enlisted. Often a business with its own PR department will use an outside source for either assistance or a second opinion. Management must carefully regularly evaluate the actions of their public relations department.

PART IV

Accounting

CHAPTER 24

Principles and Procedures

Assets

The economic resources or properties of a business or person are called assets. They hold value because they can assist the person or company sometime in the future. Types of assets are:

- Cash.
- Accounts receivable (moneys owed from sales or services).
- Inventory (merchandise held by a business).
- Land.
- Equipment.
- Building(s).
- Rights by a patent or copyright.

Liabilities

The amounts owed to others by a business or person are called liabilities. Types of liabilities are:

- Accounts payable (moneys owed to creditors for buying goods and services).
- Taxes payable.
- Mortgages payable.
- Notes payable.
- Moneys owed to employees (wages and salaries).

Owners' and Stockholders' Equity

The interest of the owner(s) in a business after the liabilities have been satisfied from the assets is called the *owners' equity*. Corporations display a section called shareholders' equity on their balance sheets. In determining this number the following information must be known:

Paid-in capital (or contributed capital)—It is the amount invested by the shareholders and equal to the assets contributed by the corporation.

115

Retained earnings—Funds obtained from profits that are retained by the company. Any losses are debited to this section and a debited balance in this area is called a deficit.

Ralpho Corporation:

Paid-in Capital	$500,000.00
Retained Earnings	(9,000.00)*
Stockholders' equity	410,000.00

*( ) indicates a loss

Revenue

The amount that is obtained from services provided and goods sold is called *revenue*. Revenues are produced in different ways by various companies and individuals. Examples are: physician—revenue from treating patients; shoe store—revenue from selling shoes.

Expenses

The amount of assets utilized or liabilities received while obtaining revenue is called *expense*. An example is a music shop—expenses from rent, instruments, electricity, sheet music, salaries, insurance, and so on.

Income

The excess of moneys received after expenses is called *income*. *Net income* is the amount of moneys received that exceeds expenses. *Net loss* is the amount of expenses that exceeds the moneys received.

ACCOUNTING CYCLE

Analyzing Transactions and Recording

Prior to recording of any transaction in accounting, a careful examination must be performed by the individual responsible for this function. Each transaction must be investigated thoroughly to determine where and what should be transcribed.

It is essential that all businesses (as well as the government) keep accurate records of their transactions. Directly and indirectly, these records are necessary for making objective business decisions and setting present and future objectives. Recording of transactions must also be performed by individuals for tax purposes and for sound financial management. An accountant must analyze all transactions carefully and then perform a professional and accepted method of recording this data.

Posting

The process of transposing or recording information from a journal to a ledger is called *posting*. The ledger contains the accounts for the company and is usually performed on a daily or continual basis. Information recorded when posting in a ledger includes the following:

- Date of the transaction.
- Amount of the transaction (either credit or debit).
- Page number of the journal where the transaction is entered.
- Ledger account number, placed in the Posting Reference column to act as a cross-reference.

The posting procedure does not involve any analysis of the transaction; it is only the writing of the transaction in the ledger.

Trial Balance

Once posting is finished and the balances for all accounts are revealed, it is beneficial to see if the ledger debits equal the ledger credits. The *trial balance* is a test of all the accounts to see if they are in balance. It will show the title and balance of every account and is most useful in preparing balance sheets and income statements. It is not a formal report and is generally never observed by anyone other than an accountant or bookkeeper. The trial balance will not prove that no mistakes or errors have been made; it merely records what is actually written.

Work Sheet

In order to expedite the financial statement, an accountant usually develops a work sheet. (It is a large piece of paper with columns.)

Using a completed work sheet facilitates:

- Locating and correcting errors easily.
- Preparing financial statements.
- Calculating net income.
- Closing the entries of a journal.

Typical Worksheet

Account	Trial		Adjustments		Adjusted Trial Balance		Income Statement		Balance Sheet	
	Dr.	Cr.	Dr.	Cr.	Dr.	Cr.	Dr.	Cr.	Dr.	Cr.

Dr. = Debits   Cr. = Credits

Each column is completed by the accountant with the correct amounts posted properly.

Financial Statements

Records that provide financial data to a user are called financial statements. They can be utilized in several ways. The four main financial statements are:

1. *Income statement*—Shows the outcome of a business, person, for a set amount of time (yearly, monthly, quarterly).

SUSAN THOMAS GIFT SHOPPE
INCOME STATEMENT
FOR THE MONTH OF DECEMBER, 19XX

Revenues:

Sales of gift items	$12,000.00	
Sales of pictures	10,000.00	
Sales of antiques	15,000.00	
Total Revenue		$37,000.00

Expenses:

Salaries	$14,000.00	
Rent	1,000.00	
Utilities	500.00	
Insurance	1,000.00	
Advertising	500.00	
Costs of gift items	5,000.00	
Costs of pictures	5,000.00	
		$27,000.00
Net Income		$10,000.00

---

2. *Balance sheet*—Shows financial status on a particular date. This is usually done at the end of each business day and is often called the statement of financial position.

SUSAN THOMAS GIFT SHOPPE
BALANCE SHEET
AS OF DECEMBER 31, 19XX

ASSETS		*LIABILITIES*	
Cash	$25,000.00	Accounts payable	$9,000.00
Gifts	20,000.00	Owner's equity	
Antiques	42,000.00	Susan Thomas, Capital	
Pictures	15,000.00		45,000.00
Supplies	5,000.00		
Furniture	6,000.00		
		Total liabilities	
Total Assets	$113,000.00	and owner's equity	$54,000.00

---

3. *Statement of changes in financial position*—Shows changes of a financial position during a particular time.

SHARONMAR COMPANY
STATEMENT OF CHANGES IN FINANCIAL POSITION
FOR THE YEAR ENDED DECEMBER 31, 19XX

Sources of Working Capital	
From Operations:	
Net Income	$150,000.00
Land Sales	140,000.00
Total sources of working capital	$290,000.00
Uses of Working Capital	
Purchase of equipment	89,000.00
Building construction	100,000.00
Total Uses of working capital	189,000.00
Net Increase of Working Capital	$101,000.00

4. *Statement of owners' equity*—Shows data concerning how an owner's equity has changed over a period of time.

CHARON PERTAL LAW FIRM
STATEMENT OF OWNER'S EQUITY
FOR MONTH ENDED DECEMBER 31, 19XX

Charon Pertal, Capital, December 1, 19XX		$25,000.00
Additional income		45,000.00
Total investment		65,000.00
Add: Net income for December	$85,000.00	
Less: Withdrawals for December	50,000.00	
Increase of capital		35,000.00
Charon Pertal, Capital, December 31, 19XX		$100,000.00

Adjusting and Closing Entries

Entries made in a journal show results of the numerous transactions that contribute to a company's financial status. It is not considered practical to keep these accounts to demonstrate all daily changes. Therefore, in order to obtain an accurate end-of-period statement, certain accounts may have to be adjusted to show any items not recorded in the transaction entries. They are usually done on the final day of a financial period and are called *adjusting entries*. Without adjusting entries, financial statements would be incorrect.

Adjusting entries must be performed to account for the following:

- Costs that must be recorded in two or more accounting periods (prepaid rent, supplies, and insurance as well as depreciation expenses for fixed assets).
- Revenue received in advance (deferred or unearned revenue) must be placed in a liability account until the service or products are delivered.
- Expenses that have occurred but will not be paid during an accounting period (accrued expenses).
- Revenues earned but not received during a particular accounting period.

When using a work sheet, adjusting entries are usually shown, but not necessarily in the journal (if less than one year). All adjusting entries situated on an annual work sheet must be recorded in a journal.

Closing entries are performed to allow one to observe any alterations in an owners' equity account and to start temporary accounts with a balance of zero at the beginning of a new accounting period.

In order to close entries, the following must be accomplished:

- Revenue and expense accounts are cleared. They are closed and their balances moved to an Income Summary Account.
- At the Income Summary, these balances are summarized and then transferred to the owner's Capital Account.

Date	Account Titles & Explanation	Post. Ref.	Debit	Credit
19XX				
Dec 31	Sales		2800.00	
	Income Summary			2800.00
	To close the revenue account			
31	Income Summary		2000.00	
	Salary expense			875.00
	Depreciation Expense			125.00
	Rent Expense			1000.00
	To close to expense accounts			
31	Income Summary		5000.00	
	James Smith, Capital			5000.00
	To close net income to capital			
31	James Smith, Capital		2500.00	
	James Smith, Drawing			2500.00
	To close withdrawals to capital			

Posting-Closing Trial Balance

Since it is quite simple to make mistakes in adjusting and closing entries and accounts, a trial balance is performed to retest the numbers of the accounts. This procedure is called a posting-closing trial balance. It is the final check and insures that the ledger is balanced.

KIMBERLY FARINA REAL ESTATE
POSTING-CLOSING TRIAL BALANCE, Aug 31, 19XX

	Debit	Credit
Cash	$ 2,000.00	
Accounts receivable	6,000.00	
Prepaid rent	800.00	
Office supplies	200.00	
Office equipment	1,000.00	
Accumulated depreciation (office equipment)		100.00
Accounts payable		4,000.00
Salaries payable		4,000.00
Kimberly Farina, capital		1,900.00
	$10,000.00	$10,000.00

ACCOUNTING AND COMPUTER SOFTWARE

Many companies are utilizing computers to streamline the work generated by their accounting and bookkeeping departments. By using the proper accounting software, many reports and routine operations can be handled in a more efficient and timely manner.

Some of the many features that software can accommodate are:

- *Payroll*—Generates payroll checks automatically; prints checks and W-2 forms; adjusts for employee overtime, vacations, sick leave, and so on.
- *Accounts receivable*—Handles credit limits, payment discounts, and status of accounts in collection; produces mailing labels; and establishes invoices and/or balances.
- *Accounts payable*—Automatically updates inventory and general ledger, prepares payments, computes discounts, and processes debit and credit memos.
- *Inventory*—Supports LIFO (Last in–First out), FIFO (First in–First out), and weighted averages.
- *Manages reports*—Produces graphs and other detailed reports, assists management in accurate business decisions by forecasting techniques, and even checks spelling.

These represent only a small sampling of the entire range of computer software features that are available. As with any management decision, great care should be exercised in the selection. A wrong decision can cost a business a great deal of money and a tremendous loss of time. Many computer stores offer excellent support systems; therefore, care should also be exercised in selecting the one from whom to purchase your program(s).

CHAPTER 25

Balance Sheet Accounts

ACCOUNTING FOR CASH RECEIPTS AND DISBURSEMENTS

Cash Receipts

Items Deemed Cash Receipts

The term *Cash Items* or *Cash Receipts* refers not only to coins and currency but also to checks, drafts, and money orders that are payable to a company. The balance of a cash account as well as the cash on a balance sheet include the total of the checking account and the cash actually on hand.

It is extremely important that correct accounting procedures be utilized for cash receipts. Care must be taken to prevent errors as well as stealing. One method is to use a system that requires duplicate receipts (one copy is used to compare with the actual deposit slip and the other is given to the bookkeeper who will use it for the recording process).

In many retail operations, the cash register will record all transactions, and its tape can furnish a listing of all that has taken place. Another method is a twofold receipt system. One receipt is given to the customer while the other is kept for accounting procedures. In many cases the bookkeeper will not actually handle the cash but rather only the cash receipts. Mail receipts must be treated in a similar fashion.

Cash Receipts Entries

Date	Account	Explanation	Amount
19XX			
Feb. 1	Martin Bass	Check	$175.29
Feb. 1	Sally Smith	Check	554.90
Feb. 1	Catherine Sherwood	Cash sales	32.89
Feb. 1	Sandra Thomas	Bank draft	433.75
Feb. 1	Rose Benjamin	Postal money order	566.75
Feb. 1	Millie Ferranto	Cash sales	61.48
Total Cash Receipts			**$1825.06**

Internal Controls

As growth occurs in any company, its owner(s) find that it is impossible to supervise all aspects of the business. At some point during this expansion, a decision must be made to delegate responsibilities to others and to institute an internal control system to help management.

An internal control system that is selected must be able to secure and protect assets, produce correct accounting information, enhance management's capabilities, and conform to the company's administrative doctrine. Both accounting and administrative supervision is essential if any control system is to work. Management, however, is ultimately accountable and obligated to develop and sustain a good healthy method of internal control.

Public companies are regulated by the Securities Exchange Act (SEC) and by the Foreign Corrupt Practices Act. These businesses' accounting systems require that tight internal control methods be utilized at all times.

Internal control must accomplish the following:

- Delegating responsibility to key personnel.
- Developing, maintaining, and updating of accounting policy and procedure manuals.
- Allowing assorted personnel to perform action(s) on a transaction.
- Employing good personnel and performing internal audits (including separate and independent checks and balances).
- Utilizing good accounting procedures and maintaining proper security for documentation and assets.
- Considering use of computers and cost factoring.
- Constantly evaluating the internal control system and making essential alterations.

One-Write System

Many businesses utilize a one-write system. It is also called a pegboard system because a pegboard is used to hold the forms in alignment.

With this system, an error cannot be performed in moving figures from one page to another since the journal and subsidiary ledger are the same as the check or receipt. The system can also be useful for payroll and purchasing goods.

Cash Disbursements

Cash Disbursements Records

The journal utilized for cash receipts is somewhat similar to that for cash disbursements. Obviously, accurate bookkeeping is essential for any business concerning its purchases or disbursements. A purchases journal and a disbursements journal differ slightly but not significantly. The cash disbursements journal records all disbursements by check. The larger the corporation, the more staff is required by the accounts payable department to handle the tremendous number of checks written by the company.

Purchases Journal

Date	Account	Date of Invoice	Terms	F	Amount
19XX					
Nov. 5	Ajax Company	11/3	n/30		$750.00
5	Mike White	11/3	n/30		125.00
9	John Paul Co.	11/8	n/10		24.50
15	Liza Pam Co.	11/12	n/30		654.99
26	Harold Gordon	11/24	n/20		34.00
30	Total—Purchases				$1588.49

Cash Disbursement Journal

Date	Ch. No.	Payee	Account Debited	F	Other Accts. Debit	Accts Pay. Debit	Pur. Disc. Cred.	Cash Cred
19XX								
Nov.								
6	21	Gen. West	Purchases		20.25			20.25
8	22	J.T. Co.	J.T. Co.		5.25			5.25
17	23	Foe Corp.	Foe Corp.			24.50		24.50
25	24	Max Mayra	Salary		35.00			35.00
29	25	Giff & Co.	Giff & Co.			22.85	.85	22.00
30					60.50	47.35	.85	107.00

Trade and Cash Discounts

A reduction off the list price (standard retail or catalog price) is a trade discount. It is usually utilized by producers and wholesalers when selling to retailers. Trade discounts can run as high as one-hundred percent and are used to save the costs of reproducing new catalogs. This type and amount of discount can vary from customer to customer (jobbers, retailers, and wholesalers).

This system permits a retailer to give customers a copy of a catalog without exposing the true costs. The discounts can be either singular (e.g., forty percent) or in a progress or chain.

Trade Discounts

Gross of invoice	. . . .	$200.00
Less 40%	. . . .	80.00
Net amount	. . . .	$120.00

Gross of invoice	. . . .	$200.00
Less 20%	. . . .	40.00
Balance	. . . .	160.00
Less 10%	. . . .	16.00
Balance	. . . .	144.00
Less 10%	. . . .	14.40
Net amount	. . . .	129.60

Trade discounts are not entered in the account of the buyer or seller. It only is a decrease in the price of the merchandise.

Cash discounts are decreases of the price of the merchandise for paying the moneys owed quickly. When a company utilizes the cash discount method, it appears on the invoice and is a section of the credit terms. Cash discounts are the following:

3/10, n/30—If a bill is paid within ten days (the discount period) of the date on the invoice, the purchaser can deduct three percent off the price. If it is not paid within the ten days, then the buyer must pay the full amount within thirty days (n = net).

4%/E.O.M., n/90—If the bill is paid by the end of the month (E.O.M.) of which the invoice is dated, then the purchaser will receive a four percent discount of the gross price. After that time, no discount is given and the bill must be paid within ninety days of the date of the invoice.

3/20/E.O.M., n/90—The payment is due within ninety days of the date of invoice and a three percent discount will be given if paid within twenty days of the end of the month in which the invoice is dated.

The benefit of a cash discount is twofold. It saves the purchaser money by paying the invoice within a stated period of time and it allows the seller to obtain money faster.

Sales discounts (seller's name for a cash discount) are recorded in the manner illustrated in the following example:

A manufacturing company sells $500.00 worth of toys to a retail customer on June 12. The credit terms were 4% E.O.M., n/60. If the buyer pays by the end of the month of the invoice, it is recorded as follows:

June 15 Cash	$480.00	
Sales Discounts	20.00	
Accounts Receivable		500.00
Received payment for		
sale of June 12 less		
the discount		

If the customer does not pay within the discounted period, it is recorded as follows:

August 15   Accounts Receivable $500.00
              Sales   500.00
              Sold toys on credit,
              terms 4% E.O.M., n/60.

Imprest Petty Cash

Many companies establish a petty cash fund so that small amounts of money can be paid easily for minor expenses. Items such as stamps, small office supplies, shipping costs, and telegrams are often covered by the petty cash fund. By developing such a fund, time and additional expenses are saved (eliminates the need for many checks made out for small amounts). The best method for controlling a petty cash fund is when it is established as an *imprest fund*.

Imprest funds are characteristic by the following:

- They contain a fixed amount of capital which is replenished regularly from other sources.
- They are supervised by one individual who is responsible for the fund.

Establishing Petty Cash Funds

A sound manager will estimate the amount of capital required to establish an imprest fund. It is better to budget a greater sum so that the potential for running short is diminished. This amount should be adequate for the prearranged period (generally for two weeks to one month) until the fund is again replenished.

The petty cash custodian or cashier is normally someone not handling other cash and negotiable instruments or assets. Once selected a check is written out to the Petty Cash account and the cash is then given over to the Petty Cash cashier.

Journal Entry for Petty Cash

Petty Cash $125.00
     Cash   125.00
To establish a Petty Cash fund

The money is usually stored in a secured container (a locked box) and every time a payment is made, a petty cash voucher or receipt is filled out by the Petty Cash cashier. Though vouchers differ, most contain the signature of the individual receiving the money, the cashier's signature, and the reason for the withdrawal or payment.

Utilizing this method, the total amount of capital in the fund should equal the cash plus the sum of the vouchers. As each voucher is added, the amount of money left in the fund decreases. All vouchers should be completed in ink.

Example of a Petty Cash Voucher

PETTY CASH VOUCHER

No. 123   **Amount $3.25**

Date: Aug. 12, 19XX

Reason for expense: Postage

John Doe   *Jane Smith*
Petty Cash Cashier   **Received by**

Replenishing Petty Cash Funds

The need to replenish petty cash funds is twofold. First, the accounting period is terminating; and second, the amount of capital within the fund is nearing depletion.

A check is drawn out to the Petty Cash custodian for the total of all the paid but uncanceled petty cash receipts or disbursements made since the previous time of the fund's replenishing. Journal entries are established and recorded. Expenses are debited where indicated as cash accounts are properly credited. In many cases, before the Petty Cash custodian can cash the check to refill the fund, he or she must hand over to another delegated individual all the uncanceled petty cash receipts. The vouchers are then identified by a marking and are kept for other accounting procedures. Once this is completed, the fund can be replenished by the check.

Example of Journal Entries for Replenishing Petty Cash

Supplies	$2.50
Stamps	3.50
Bus fare	1.75
Cash	7.75
Replenish the petty cash fund	

Petty Cash

| | | | | 1 | 2 | 3 | DEBIT — 4 | 5 |
	DATE	EXPLANATION	Vou No	TOTAL	POSTAGE	OFFICE EXPENSE	MISC. ACCOUNT	EXPENSES AMOUNT
1	Jan 4	START FUND (CH #66)		500.00				
2	Jan 8	STAMPS	1	20.00	20.00			
3	Jan 9	J. Kelly	2	10.00		10.00		
4	Jan 10	Snow Plowing Inc	3	53.00			Snow Plowing	53.00
5	Jan 20	P.L.T.	4	12.50			Delivery Exp.	12.50
6	Jan 21	Postman	5	1.25	1.25			
7	Jan 21	S.V. Stationary	6	7.45		7.45		
8	Jan 25	Fix-It Inc	7	24.95			Window Repair	24.95
9		TOTALS		129.15	21.25	17.45		90.45
10								
11	Jan 30	BALANCE		370.85				
12		30	Replenish Acct (CH #117)	129.15				
13								
14								
15								

Reconciling Petty Cash

Occasionally errors are made by those responsible for handling the imprest petty cash fund. Entries into the journal for shortages are handled by utilizing the *Cash Over and Short Account.*

Example of Reconciling Petty Cash

(A shortage of $10.00 in the petty cash fund)

Stamps	$12.50	
Paper	10.50	
Telegram	5.00	
Cash Over and Short		10.00
Cash		38.00

Replenish the petty cash fund

Types of Checks and Check Registers

A checking account can easily be opened by either an individual or company by merely going to a financial institution (such as a bank) that provides this service and filling out an application. Besides maintaining records for each account the bank will also offer other services such as collections, and loans automatically withdrawn from the account.

Since there are so many different types of checking accounts, great care should be taken before the actual selection is made. Compare the features of each account and examine the costs. In order to attract a new company, the bank may elect to avoid a service charge. The best checking account is one that works well for your particular situation.

When opening an account, an application must be filled out. It will include your name, address, occupation, social security number, place of work, and so on. In some regions, a corporation cannot open an account without providing certain legal documents at the time of application.

Signature cards must also be filled out. They will serve to verify the customer's signature if and when necessary. Anyone permitted to utilize the account must sign the signature card. At the time of opening the account, some form of revenue will be required as the initial deposit (cash, bank drafts, checks are all acceptable).

The customer will be provided with temporary checks and deposit slips until the personalized printed checks arrive. Always examine the numbers on the bottom of the check and deposit slips (MICR bank code and account number) to make sure the numbers are correct.

The process in which a check is signed or stamped on its back is called an *endorsement.* Every check must be endorsed as the name appears on the front. Three types of endorsements are as follows:

Restrictive endorsement—restricts how the check can be handled, e.g., "for deposit only".

Special endorsement—Checks can be given to someone else to cash or deposit, e.g., "pay to the order of . . . ."

Blank endorsement—Signature of payee on back.

Types of Checks

Besides the standard checking account, other special checks do exist. The most common are the following:

- *Cashier's check*—This kind of check is written by the financial institution itself. The check is drawn on the institution's own assets, thereby assuring payment. It is widely accepted and used often for payment through the mail.
- *Certified check*—A check which includes the name of the payee and the amount, is certified by the financial institution. It basically states that there are adequate funds to cover the amount written on the check. The word "Certified" is placed directly on the check. Funds are taken from the account when the check is certified and the payment is guaranteed by the certifying agency.
- *Traveler's check*—A check designed specifically for an individual and usually used for travel. When stolen or lost, checks can easily be replaced (provided that the serial numbers are known and reported) and they are readily accepted when away from one's home base of operation. American Express and Barclays Bank are some of the companies offering this type of check.
- *Money order*—This form of payment can be obtained from the United States Post Office or from other financial institutions. They are commonly used for sending funds through the mail and are purchased for a specific amount.
- *Money funds or money-market checks*—Whether offered by a bank or large mutual fund group, many supply their investors with a checking account that will allow withdrawal from the capital of the specific account. Some have certain restrictions upon the use and amounts of the checks that can be written.

It should be noted that a NSF (Not Sufficient Funds) check indicates that there are not enough funds in the account to cover the amount written on that check. A dishonored check is one that the institution will not pay; a postdated check is one that is dated following the date of issuance of the check.

Check Registers

Instead of using a Cash Disbursement Journal, many companies utilize a *check register* to put on record any voucher payments. It is a recording method for checks written and offers greater ease for personnel responsible for handling vouchers and checks within the business.

Check Register

	DATE	PAYEE	CHECK NUMBER	VOUCHER NUMBER	VOUCHER PAYABLE (DEBIT)	PURCHASE DISCOUNTS	CASH
			1	2	3	4	5 CREDIT
1	19XX						
2	Feb 1	Peter Weiss	161	452	18.00		18.00
3	4	Sax Company	162	453	125.00	25.00	100.00
4	8	R.V. + Co.	163	460	8.00		8.00
5	12	Russell Corp.	164	465	100.00		100.00
6	19	Kane + Kane	165	470	50.00	10.00	40.00
7							
8							
9							

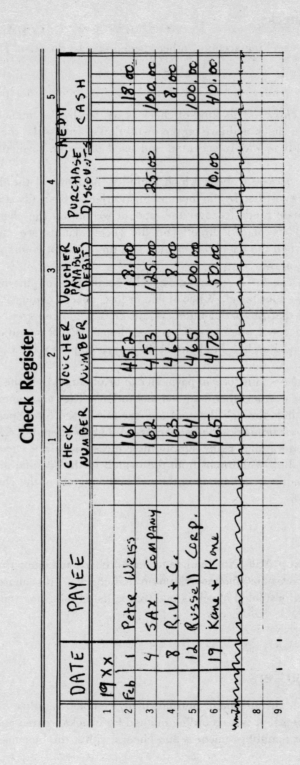

Voucher System and the Recording of Accounts Payable

When a business grows to a point where its owner(s) cannot fully control the flow of disbursements, a voucher system is usually instituted. Utilizing this method, all cash disbursements are handled effectively and with adequate controls. Funds and disbursements from petty cash are generally exempt from the voucher system.

The key to this system is the voucher (a paper containing facts of a particular transaction and the signature of the individual authorizing it). Prior to every cash disbursement, a voucher should be completed and authorized. Vouchers differ among businesses; however, some of the information that might be presented are:

- Invoice facts (date, seller, numbers, prices).
- Signature of person authorizing payment.
- Facts on means of payment.

A Voucher

CROWLEY CORP. Voucher No: 851
WYCOW, NEW JERSEY DATE: 5/11/XX

PAY TO: LIZAR COMPANY
88 RAWLEY CT.
SPRING VIEW, NEW YORK

DATE	DETAILS	TERMS	AMOUNT
4-15-XX	INVOICE NO. P645	3/15, n/60	$59.95

Accounts Debited: Freight expense
Accounts Credited: _____
Order Checked By: S.L.A.
Goods Received By: N.G.
Invoice Checked By: M.D.R.

Date Paid: 6/28/XX

Amount: $59.95
Method of Payment: Check #554

Payment Approved by:
Franz Goldman
_____

By using the voucher system, increased control is obtained over cash disbursements. The ability to incur debt is delegated to certain persons or areas of the company and specific guidelines and checks and balances are developed to control the situation closely. In order for payment to be rendered, all verifications, record keeping, and authorizations must be fulfilled and checked.

Under the voucher system, Vouchers Payable is used instead of Accounts Payable. When a voucher is paid, the payment is recorded as a debit to Vouchers Payable and a credit to Cash. A voucher for merchandise (bought) results in a debit to Purchases and a credit to Vouchers Payable.

All vouchers should be recorded on a Voucher Register. As expected, registers differ from company to company. The Voucher Register is really a book for transactions that will lead to cash payments. Once the voucher has been recorded, it is then placed in the unpaid voucher file and it remains there until payment is received.

Outline of the Voucher System

Formulate the Voucher
•
•
Record in the Voucher Register
•
•
Place Voucher in Unpaid Voucher File
•
•
Record in the Check Register
•
•
Place in the Paid Voucher File

Example of a Voucher Register

VOUCHER REGISTER

	DATE	VOU. NO.	PAYEE	PAID DATE	PAID CHK NO	VOUCHERS PAYABLE Credit	PURCHASES DEBIT	ADVERT. DEBIT	DELIVERY Debit	SUNDRY ACCOUNTS Account	SUNDRY ACCOUNTS Amount
						2	3	4	5	6	7
1	19XX										
2	Oct 1	541	Smith & Co.	10/6	621	500.00	500.00				
3	6	542	Frey Brothers	10/7	622	10.00				Office Equipment	10.00
4	9	543	Shane + Weiss	10/8	623	25.00		25.00			
5	10	544	M.M.&J.	10/9	624	15.00		15.00			
6	18	545	V. Vakassian	10/17	625	12.00			12.00		
7	25	546	S. Pilmer	10/22	626	670.00	670.00				
8	30	547	Zena Realty	10/30	627	54.00				Future	54.00
9						1286.00	1170.00	40.00	12.00		64.00
10											

Internal Controls

The nature of the voucher system lends itself to internal control. The division of duties and responsibilities assists in reducing the chance for errors during cash disbursement. Not until everything is checked can a check be written as payment for a particular voucher. The voucher register and the general ledger also insure further internal controls over any cash disbursements.

BANK STATEMENTS AND CASH BALANCE

Once during every month, a bank sends its customers statements regarding their checking accounts. The statement reviews and outlines all the transactions that occurred in the customer's account. Items appearing are the following:

- Name of customer and financial institution.
- Specific bank branch, if applicable.
- First and last date that the statement covers.
- Total of moneys deposited and withdrawn.
- Service charges.
- Returned checks.
- NSF (Not Sufficient Funds) checks and other bank fees.
- Checks written and paid.
- Balance of funds at the first and last day of the statement.
- Listing of debits, e.g., mortgage payment.

Bank Statement

BIG CITY BANK
Any town, Any State

Account No.: 12345   Branch No.: 63   Date: Feb. 28, 19XX

STATEMENT

CREDITS (DEPOSITS)	DEBITS (CHECKS)	DATE	BALANCE
	STARTING BALANCE	1/31/XX	$500.00
$ 50.00		2/05/XX	550.00
$100.00		2/10/XX	650.00
	$200.00	2/15/XX	450.00
	$100.00 (NSF)	2/20/XX	350.00
$200.00		2/25/XX	550.00
	$ 25.00 (SC)	2/28/XX	525.00

Starting Balance: $500.00   Total Credits: $350.00
Total Debits: $325.00   Final Balance: $525.00

When the financial institution sends the monthly bank statement to the owner of the account, other objects may be included (canceled checks, debit or credit memos).

Reconciliation

Upon receiving the bank statement, one possibly may observe that the balance exhibited by the bank statement is different from the balance on the depositor's records. In order to determine the accuracy of both sets of records, one must reconcile the two and specify their disparities.

Common items that can cause a difference between the bank and depositor's balance are: outstanding checks, deposits that were not present (may be in transition), service charges, errors by either party, and credit or debit notations. When reconciliation (to reconcile is to cause the two balances to concur) occurs one is making the banks's balance conform to the depositor's balance.

Detection and Correction of Errors

In order to detect and correct mistakes in one's checking account, reconciliation must be performed. The following procedure implements this task.

- *Ascertain the number of deposits in transit*—A comparison of the deposits shown on the bank statement and those in the depositor's records will indicate any errors or deposits in transit. Any differences are itemized.
- *Evaluate if any checks are still outstanding*—The canceled checks should be compared with those detailed on the bank statement (it is wise to retain the canceled checks that are returned with the statement in the order that they are received for this process). Once this is performed, the checks should be organized and arranged by number in the sequence in which they were actually written). One should find out if any outstanding checks from the last month's reconciliation are currently missing. Check to see if any unrecorded deposits from the last statement appear on the most current statement. Any and all differences from the above should be noted.
- *Confirm that all transactions located on the bank statement are entered on the depositor's books*—Check both the Cash Disbursements Journal or the Check Register and note any item that is not recorded.
- *Develop a reconciliation of the balances from the bank statement and the depositor's books.*
- *Make any necessary journal entries or modify any corrections that are found.*

Reconciling A Bank Statement

BIG DIPPER CANDIES
BANK RECONCILIATION AS OF JANUARY 31, 19XX

Balance of bank statement	**$259.00**	**Balance of book**	**$175.00**
Plus:		**Plus:**	
Bank error	121.00	Book error	325.00
Deposit in transit	50.00	Collection by	
	$630.00	bank minus note	25.00
			$625.00

Minus:				
Outstanding checks		**Minus:**		
No. 352	100.00	NSF check	$95.00	
No. 502	65.00	Returned		
No. 775	35.00	200.00	check	100.00	$195.00

Adjusted balance	**$430.00**	**Adjusted balance**	**$430.00**

Journal Entries To Record Reconciling Errors

Once the bank reconciliation is performed, one must enter any alterations into the journal. This will enable the balance of the company's Cash account to then be identical to the adjusted book balance.

Journal Entries For Reconciling Errors

1) Oct. 3, 19XX   Cash   1,250.50
                      Notes receivable $1,250.00
                      Note Collected by institution

2) Oct. 3, 19XX   Accounts Receivable $45.00
                      Squate Company
                      Cash $45.00
                      To record the return of
                      the NSF check

ACCOUNTING FOR INVESTMENTS

Real Estate

Land is a commodity with a limited or set quantity. As with any other investment, its price is governed by supply and demand. With the exception of several regions, land and housing values have tended to rise over the years. For example, in one New York City suburb a home purchased for $42,000.00 in 1970 is worth $150,000.00 today. On the other hand, an oversupply of condominiums in various sections of the country has caused a decrease in their selling price.

It must be remembered that land cannot be depreciated. Since it does not possess a useful lifetime, no journal entry is recorded for depreciation. Generally, the cost of land is displayed independently on a balance sheet when purchased with a building on it. Nonpermanent betterments are recorded on a separate account (they are depreciated) while the price of any permanent changes is added to the expense of the land.

There are many deductions available to those purchasing real estate as an investment. Some of these are:

- Accrued interest on mortgage.
- Annual state, town, county, and school taxes.
- Survey costs.
- Title search and insurance.
- Termite and engineering inspection.

For those investors who desire to own real estate as an investment, there are also other avenues to take besides actually purchasing the land or house directly. One can pool capital with others and form a *real estate syndicate*. Those investing are usually limited partners and leave the actual management to the general partners. The limited partners will enjoy both the profits (if any) and the tax benefits from this relationship.

Another method of investing in real estate is through the purchase of real estate investment trusts (REITs). Property is bought through capital raised by selling stock and moneys earned by each shareholder are taxable.

Bonds and Interest Income

Bonds are issued by corporations (or the government) to raise capital. They are pledged (promissory) notes distributed to lenders. Usually bonds are issued in increments of $1,000.00 and assist companies in raising large sums of money.

A written contract, called an *indenture*, between the company and the purchaser of the bond encompasses the conditions of the borrowing. It will often spell out amounts of capital to be borrowed, terms, and any restrictions.

Terminology Associated With Bonds

Principal—Amount to be paid at maturity date of bond.
Registered bond—Issued in specific name.
Bearer bond—Issued to no particular individual.

Mortgage bond—Safeguarded by the tangible assets of the corporation (senior and junior types).

Debenture—Not safeguarded by assets of the company.

Coupon rate—Yearly interest divided by the face rate.

Serial bond—Individual bonds maturing on various times.

Coupon bond—Bonds with coupons which will provide the interest on a specific date.

Callable bond—Bond can be paid off prior to maturity date.

Call—Permits a company to pay off bond before maturity date.

Convertible bond—Can be exchanged for stock.

Maturity—Life of a bond until a specific date.

Trustee—Protects bondholders and monitors indenture.

Bond value—Rate at which the corporation will purchase bond back.

Municipal bond—Issued by states, cities, turnpike authorities, and government agencies; tax-exempt from either or all federal, state, or local taxes.

General obligation bond—Municipal bond protected by ability to tax.

Junk bond—Non-investment grade bonds.

Current yield—Annual rate of interest divided by present price.

Sinking fund—Moneys used to retire the bonds.

Revenue bond—Municipal bond protected by specific supplies of income.

Bonds are often bought as an investment vehicle. When a bond is mentioned at a particular price, it usually includes the accrued interest.

Buying of Bonds

Cost of bond	$10,000.00
Fees and taxes	25.00
Price of bonds	$10,125.00
Interest (accrued)	500.00
Total amount paid	$10,625.00

Entry For An Investment Of Bonds

June 5, 19XX	Sullivan Corporation Bonds	$7,380.00	
	Interest earned	250.00	
	Cash		$7,630.00
	Bought seven bonds at $104.00 plus interest and $100.00 commission		

Recording Interest of Bonds

Sept. 8, 19XX	Cash	300.00	
	Interest earned		300.00
	Interest received from Teisch Corporation		

Selling a Bond

	Temporary Investment		
Oct. 9, 19XX	Cash	$20,900.00	
	Gain from bond sale		$100.00
	Investment in Karp bonds		20,400.00
	Interest received		150.00
	Income from interest		300.00
	Record the sale of Karp		
	Company Bonds		
	Long-term Investment		

When accounting for long-term investments of bonds, amortization must be considered. A part of the premium or discount is amortized whenever interest is received.

Initial Entry for Purchase of Bonds

Sept. 7, 19XX	Bond Investment	$732.00	
	Income from bond interest		$732.00
	Record amortization to date		
	of purchase		

Entry for Sale of Bonds

Nov. 12, 19XX	Cash	$11,900.00	
	Feiler Corporation Bonds		$11,900.00
	Gain on sale of investment		550.00
	Record the sale of Feiler Corporation		
	Bonds at $100 minus $100.00 commission		
	and additional expenses		

Stocks and Dividend Income

A share of stock represents ownership of a company. These *equity securities* include both common and preferred stocks. The owners of stock are called *shareholders* or *stockholders*. If Cosenza Corporation has one million shares, each shareholder holding one share owns one millionth of the company. The more shares one owns, the higher the percentage of ownership of the company.

Terminology Associated With Stocks

Treasury shares—Shares repurchased by the company.
Issued shares—Shares issued and purchased by investors.
Outstanding shares—All shares issued minus any treasury shares.
Authorized shares—The number of shares that a company can issue.
Book value—Amount of a company's assets less its liabilities. Book value per
    share is the book value divided by the shares outstanding.
Par value—Value of a single share of stock.
Market value—Price that one must pay for a share of stock.

Preferred stock—A cross between a stock and bond. Dividends are usually rigid with no set maturity time. Usually accompanied by many of the rights of common stock.

Earnings per share—Net income of a company divided by the total number of shares outstanding.

Cash dividends—Net income distributed to the company's owners (shareholders).

Stock dividends—Dividends given as shares of stock.

Cumulative preferred stock—Receives dividends before common shares can be paid (includes any dividends paid years before).

Callable preferred stock—Preferred stock that can be reclaimed by the company at any time.

Stock split—Any dividend of stock greater than twenty-five percent. The par value decreases proportionally with the increased shares outstanding.

Entry for Selling Stock (Corporation)

March 2, 19XX	Cash	$500,000.00	
	Common stock		$500,000.00
	To record selling and issuing of 500,000 common shares at $1.00 each		

Entry for Swapping Stock for Other Assets

April 5, 19XX	Land	$25,000.00	
	Building	25,000.00	
	Common stock		50,000
	To record the swapping of 10,000 shares of common stock for land and building		

Dividend Income

Dividends are generally paid to shareholders in cash. It should be remembered that dividends decrease the company's net assets and retained earnings. Prior to paying dividends, the board of directors must consider some of the following:

- Overall financial status of the company.
- Capital needs for the future.
- Current debts.

Only shareholders as of a certain date are eligible for dividends. Therefore, the exact dates of the payment and declaration for payment by the board are extremely important.

Entry for a Dividend (Corporation)

May 11, 19XX	Dividend reported	$100,000.00	
	Dividend payable		$100,000.00
	Dividend announced		
	by board of directors		
June 1, 19XX	Dividend payable	$100,000.00	
	Cash paid		$100,000.00
	Paid dividend		
	of May 11, 19XX		

When an individual calculates federal and state income taxes, the income from dividends must be included. These dividends are not limited to stocks and bonds but also can come from insurance policies, limited partnerships, and other sources of investment. With changes in the tax laws occurring continually, one must constantly be aware of the new statutes that govern dividends and how they affect one's overall income.

Inventories

Since inventory is essential in defining one's true assets or income, it is crucial that financial statements reflect a true picture of its worth. This evaluation entails counting the stock on hand and determining the value of the items (damage and obsolescence must be considered). You must realize, however, that different approaches can be followed to determine the cost of inventory and that one is really making suppositions on its value.

Pricing

Once the number of items (inventory) has been established, the cost must be determined. Since many items are purchased at different times and at assorted prices, the situation becomes complex. In order to solve the problem, management can utilize one of many different bases of costing. Three regularly used methods are the following:

Last in–First out (LIFO)—A method of pricing inventory that theorizes that goods acquired last sell first. Therefore, the last merchandise is valued at the prices of the first goods received. The costs of the last items received are matched with the capital from sales. This method often represents the cost of restocking the goods actually sold.

Many companies tend to keep a minimum stock, which is really a long-lived asset. LIFO is well suited because it commits the original price to the inventory. Also during an economic period when prices tend to rise, net income is reduced by using LIFO rather than other methods of inventory pricing. Therefore, this method will decrease the company's income tax.

LIFO

Total costs of 60 cots for sale		$630.00
Minus final inventory based on LIFO		
10 Cots (Inventory from March 1)	@ $10.00 = $100.00	
15 Cots (Purchases from April 5)	@ $11.00 = $165.00	
25 Cots (Final Inventory)		$265.00
Cots for sale		$630.00
Minus: Final Inventory		265.00
Costs of Cots sold		$195.00

First in–First out (FIFO)—A method of pricing inventory that theorizes that goods are sold in the sequence in which they are obtained. Many businesses attempt to sell items in the order in which they are purchased by them. This is especially true of perishable goods or trendy items. Inventory is valued at the cost of the last purchased goods. FIFO is utilized because it is generally works in accord with what is actually occurring and because it allocates the most recent costs to the final inventory.

FIFO

Total costs of 45 hats for sale		$495.00
Minus final inventory based on FIFO		
12 Hats (Inventory from Feb. 24)	@ $10.00 = $120.00	
7 Hats (Purchases from June 23)	@ $12.00 = 84.00	
19 hats (Final inventory)		$204.00
Hats for sale		$495.00
Minus: Final Inventory		204.00
Costs of hats sold		$291.00

Weighted average—This method uses a system of average cost of units. Both quantities and unit costs are considered. It gives a cost between the items sold and those on hand. Weighted average cost is determined by dividing the costs of merchandise available by the number of units.

Prices of every unit (starting inventory and those added by each purchase) are weighted by the sum of the units (from starting inventory and those added by each purchase). They are averaged to determine the weighted cost per unit.

Weighted Average

13 Units	@ $15.00	=	$195.00
12 Units	@ 10.00		120.00
22 Units	@ 8.00		176.00
18 Units	@ 12.00		216.00
65			707.00

$707.00 \div 65 = 10.877 (weighted average of cost per unit)

Total cost of 65 units for sale	$707.00
Minus final inventory based on the weighted average cost	
(15 units @ $10.877)	163.16
Cost of units sold	$543.84

Applying Lower of Cost or Market Theory

Throughout the years, it has been customary for inventory pricing to be the lower of either cost or market (cost representing the price paid for the goods when bought and market being the price that would have to be paid on inventory date to replace or buy the goods). This theory was utilized because it presented a conservative number for inventory.

The LCM (lower of cost or market theory) can be employed to separate goods in the inventory; the whole inventory; segmented departments or sections.

Using LCM has a definite advantage. If the replacement price of a particular piece declines, the selling price would generally be reduced. This situation could lead to a loss. That loss should have been expected or forecasted and obtained in the year of the declining price. Theoretically, the utilization of LCM should apply to the above scenario; however, cost and selling prices do not necessarily fall precisely together.

The theory has been altered somewhat to allow for certain exceptions. Some of the modifications are:

- If no decline in selling price has occurred or none is anticipated, merchandise should be taken into inventory at cost (even if replacement cost could be lower).
- Occasionally, items should be put into inventory at a cost between their cost and the replacement cost.
- Periodically, items should be placed in inventory below replacement price.
- Inventory should be maintained at a point to keep a profit (which one considers normal) when the replacement price declines more than the selling price.

Determining Cost of Goods Sold

The size and nature of every business determines how many times and when the costs of goods sold are calculated. For example, it is not practical for a large grocery store to keep a daily record of the costs of all the items sold. Usually, at the end of every accounting period, a physical inventory is performed. From this inventory and accounting records, they can find the costs of goods sold during that particular period. These are called *periodic inventories* and the system is called a *periodic inventory system*.

A small car dealer may keep a daily record of the costs of the cars sold. This is called a *perpetual inventory record* and the end results is called a *perpetual inventory of accounting for goods on hand and sold*.

When utilizing the periodic inventory system, one must have the following data:

- Costs of goods at the start of the period.
- Costs of goods bought during the period.
- Costs of all remaining goods at the end of the period.

Determining Costs of Goods Sold

Costs of goods (at start of period)	$25,000.00
Costs of goods bought (during the period)	$15,000.00
Total amount of goods for sale (during the period)	$40,000.00
Costs of goods remaining (at the end of the period)	$17,500.00
Costs of goods sold (during the period)	$22,500.00

It is often difficult to designate a cost at inventory. One must determine a price for every item and calculate the number of items present. After the inventory is completed, the price for every item must be established. Great care must be taken in order to avoid any mistakes or errors during inventory. These can cause misstatements in accounting and can be carried over from period to period.

Evaluating Effect of Inventory on Net Income

It is possible to increase or decrease a corporation's net income by the selection of either inventory pricing method. With this fact in mind, it is understandable why an accountant demands that a company constantly adhere to the selected method. Frequent changes in inventory valuation methods could pave the way for net income manipulation.

Usually, there are many different possible procedures for a transaction. The accountant utilizes an acceptable method or procedure that shows periodic income. Once established, it will be used with consistency and will enable financial statements to be compared easily and on par with one another.

It should be noted that the starting inventory and net income are inversely related. If the starting inventory is understated by the company, its net income will be overstated. Conversely, if the starting inventory is overstated by the company, its net income will be understated.

When determining which method to use, many aspects should be considered. You must decide whether the company desires to show increased stress on the income statement or on the balance sheet. Tax considerations must be weighed; the method chosen can and will affect the revenues and tax consequences. Some businesses attempt to select their inventory valuation with their movement of goods and merchandise.

PROPERTY, PLANT, AND EQUIPMENT RECORDS

A company may acquire an asset in hopes of keeping it for a number of accounting periods. Such an asset is called a *long-lived* or *fixed asset*. These items are usually purchased so that the company can perform its operations (desks, machinery, trucks). Once, however, a piece of equipment is withdrawn, it is no longer a plant asset. If the item is used for less than one accounting period, it is generally considered a supply rather than a fixed asset. The asset placed in the plant and equipment category must be utilized in the daily and regular operations of the firm.

The term *plant and equipment* is often called operating assets, property (real—land and all things on the land and personal—all things possessed other than real property), plant, and equipment. The *useful life* of any plant asset is the time during which the company anticipates usage.

Acquisition

The original cost of an asset is a total of all expenditures of purchasing and preparing an asset for use. These costs must be both essential and within reason. Such expenses as sales tax and the costs of installation are generally considered acceptable. Any discounts obtained from cash must be deducted from the original cost. Whenever a fixed asset is purchased, the accountant must debit the asset account for the original cost.

If a plant asset requires repair before actually being utilized, the expenses cannot be charged to the asset account (it is charged to an expense account). Actual depreciation cannot begin until the asset is ready to be utilized by the company. If the business itself is building its own plant asset, costs can include insurance *during* the actual construction, materials, and labor.

Land is often purchased for a construction site. In this case, commissions, legal fees, and landscaping are included in the cost. Any assessments must be debited to the land account. If a building must be removed from the land purchased (in order to put a new one in its place), the amount is charged to the land account.

Purchase of a Piece of Equipment

Regular price		$100,000.00
Minus: discount (5%/10)		5,000.00
Net price		95,000.00
Add: Shipping	$2500.00	
Uncrating	500.00	3,000.00
Total cost of equipment		$98,000.00

When both land and a building are purchased together, each one must be individually allocated. Usually this is based on an appraisal value (price determined by an expert) or the tax-assessed rate.

Allocation of a Building—Land Purchase

	Appraised Value	Percent of Total	Apportioned Cost
Land	$ 60,000.00	30%	$ 54,000.00
Building	140,000.00	70%	126,000.00
Totals	$200,000.00	100%	$180,000.00

Journal Entry for a Building—Land Purchase

Land	$35,000.00	
Building	45,000.00	
Cash		$80,000.00
For the purchase		
of a building and land		

Allocation of Costs (Depreciation, Depletion)

Many fixed assets are depreciated. This means that the cost of the plant and equipment is allocated over a period of time (generally over their expected useful lifetime). Depreciation has little to do with the resale value of an object and not with valuation—only allocation. Any asset without a limited useful lifetime cannot be depreciated (example—land).

Journal Entry for Depreciation

Depreciation Expense—machine	$250.00	
Accumulated Depreciation—machine		$250.00
To record depreciation for		
machine		
for one year		

Each and every plant and equipment asset must have an individual Depreciation Expense account and an Accumulated Depreciation account. Individual accounts permit the correct allocation of expense among the accounting requirements and in the management sectors where necessary.

Whenever depreciation is recorded, the asset account is not credited. The Accumulated Depreciation account is considered as a contra-asset account (saves the initial price of the asset). It is subtracted from the associated asset located on the balance sheet. By subtracting it from the asset account, the *book value* (differentiation separating the asset account and the associated Accumulated Depreciation account) is exposed. Depreciation will not increase the amount of cash within the company nor will it influence the present assets or liabilities. Generally, depreciation figures are shown regularly on many financial statements.

Accumulated Depreciation

Tice & Bass, Ltd.
Balance Sheet
January 31, 19XX

ASSETS:			
Cash		$25,000.00	
Receivables		30,000.00	
Present Assets			$55,000.00
FIXED ASSETS:			
Land		75,000.00	
Machinery	32,000.00		
Minus: Accumulated			
Depreciation	26,000.00	6,000.00	
Total Fixed Assets			81,000.00
Total Assets			$136,000.00

As with many other accounting methods, an accountant can select one of several methods for determining depreciation. You must attempt to determine the possible life expectancy of the asset and the value of the asset when its usefulness has ended (often called the scrap, salvage, trade in, or residual value).

Common Methods of Determining Depreciation

Straight line—Depreciation is allocated uniformly over the expected life of the asset. The following method is used:

$$\text{Annual Depreciation} = \frac{\text{Cost} - \text{Residual Value}}{\text{Estimated Life}}$$

The following example illustrates how to calculate straight line depreciation.

$$\$15,000.00/\text{year} = \frac{\$100,000.00 - 25,000.00}{5 \text{ years}}$$

Units of production—Depreciation is linked to the estimated productive capability of the asset (measured in a unit of production). The following method is used:

$$\text{Depreciation (unit)} = \frac{\text{Cost} - \text{Residual Value}}{\text{Approximated units of output}}$$

The following example illustrates how to calculate depreciation through units of production.

$$\$1.00/\text{hour} = \frac{\$20,000 - 6,000.00}{14,000 \text{ hours}}$$

The next methods discussed are called *accelerated methods of depreciation*. They tend to put greater depreciation in the beginning years of an asset's expected life (for possible reduction of one's income tax). The costs of maintenance and repairs are important aspects and are considered when selecting this accounting method.

Declining balance—Depreciation is determined by using a preset rate to a decreasing asset's book value (includes the residual value).

Double-declining-balance—A method of depreciation that utilizes a double straight-line rate. Before any numbers are used, the previous year's depreciation is subtracted from the cost of the asset. The residual value is not deducted while using this method and the cost of the asset cannot depreciate below the residual value of what is considered reasonable. Sometime during the course of using the double-declining-balance method, it must be altered to the straight-line method.

$$\begin{array}{ccc} \text{Double} & \text{Decreasing} & \\ \text{Straight-line} \times & \text{Book Value} = & \text{Annual Depreciation} \\ \text{Rate} & & \end{array}$$

Double-Declining-Balance

Year	Yearly Depreciation	Expense (Yearly Depreciation)	Left over Book Value
1	$20,000 (40%)	$8,000.00	$12,000.00
2	$12,000 (40%)	$4,800.00	$ 7,200.00
3	$ 7,200 (40%)	$2,880.00	$ 4,320.00
4	$ 4,320 (40%)	$1,728.00	$ 2,592.00
5	$ 2,592 (40%)	$1,036.80	$ 1,555.20

Sum-of-the-years'-digits—By using a series of fractions every year, the depreciation is determined. The residual value is subtracted from the cost of the asset before starting. The sum of the asset's useful or expected life is the denominator. The fractions decrease every year and the numerator represents the years left of useful life.

$$\text{Cost minus residual life} \times \frac{\text{Remaining years}}{\text{Total of useful years}} = \text{Annual Depreciation}$$

Sum-of-the-Years'-Digits

Year	Yearly Depreciation	Yearly Depreciation Expense
1	$12,000.00 (5/15)	$4,000.00
2	$12,000.00 (4/15)	$3,200.00
3	$12,000.00 (3/15)	$2,400.00
4	$12,000.00 (2/15)	$1,600.00
5	$12,000.00 (1/15)	$ 800.00
Full depreciation		$12,000.00

By using any of the methods described, the depreciation will be equal. How you disperse the useful life of the asset can differ among those available.

Depletion

Companies dealing with natural resources (mining of ores or harvesting trees) use depletion as an accounting procedure. It can be defined as utilizing a part of a natural resource's cost to the amount of resources (trees or ore) extracted or harvested during that time.

Entry on Depletion

Depletion—Consolidated Gold Mine $150,000
    Accumulated Depletion $150,000

The term *percentage depletion* is recognized by the Internal Revenue Service for tax reasons. It represents a specific percentage of revenue and can differ with the kind of material involved.

Amortization

Many businesses have intangible assets. Patents and copyrights are two types of intangible assets. When bought, the cost is allocated over the useful life of this type of asset. This process is systematically done and is called amortization. Contra accounts are not utilized in the recording of accumulated amortizations. On the balance sheet, the unamortized balance is registered as an intangible asset.

Entry for Amortization

(On Jan. 15 a copyright was purchased for $17,000.00)

Jan 15, 19XX	Copyright	$17,000.00	
	Cash		$17,000.00
	Purchase of copyright		
Dec 1, 19XX	Amortization Expense—copyright $1,000.00		
	Copyright		$1,000.00
	Record copyright amortization for one year		

Replacements and Repairs

Most, if not all, machinery during its useful lifetime requires repair or replacement. This category can be broken down to two sections: routine and regular repairs and replacement and extraordinary repairs and replacement.

Routine repairs and replacement are those expenses that are required to maintain the machinery (asset) in working order, e.g., painting, replacing small parts. This type of expenditure is a present or current expense and must be manifested on the present income statement (a deduction from the company's revenues). Maintenance expenses such as cleaning and adjustments are likewise considered a present expense and are frequently merged with present repairs for accounting functions.

Extraordinary repairs and replacements are those whose purpose is to keep machines (assets) running past their useful life expectancy. It is transcribed as a debit to Accumulated Depreciation.

Entry for Extraordinary Repairs

Cost	$16,000.00
Minus: Accumulated Depreciation	12,000.00
Book Value	4,000.00

NOTE: A major repair is performed for $4,200.00 that will add increased life to the asset.

Feb. 14, 19XX	Accumulated Depreciation (machine)	$4,200.00	
	Cash		$4,200.00
	Record extraordinary repair to a machine		

The following calculates annual depreciation.

Book Value prior to extraordinary repairs	$4,000.00
Extraordinary repair	4,200.00
Total	$8,200.00
Depreciation (annual) for 4 years left	$2,050.00

DISPOSITION OF PROPERTY ITEMS

All assets (with the exception of land) possess a limited lifetime. There comes a time when the asset wears out or has no further use to the company. At this point, the asset will either be sold, traded, or scrapped. It is considered *fully depreciated* when the accumulated depreciation is equal to the asset's cost.

Sale of An Asset (Plant and Equipment)

Assets are either sold at a loss, gain, or at current book value. The differences between the current book value and the selling price will determine if a loss or gain is present.

Recording At Book Value

Cash	$4,200.00	
Accumulated Depreciation	4,800.00	
Machine		9,000.00
Record sale of		
machine at book value		

Recording At Less Than Book Value

Cash	$3,000.00	
Accumulated Depreciation	4,800.00	
Loss on sale	1,200.00	
Machine		9,000.00
Record sale of		
machine less than book value		

Recording At More Than Book Value

Cash	$5,100.00	
Accumulated Depreciation	4,800.00	
Gain on sale		900.00
Machine		9,000.00
Record sale of machine		
more than book value		

Exchange of Plant and Equipment Assets

Periodically, plant and equipment assets must be exchanged for another piece (either equivalent or different). It is quite usual for this to occur with office and automotive equipment. Since many dealers offer a trade-in allowance on an older asset, it is common practice to not receive full or fair market value during the transaction. When no trade-in is involved, one usually purchases the new equipment for list or below list price. Think about buying a new car from a dealer to fully comprehend this concept.

Trade-In Allowance

You can purchase a new car at the list price of $20,000.00. You can trade-in your old car (book value of $3,000.00) and pay $15,000.00 in cash. Otherwise, you could pay $19,000.00 cash with no trade-in.

The following example illustrates how to determine the trade-in allowance of the old car (automobile purchased at list price).

List price of Automobile	$20,000.00
Minus: Cash paid with trade-in	15,000.00
Trade-In Allowance	$5,000.00

The cash price without a trade-in will give you the fair market price of the automobile. Using the method below, you can determine that the old car's fair market value is $4000.00.

Fair market value of automobile	$19,000.00
Minus: Cash paid with trade-in	15,000.00
Fair Market Value of old car	$4,000.00

In most cases, the gain or loss for exchanges of similar assets is not recognized but the gain or loss is assimilated into the cost of the new asset. When an exchange occurs of different assets with unlike purposes, a gain or loss must be recognized.

Entry For Different Assets

Drying machine	$50,000.00	
Accumulated Depreciation (printing machine)	35,000.00	
Gain on Exchange of Asset		2,500.00
Printing machine		47,500.00
Cash		40,000.00
Record gain of exchange of different assets		

The following example illustrates the method of determining the gain.

Fair Market Value of Drying Machine Exchanged (Cash price—cash)	$10,000.00
Minus: Book value of Drying Machine Exchanged (Cost—accumulated depreciation)	7,500.00
Gain	2,500.00

When an exchange occurs with equivalent assets, the gain or revenue is recognized if two things happen. First, the actual exchange must materialize. Second, the earnings procedure must be considerably implemented.

Entry For Similar Assets

Fair Market Value—old machine	$11,000.00
Minus: Book value—old machine	7,500.00
(Cost—Accumulated Depreciation)	
Gain	$3,500.00

No gain is recognized, therefore, the following is performed:

New Machine (Old book value + new cost)	$19,000.00	
Accumulated Depreciation	13,750.00	
Old Machine		$21,250.00
Cash		11,500.00
Record exchange		
of equivalent assets		

Losses would be handled in a similar manner. During a trade-in situation, any additional moneys paid (cash or note) is termed *boot*.

Abandoning An Asset

Often a business is forced to scrap or retire an asset. Sometimes it cannot be sold or used for trade. When the asset is fully depreciated (accumulated depreciation is the same as its cost), the entry is a debit to Accumulated Depreciation and a credit in the asset account. The book value is then nil.

Entry For An Abandoned Asset

Accumulated Depreciation	$750.00	
Machine		$750.00

Record abandon of a machine. If the machine is not fully depreciated then the following entry is made:

Accumulated Depreciation	$900.00	
Loss on Abandonment	100.00	
Machine		$1,000.00
Record abandonment of machine		

Since the laws are different for displaying losses on financial statements and income taxes, two sets of books are usually maintained. The expense of keeping separate books is generally compensated by the losses incurred. Depreciation must be brought up to the date of abandonment or removal from service.

Price-Level Indexing

Before one can objectively compare and assess a company's financial statements throughout the previous several years, price level changes (alterations in the relationship or ratio between the purchasing of goods and services and capital) must be considered.

These changes can influence both the income statement and balance sheet. By utilizing a price-level index, one can attempt to take into consideration the influence of inflation and deflation upon the figures on the accounting sheets.

Price-level changes can either be *general* or *specific*. Specific relates to one particular item, whereas, the general price-level changes refers to the buying capacity of an average number of items.

When one considers price changes in accounting, two approaches are commonly used:

- *Constant*—Dollar accounting conveys amounts expressed with a constant dollar buying capacity.
- *Current*—Cost accounting utilizes recent dollars for any assets or expenses.

The Consumer Price Index (CPI) is the most widely used index and is released monthly by the United States Government.

OTHER ASSETS

Receivables

Notes Receivable

A note receivable is a signed note by a client or customer promising to pay the amount due. It usually specifies to reimburse a set amount by a certain time. It is an asset that can be transferred to a financial institution for cash or to another person or company.

Payee—One to whom the note is payable.
Maker—One who is making the pledge to pay.

The business or person receiving the note records it in an asset account entitled Notes Receivable while the maker of the note records it in a liability account called Notes Payable. If interest is to be paid from the first to the final dates, it is called an interest-bearing note. If none is designated, then it is called a non-interest-bearing note.

Interest and Non-Interest-Bearing Notes

Interest Bearing-Note

$5,000.00 Newark, New Jersy *May 15* 19 *XX*
60 days After Date *1* Promise to pay to
The order of *Kathie Wertalik*
Five thousand and 00/100 ———————— Dollars
Payable at *First Federal Bank of Monsey*
Value received with interest at *12.5* %
Sheryl Loreng

The following is the procedure for determining interest on a note.

$$Total = Principal \times Rate \times \frac{Days}{360}$$

The following example illustrates this procedure.

$$Total = \$1,000.00 \times 10\% \times \frac{90}{360}$$
$$Total = \$25.00 \; interest$$

Another way to determine interest is called the sixty-day, six percent method. Whenever an interest rate of six percent is charged for sixty days, you merely have to multiply the principal by .01 or one percent to get the amount of interest.

To ascertain the exact date when a note is payable one can simply perform the following, assuming a thirty-day note taken on February 1, 19xx:

Total days of note		30
February (days)	28	
Minus: Date on note	1	
Remaining days	27	
Sum		27
Date due of note		March 3

Entries For Interest-Bearing Notes

Buying an asset with a note:

April 2, 19XX	Office machinery	$1,200.00	
	Notes payable		1,200.00
	Bought office machinery		
	with a 90 day, 10% note		

Sheryl Stanley Enterprises gave a note on a $25,000.00 loan at 12% for 60 days:
Sheryl Stanley Enterprises (debtor)

April 5, 19XX	Cash	$25,000.00	
	Note Payable		$25,000.00
	Recording a note		
	payable at 12% for 60 days		

Bank (creditor)

April 5, 19XX	Notes Receivable	$25,000.00	
	Cash		$25,000.00
	Recording a note		
	receivable to Sheryl Stanley Enterprises		

Upon payment, the entries are as follows:
Sheryl Stanley Enterprises (creditor)

June 4, 19XX	Notes Payable	$25,000.00	
	Interest paid	500.00	
	Recording note		
	payable to bank		

Bank (creditor)

June 4, 19XX	Cash	$25,000.00	
	Notes Receivable		$25,000.00
	Income from interest		500.00
	Recording note		
	receivable from Sheryl Stanley Enterprises		

It is common practice for a financial institution to loan money to a company when notes (receivable) are involved. Interest-bearing notes are transferred to the institution (endorsing them to the bank), enabling the holder to obtain funds. Interest is often levied by the institution from the transfer date to the maturity date. Non-interest-bearing notes are generally discounted (those not mentioning any interest) below maturity value. The amount received is equal to the full value of the note at maturity minus the discount.

Entry For a Non-Interest-Bearing Note

April 12, 19XX	Notes Receivable	$2,550.00	
	Accounts Receivable-		
	Eric Marc, Inc.		$2,550.00
	Recording a		
	60-day, non-interest-bearing note		

Entry For an Interest-Bearing Note

April 12, 19XX   Notes Receivable $2,550.00
                         Accounts Receivable-
                             Eric Marc, Inc. $2,550.00
                         Recording a 60-day, 12% note

Discounting

When a financial institution retains money from the maturity value of a non-interest-bearing or interest-bearing note, the portion is called a *discount*. In essence, the lender is charging interest or a fee on the transaction and provides the company with the balance of the funds. The rate that is utilized by the bank for this transaction is called the *discount rate*. Discounting (switching a note for cash) does have a risk to the borrower (unless the note has a "without recourse" statement). Should the debtor fail to repay the amount, the endorser would be responsible to the bank for the amount due. The maturity value is equal to the interest due and the face value of the note.

Accounts Receivable and Bad Debts

When a business provides a service or sells products and goods on credit, it is conceivable that a customer may not pay the moneys owed. If collection of this amount is not possible, the amount due is called a *bad debt*. As long as the number of bad debts is not too sizable, many firms actually consider them simply part of doing business.

There are two procedures that are commonly used in accounting of bad debts. It must be remembered that when a bad debt occurs, an entry must be made to record the transaction. Of the two methods, the direct write-off is the simplest but it is not fully acceptable.

> *Direct write-off*—You must make all attempts to retrieve the moneys owed before using this method. At that time, an entry is made for the bad debt and the Accounts Receivable is then credited. It should be noted that this procedure offends the Matching Principles rule (both the expense and revenue are to be matched during the same period).

Entry For a Direct Write-Off

Dec. 1, 19XX   Bad Debts Expense $2,450.00
                         Accounts Receivable—
                             Jackie Nicole Corp. $2,450.00
                         To write off the bad
                         debt of Jackie Nicole Corp.

> *Allowance procedure*—This is the most common process utilized by companies for bad debts. Using the allowance procedure the bad debt is approximated during the same period of the sale. For credits, a contra account must be established.

Entry For the Allowance Procedure

Dec. 1, 19XX   Bad Debts Expense $2,450.00
                     Accounts Receivable—
                     Jackie Nicole Corp. $2,450.00
                     To write off the bad
                     debt of Jackie Nicole Corp.

One of the most formidable tasks is to correctly judge figures of the entry for the bad debt. Several techniques are the following:

- Proportion of credit sales.
- Proportion of net sales.
- Proportion of accounts receivable.
- Aging accounts receivable.

Prepaid Expenses

Any expenses that are paid in advance or ahead of the time that they are due are called *prepaid expenses*. In the beginning, this type of expense is debited to the asset account. Later, it must be replaced in the expense account. Insurance is an example of a prepaid expense.

An Entry For a Prepaid Expense

Feb. 1, 19XX   Prepaid Insurance $600.00
                     Cash $600.00
                     Record the acquisition
                     of a six-month policy

After one month, the following entry is put in the expense account:

March 1, 19XX   Insurance expense $100.00
                     Prepaid insurance $100.00
                     Recording one month's
                     expense for insurance

Intangible Assets and Amortization

An asset that possesses no inherent worth but whose true value comes from the rights of possession is called an *intangible asset*. It has no physical being or substance.

Several intangible assets are patents, copyrights, trademarks, and goodwill.

This kind of asset is recorded on the balance sheet under an intangible asset section. All intangible assets are amortized over their expected useful lifetime.

Amortization is best defined as a orderly allocation (over an expected useful lifetime) of an intangible asset's cost. Forty years is the maximum number that an intangible asset can be amortized.

DEBT EQUITIES (LIABILITIES)

Debts that must be paid or moneys owed by a company are called *liabilities*. They can be of two types *current* or *long-term*. Current obligations are debts that must be paid in less than one year whereas long-term obligations have a payback of longer than one year.

Liabilities occur from actual transactions and not from pledges to undertake these transactions. Liabilities include customers paying in advance for goods or services, gathering taxes from customers or employees, and product and service guarantees and warranties. They can be classified in one of two ways:

> *Short term*—Notes and accounts payable, wages owed to employees and unearned rent.
>
> *Long term*—Mortgage, bonds, and long-term payables.

Short-Term Obligations

There are various kinds of notes payable, as described in the following.

Interest-Bearing (Simple and Add-On Interest)

Notes are negotiable instruments (promissory obligations) that can require the maker to be responsible for both the money owed and any interest due. A set interest rate is designated to be paid at the date of maturity.

If the principal is not paid before or on the maturity date, the borrower may request an extension. The creditor must approve all the terms and is entitled to additional interest for the extended period of time.

Entry for an Extension of Note*

Dec. 1, 19XX	Note payable (old)	$775.95	
	Interest	50.00	
	Cash		150.95
	Notes Payable (new)		675.00

Check issued for $150.95 and a note for $675.00 to repay a note of $775.95 and interest due

*Note is Renewed at Maturity Date.

In order to record and keep track of the notes issued by a company, a notes payable register is utilized. The data for the register is taken directly from the note or from the note stub.

Notes Payable Register

NOTES PAYABLE

19XX			19XX		
Oct. 12 No. 1	$752.00		Sept. 1 No. 1	$543.96	
Oct. 15 No. 2	235.85		Sept. 5 No. 2	165.89	

Non-Interest-Bearing

Unlike interest-bearing notes, non-interest-bearing notes do not indicate any amount of interest to be paid at maturity. It is not uncommon, for this type of note is frequently discounted.

Entry For a Non-Interest Bearing Note

April 12, 19XX	Cash	$456.75	
	Discount to note		
	payable	45.25	
	Notes Payable		$502.00
	Recording of a		
	non-interest-bearing note		

Term

The major difference between the long-term and short-term notes is the length of time to the date of maturity. *Short-term notes* mature in less than one year or less than the corporation's business cycle. *Long-term notes* mature in a time more than one year or greater than the company's business cycle.

Principal is paid on an interest-bearing note on the maturity date while interest payments are made as designated by the note. Both the short- and long-term interest is accrued at the termination of each accounting cycle.

Often a corporation will issue notes in order to circumvent the expense of distributing bonds. Smaller companies may seek to privately place long-term notes rather than going to the public to raise capital. Accounting for long-term notes is similar to that of bonds. The balance should be reported on the balance sheet as a long-term liability.

Installment

Often sales are made to a purchaser and equal consecutive payments are made for the item. This procedure is termed installment payment. It is one of the most traditional methods used by retailers to enhance business. A contract is signed by the buyer at the time of purchase (the terms of the contract include price of the item, duration of payout, and the amount of interest to be assigned. Often a down payment is required when one signs the contract and the item does not become the possession of the buyer until the final payment is made. The accounting of installment sales can be performed either on an accrual or installment basis.

Entry for a Installment Purchase

Oct 21, 19XX	Installment Accounts Receivable	$150.00	
	Installment Purchase		$150.00
	Recording a installment purchase		

Accounts Payable

When goods and services are bought without notes and with an open account, the designation *accounts payable* is utilized. These are registered as liabilities on financial statements and careful internal controls are needed to assure that all liabilities are properly recorded and that none are forgotten.

Accruals

Statements reflecting the amount of liabilities cannot be deemed accurate unless all the interest accrued for the notes payable is determined. *Accrued liabilities* are those expenses that were not paid (they also must have been recorded). A payable register should be used to assist the record keeping. On a balance sheet, Accrued Interest Payable is listed as a liability. Vacation pay and property and income taxes are business expenses that accruals are used.

Entry For an Accrued Interest Payable

Dec. 11, 19XX   Interest Expense $234.12
                     Accrued Interest Payable $234.12
                     Recording interest
                     accrued on notes payable

Long-Term Obligations

Notes

Long-term notes are those that have a maturity date extending beyond one year or one accounting cycle. It should be observed that a long-term note is neither a current asset nor liability and it is recorded on the balance sheet as a long-term liability. Interest is paid on a long-term note according to the conditions of the note.

Mortgages

A mortgage payable is considered a long-term obligation. The company or individual borrowing the capital provides the creditor with a secured claim against the debtor's mortgage or other assets and constitutes a lien against the mortgaged property. The claim includes both payment of principal as well as interest. Failure to repay can result in either foreclosure, litigation, or the possible loss of the secured asset. A Mortgage Payable account is often utilized to record any transactions of payment and other appropriate information.

Bonds

Bonds payable are another type of long-term obligation. These are issued by a company (or government) via a certificate that can be secured or not by the debtor's assets. The different kinds of bonds grant diverse rights to the borrower; therefore, a careful analysis of each bond being offered should be performed.

OWNER'S EQUITY

The owner's equity is defined as the portion of a firm's assets that is greater than the total liabilities. An owner's net worth is his or her share of the company's assets minus all liabilities. If a business gets in trouble, the owner's equity is the amount left after all the creditor's obligations have been satisfied.

Proprietorship and Partnership

Proprietorship

When a business or company is owned by one individual, it is termed a sole proprietorship. As expected, this type of company is generally small in size and tends to be service oriented. If Mel Katzman is the only owner of the local computer store, then he is the sole proprietor of the business. Some of the things influencing the owner's equity are:

- Moneys or assets taken for personal reasons.
- Earnings achieved and expenditures acquired.

An account for each owner's equity item should appear on the balance sheet and income statement. As a transaction transpires, it is recorded in the proper place.

Proprietorship Accounts

Withdrawals—Shows when the owner withdraws money, e.g., "Stuart Daniels, Withdrawals"

Capital—Shows when the owner puts money in the business, e.g., "Stuart Daniels, Capital."

Revenue—Shows the type of revenue realized, e.g., "Revenue from Rent."

Expense—Shows the type of expense acquired, e.g., "Insurance expense."

Partnership

Except for the treatment of owner's equity, the accounting is similar to that of the sole proprietorship. Every partner must have different capital and withdrawal accounts.

Partnership Capital and Withdrawal Accounts

The following begins a Capital Account.

Dec. 1, 19XX	Cash	$100,000.00	
	Jerry Gorden		$25,000.00
	Mary Anne Cafone		25,000.00
	Leslie Crawley		25,000.00
	Marc Alan		25,000.00
	To record beginning investment of partnership		

The following illustrates withdrawal of Capital.

Dec. 12, 19XX	Jerry Gorden, Withdrawal	$20,000.00	
	Cash		$20,000.00
	To record a withdrawal by Jerry Gorden		

When the partnership shows a profit, there are several ways in which the earnings can be allocated. The Income Summary must be closed and the figures transferred to the partner's individual Capital Accounts. Should there be a loss in the partnership, the losses are distributed in the same manner. The following lists some of the possible ways to allocate earnings.

Capital invested ratio—Profits and losses are divided based on the capital invested.

Example of Capital Invested Ratio Allocation

The first entry shows the initial investment.

Feb. 12, 19XX	Nathan Daniels		
		$100,000.00	(4/5)
	Janet Cohen	25,000.00	(1/5)

Dec. 31, 19XX	Income Summary	$25,000.00	
	Nathan Daniels		$20,000.00
	Janice Teisch		5,000.00
	Closing Income		
	Summary account and		
	divide the earnings		

Fractional ratio—Profits and losses are divided on a ratio based on the partnership agreement.

Fraction Ratio Allocation

The partner agreement established the following fractions for each partner.

Partner 1 = 1/5
Partner 2 = 2/5
Partner 3 = 1/5
Partner 4 = 1/5

Dec. 31, 19XX	Income Summary	$50,000.00	
	Harold Jones		$10,000.00
	Pamela Smith		20,000.00
	Shannon Murphy		10,000.00
	Susan Edgar		10,000.00
	Closing Income		
	Summary account and		
	divide the earnings		

Salaries and Interest—Profits and losses are divided by experience, amount of time spent, capital invested, and other factors. Salary and interest of capital are considered. An example would be if one partner is working full time while the other is working only part time, and the profits must be divided in unequal amounts.

Salaries and Interest Allocation

Dec. 31, 19XX   Income Summary $10,000.00
                      Janine Spermen $6,000.00
                      Larry Siegell   4,000.00
                      Closing entry to
                      divide among partners
                      the annual net income.

The termination of a partnership can occur for many reasons. In each case, the accountant must perform certain tasks in order for the transition to go smoothly.

Sale of a partnership requires that a name be changed in the partnership books and records. A new capital account is utilized and if approved by the other partner(s), then a new partnership is prepared.

Entry For a Partnership Sale

Feb. 16, 19XX   Reggie Russel, Capital $43,000.00
                      Joan Sanderson, Capital $43,000.00
                      Transfer Russel
                      equity to Sanderson

Should a partner withdraw from the partnership, a valuation of the partnership's assets must be performed. Once this is done and everyone concerned agrees, then the accountant and lawyer can perform their duties.

Entry for a Partnership Withdrawal

April 21, 19XX   Lynne Sullivan Capital $14,000.00
                      Cash $14,000.00
                      To record the withdrawal
                      of Seller

Should all the partners agree to terminate the partnership, the following steps must be taken:

- Sell all assets of the partnership.
- Use an accepted method to distribute the profits or losses among the partners.
- Pay the liabilities owed by the partnership.
- Disburse the remaining cash among the partners.

Entry for the Termination of a Partnership

June 25, 19XX   Boris Rebnick, Capital $2,000.00
                      Eric Lawrence, Capital   456.00
                      Cash $2,456.00
                      To disburse the
                      remaining cash and
                      terminate the accounts

Capital Stock (Rights and Responsibilities)

The shares of a corporation (ownership) are called *capital stock*. The *authorized shares* are the total number of capital stock that can be issued by the corporation and those sold to investors are called *issued stock*.

Preferred and Common Stock

Common shareholders possess certain rights as owners of the corporation. They have the right to vote at shareholders' meeting and have the ability to receive a dividend (profit of the corporation). They can purchase additional shares at any time and increase their percentage of ownership accordingly. Shareholders can also sell their shares at any time.

Upon termination of a company, the shareholders are entitled to receive (proportionately to their shares) any assets remaining once the outstanding liabilities have been settled. Periodically, a corporation may issue different classes of stock (the rights of each type must be carefully evaluated before purchasing). Shareholders do not participate in the daily running of the corporation.

Preferred stock retains many or all the rights of common stock; however, some rights are either added or modified. This type of stock receives its dividends and any assets due upon liquidation before the common. As discussed elsewhere in this book, there are different kinds of preferred stock. Please refer to the appropriate section for further details.

Recording the Issue or Retirement

The corporation must keep a listing of its shareholder's names and addresses as well as the number of shares owned. This data is recorded in a shareholders' ledger and is updated as indicated. Common and preferred stocks should each have individual accounts.

Entries For Selling a Stock For Cash at Par

Jan. 16, 19XX   Cash $100,000.00
                       Common Stock $100,000.00
                       To record the sale of 100,000 shares at $1.00
                       par value at $1.00/share

The following entry is an alternative.

Jan. 16, 19XX   Cash $100,000.00
                       Preferred Stock $100,000.00
                       To record the sale of 1000 preferred shares at
                       $100.00 par value at $100.00 per share

No-par stock has no established value. Par value, on the other hand, is a value that is indiscriminately provided to the share of stock. Stocks can be sold at that amount and for more or less. The par value is the amount that is recorded in the capital stock account.

Entry For a No-Par Stock

Feb. 17, 19XX   Cash $750,000.00

            Common Stock $750,000.00

            To record the sale of 750,000 no-par shares
at $75.00 per share

Entry for Selling Stock for an Asset

Feb. 17, 19XX   Land $100,000.00

            Common Stock $100,000.00

            To record a switching of land for common stock

Entry for Stock Sold at a Premium

Feb. 17, 19XX   Cash $130,000.00

            Common Stock $100,000.00

            Premium on Common Stock   30,000.00

            To record the sale of 100,000 common shares
at $1.00 par value for $1.30 per share

Entries for a Stock Sold at Discount

Feb. 17, 19XX   Cash $500,000.00

            Discount on
Preferred stock $100,000.00

            To record the purchase of preferred stock at
a discount.

The following entry is an alternative.

Feb. 17, 19XX   Cash $500,000.00

            Discount on
Common Stock $100,000.00

            To record the purchase of common stock at a
discount.

Entry for Retiring a Preferred Stock

Feb. 17, 19XX   Preferred Stock, $100 par value $10,000

            Premium on Preferred stock   10,000

            Retained earnings   2,000

               Cash $22,000

            To record the calling of preferred stock

Entry for the Retirement of Stock

Feb. 17, 19XX   Common Stock $500,000.00

                         Premium on Common Stock   100,000.00

                         Cash   600,000.00

                         To record the purchase and retirement of
100,000 common shares at $6.00 per share.

Dividend Payments

A *dividend* is a distribution of a corporation's assets to its shareholders. A *cash dividend* is the distribution of cash to the shareholders while a *stock dividend* means that shares of stock are distributed to the shareholders of record. Dividends can also be in the form of other assets of the company, e.g., one mining company provides bars of silver as a dividend to its shareholders. Dividends are usually paid on a per share basis. Dividends paid by a company are registered in a Dividends Account.

The final decision to provide the existing shareholders with a dividend must come from the Board of Directors. The Board must decide the following:

- *Date of declaration*—Date that the Board of Directors approves the dividend.
- *Date of record*—Date that one must own the stock in order to receive the dividend.
- *Date of payment*—Date that the checks are sent out to the shareholders.

It must be remembered that a cash dividend will decrease the retained earnings of a corporation. In order for the Board of Directors to declare a dividend, the company's financial overall status must permit it to do so. On the balance sheet, it should be noted that Dividends Payable is recorded as a liability. Once declared, the dividend (liability) must be paid to the shareholders of record.

Entry For a Declared Dividend

March 14, 19XX   Retained Earnings $100,000.00

                         Common Stock Dividends Payable $100,000.00

                         To record the declaration of a $.10 per share
dividend for the outstanding common shares.

April 14, 19XX   Common Stock

                         Dividends Payable $100,000.00

                         Cash $100,000.00

                         To record the payment of a cash dividend
declared on March 14, 19XX.

Though shareholders are owners of the company, they are not entitled to any of the assets until the Board of Directors declares a dividend. Sometimes a corporation elects to pay its shareholders a dividend in the form of stock rather than cash (a stock dividend). It should be remembered that a cash dividend will reduce the shareholder's equity and corporate assets while a stock dividend does not affect any of these. Total capital is also not influenced by a stock dividend.

Entry For a Stock Dividend

Dec. 11, 19XX   Retained Earning $30,000.00
               Common Stock Dividend Distributable $20,000.00
            Premium on Common Stock   10,000.00
            To record the declaration of a stock dividend

Feb. 15, 19XX   Common Stock Dividend
            Distributable $20,000.00
            Common stock   20,000.00
            To record a stock dividend

Treasury Stock

Stock that is purchased by the corporation through outright acquisition or obtained by donation is termed *treasury stock*. The stock has been issued and then reacquired. Treasury stock can be reissued at a discount (unlike unissued stock).

When determining the book value of a stock, treasury stock must be subtracted from the authorized stock to find the number of shares outstanding. The treasury stock receives no dividends nor can it have the right to vote.

Entry For The Purchase of Treasury Stock

June 17, 19XX   Treasury stock—Common $50,000.00
            Cash   50,000.00
            To record the purchase of 50,000 shares
            of treasury stock at $1.00/share.

An Entry For The Donation of Treasury Stock

June 17, 19XX   Received from shareholders as a donation
            100,000 shares of common stock

Securities Markets

As discussed in other sections of this book, stocks are traded in securities markets. Not only are stocks bought and sold, but also bonds, commodities, and other financial instruments. Besides the United States, securities markets are found in many other countries.

A corporation may elect to sell its shares to the public via an underwriter. Numerous companies are listed on the many exchanges that exist (e.g., New York Stock Exchange, American Stock Exchange) or are simply listed on the huge over-the-counter marketplace. Regardless of where the company shares are traded, specific regulations of the Securities and Exchange Commission (SEC) must be followed.

Since the expense of "going public" is quite costly, many smaller corporations will seek capital through a private placement of their company's stock. This can be done by using an investment banker, stock brokerage company, other financial institution, or by the company itself. As with any other traded stock, the SEC rules and regulations must be observed. Private stock is not usually listed on any of the public exchanges and are not as easily bought and sold. It is not uncommon for a corporation to sell shares privately before seeking a public placement. Once a company has successfully gone public with its shares, many of those shares that were sold previously may not be free to be traded. Again, the SEC has specific regulations concerning private placement and when shares can be traded on the open market. A stock certificate book and stockholders ledger should be utilized by the corporation for record keeping.

Entry For Stock Issuance

Dec. 11, 19XX   Cash $2,000,000.00
                   Common Stock   2,000,000.00
                   To record the issuance of 2,000,000 shares
                   at $1.00 per share.

The following is an alternative entry.

Dec. 11, 19XX   Cash $4,000.00
                   Common stock   4,000.00
                   To record the issuance of 4 shares at
                   $1,000.00 per share.

Retained Earnings

In the course of business, it is not uncommon for a corporation to keep a portion of its earnings to reinvest within the company. This part, which is retained from the shareholders' equity and is not paid out as dividends, is called *retained earnings*.

A Retained Earnings Account is utilized to register retained earnings by corporations. In many cases, businesses will forgo a dividend and elect to maintain an extensive retained earnings in order to insure that the proceeds of the company are guaranteed. Retained earnings are essential to help finance further expansion and must be dealt with carefully and prudently by a company's Board of Directors. Just because a corporation has retained earnings does not affirm that assets are available to pay existing shareholders a dividend. Elements that can influence retained earnings are:

- Intermittent net income or losses.
- Payment of dividends.
- Modifications of past earnings.

Appropriated

When a portion of the retained earnings is designated for either a dividend or for some other lawful reason, it is called *appropriated retained earnings*. Upon assigning monies for appropriated retained earnings, a special account termed Appropriated Retained Earnings Account is established.

Unappropriated

That portion of the retained earnings that is not designated to a particular reason or dividend. Funds can be transferred from the appropriated retained earnings account to the unappropriated retained earnings account (usually by orders of the Board of Directors).

CHAPTER 26

Income Statement Accounts

The income statement is the initial statement that the accountant prepares. The statement will display the following data for a set segment of time: revenues, expenses, and net income or losses. The *fiscal period* is a time covered by the financial statement, while the term *fiscal year* refers to the statement covering twelve consecutive months. It should be noted that financial statements should list: corporation, name, date, and name of statement.

REVENUES

The amount of money or account receivables that a company acquires from the sale of a product or a service provided is termed *revenue*.

- *Net income*—Bring in more assets than utilize.
- *Net loss*—Utilize more assets than brought in.

EXPENSES

The amount of money or total assets that a company must utilize in order to obtain its revenues or income is termed *expenses*.

By using the *matching principle,* an accountant is able to compare the expenses and revenues for a given segment of time. This is very important and allows the accounting department and overall management to objectively analyze the corporation's financial status.

OPERATING EXPENSE

These are expenses that are acquired with the general running of a business. This includes such items as: salaries, commissions, and advertising.

Payroll

Salaries and wages constitute a major portion of many companies' overall expenses. Most common payroll periods (period of time of every payroll compensation) are either weekly, biweekly, or monthly. An independent contractor differs from an employee in that deductions are taken from the employee's salaries or wages, while the independent contractor provides service for a fee. A *payroll register* is utilized by an employer to record all the payroll information and deductions for each pay period.

Certain deductions must be taken out of wages or salaries before paychecks are issued. The most common decutions are: federal, state, and local taxes; Social Security (FICA) Tax; and unemployment insurance taxes. Other deductions are: union dues, savings bonds, health plans, contributions to pensions, or charitable contributions.

Payroll Taxes

Every company that hires employees is responsible for correct payroll accounting procedures. The employer must see that all the deductions are properly recorded and that every tax requirement is handled appropriately.

Federal, state, and local withholding tax systems designate the employer to function as a tax collection representative for employees. The portion of taxes retained from an employee's paycheck is based on earnings (a wage-bracket withholding table is used to determine the correct deduction). When an employee is initially hired, he or she must complete an Employee's Withholding Allowance Certificate (W-4). The information on this form will determine the amount to be deducted. All moneys collected are paid by the employer to the proper authorities. This is true of federal, state, and local income taxes.

Social Security tax (FICA) is paid by both the employee and employer. The amount reimbursed by both is based on the employee's gross earnings. Those individuals who function as independent contractors (self-employed) must pay Social Security via a self-employment tax.

Insurance

Employers must pay state and federal unemployment taxes for every employee. This type of insurance is a protection for all employees. It can be utilized when economic conditions (not by their own doing) terminate their employment. The amount paid by each employer can vary based on a variety of factors (state where the business is located, employee earnings, and so on). All moneys owed by the employer are paid to the proper authorities.

Federal Individual Income Taxes

In order for the United States Government (federal, state, and local) to have enough capital to function, a variety of taxes have been implemented to attract revenue. Income taxes on both corporations and individuals raise a substantial amount of money for this purpose. The income tax is a segment of the overall economic policy of the government and can be utilized as a instrument to either increase or decrease economic growth.

The current income tax system is incremental in structure, with those, theoretically, earning the most paying the most. The individual taxpayer completes his or her tax forms (maybe with the help of a tax preparer or other competent professional) and sends them to the government.

It appears that every year changes in the tax laws take place. Deductions may alter annually and tax courts are constantly making decisions that affect the tax status of many individual taxpayers. In order to keep abreast of all the latest rulings and laws, many publications for the tax preparer or other interested parties are available.

For those with simple returns, a short tax form is generally utilized while those individuals with many deductions must use the long form version. Taxes are due on April 15 after the termination of one's tax year.

Ordinary Income/Loss

All the income acquired by an individual (except income that is exempt under the Internal Revenue Code) is considered *gross income*.

Some of the items comprising gross income are: wages, rents, prizes, professional fees, bonuses, salaries, dividends, partnership income, commissions, tips, interest, fees, royalties, business income, and back pay.

In order to obtain one's *adjusted gross income*, certain deductions can be taken from the gross income. These deductions will be discussed later on in this section. A loss occurs when your expenses are greater than your income.

Capital Gains/Losses

In order to stimulate investments, the federal government had been lenient in taxing certain capital gains. Capital gains/losses were defined for the selling of capital assets.

Capital gains deductions, however, have been repealed with the new tax laws. Capital losses will offset ordinary dollar-for-dollar income and can be carried forward.

Deductions (Business/Personal)

As with any other aspect of income taxes, business and personal deductions can possibly change year to year. Personal deductions are taken from the adjusted gross income in order to obtain taxable income. The business income from proprietorships and partnerships was taxed individually among all the principals.

You can elect to claim standard deductions or wish to itemize deductions. Some of the more common personal deductions of the past were: real estate taxes, interest paid on a debt, and charitable contributions. Careful record keeping and receipts are required and extremely necessary in the event of an audit by the Internal Revenue Service.

Corporations are handled differently than individuals by the tax laws and regulations. Taxation is often higher for the corporation. Some of the more common business deductions of the past were:

salaries and wages, repairs, rents, interest paid, advertising, amortization, depletion, and contributions.

Income Statement

Ethel Lorenz Flower & Gift Shoppe
Income Statement for the Year Ended December 31, 19XX

Sales:		$250,000.00
Cost of goods sold:		125,000.00
Gross Profit from sales:		$125,000.00
Expenses:		
Rent	$20,000.00	
Insurance	1,000.00	
Salaries	21,000.00	
Depreciation	1,000.00	
Advertising	5,000.00	
Utilities	2,500.00	
Office Supplies	500.00	
Taxes	4,000.00	
Delivery charges	500.00	
Miscellaneous Expense	500.00	
Total operating expenditures:		56,000.00
Net Income:		$69,000.00

CHAPTER 27

Analysis and Interpretation of Financial Statements

There are many procedures for the analysis and interpretation of financial statements. It must be realized that the financial statement presents a financial picture of a business's present and past status. It also permits the company to evaluate itself compared with other similar and competing companies. By using an audit, Certified Public Accountant (CPA) firms can analyze a business and report objectively on the company's condition. All publicly held companies must be audited by an independent CPA firm at least once a year. Analysis of financial statements is utilized in union negotiations, applications for credit and borrowing, attracting investors, and for a whole host of other business relationships and dealings.

A CPA reviews, investigates, and appraises a company's financial statements in order to insure that the company's data meets legitimate accounting procedures and principles. It is common protocol for footnotes describing the accounting methods to accompany the financial statement. Comparisons of financial statements can be made by either dollars or percentages.

BALANCE SHEET

The analysis of a balance sheet(s) is important. Using the following methods, the CPA can determine a great deal about the business or corporation.

The current ratio, working capital ratio, and acid-test ratio deal with a company's short-term or current status, whereas the concern its long-term position. The latter assist the business with debt management.

Current Ratio

The current ratio is the ratio of the current assets to current liabilities. It gives the number of times a company's current liabilities can be repaid with its current assets by dividing the total current assets by the total current liabilities. It is often called the working capital ratio and is utilized quite frequently.

Current Ratio

$$\frac{\text{Current Assets}}{\text{Current Liabilities}} = \text{Current Ratio}$$

$$\frac{\$150,000.00}{\$50,000.00} = 3:1$$

Working Capital

It is really not a ratio but rather it measures the amount of current assets remaining if every current liability is paid by the current assets. It demonstrates the business's short-term financial adequacy and ability to function.

Working Capital

	Current Assets	$75,000.00
−	Current Liabilities −	50,000.00
	Working Capital	25,000.00

Acid-Test Ratio

The acid-test ratio is the business's capability to repay its current liabilities with its liquid current assets. It is also called quick ratio or quick current ratio. Quick assets include cash, marketable securities, accounts receivable, and short-term notes receivable. Inventory and prepaid expenses are not incorporated in this category.

Acid Test Ratio

$$\frac{\text{Quick assets}}{\text{Current Liabilities}} = \text{Acid Test Ratio}$$

$$\frac{\$50,000.00}{\$25,000.00} = 2:1$$

Debt-Asset Ratio

This ratio demonstrates the association between debt (liabilities) and total assets. It is also called debt ratio and it assists creditors in evaluating the company.

Debt Asset Ratio

$$\frac{\text{Total Liabilities}}{\text{Total Assets}} = \text{Debt-Asset Ratio}$$

$$\frac{\$250,000.00}{\$1,000,000.00} = 25\%$$

Equity-Asset Ratio

This ratio is owners' equity divided by the company's total assets and reveals fiscal stability.

Equity-Asset Ratio

$$\frac{\text{Total Owner's Equity}}{\text{Total Assets}} = \text{Equity-Asset Ratio}$$

$$\frac{\$750,000.00}{\$1,000,000.00} = 75\%$$

Debt-Equity Ratio

This ratio shows the relationship between total liabilities and owner's equity.

Debt-Equity Ratio

$$\frac{\text{Total Liabilities}}{\text{Owner's Equity}} = \text{Debt-Equity Ratio}$$

$$\frac{\$250,000.00}{\$1,000,000.00} = 25\%$$

OPERATING STATEMENTS

In order to compare one's business with another or with itself from a previous year, the owner(s) must utilize percentages. The owners are also interested in whether the company is losing or making money, therefore, analysis of the operating statements is most important in providing this information. Some of the more common ratios that are used are shown in the following formulas:

$$\frac{\text{Expenses of Merchandise Sold}}{\text{Total Sales}} \times 100\%$$

$$\frac{\text{Administrative Expenses}}{\text{Total Sales}} \times 100\%$$

$$\frac{\text{Net Profit}}{\text{Total Sales}} \times 100\%$$

$$\frac{\text{Cost of Items Sold}}{\text{Total sales}} \times 100\%$$

RETAINED EARNINGS STATEMENT

The retained earnings statement exhibits a company's retained earnings for the fiscal year. When a dividend is declared, the retained earnings account must credit the retained earnings account as well as having enough cash on hand to pay the dividend.

Upon examining a retained earnings statement, you may observe that a company has a rather considerable quantity of capital in the retained earnings account and yet it may elect not to declare a dividend. In many cases, the entire amount of money in this kind of account may be needed to actually run the business. It is often considered good business sense to retain capital in this account for possible emergencies or expansion and not use it all to pay the shareholders' dividends.

In order to fully understand how a company utilizes its retained earnings, a careful analysis of the retained earnings account must be performed. Dividends (stock and cash), appropriated funds for expansion, and the purchase of treasury stock are a few of the entries commonly found in a retained earnings account.

STATEMENT OF CHANGES IN FINANCIAL POSITION

This statement will permit you to observe if there have been any changes (either increase or decrease) in a company's working capital. Any alteration of a noncurrent account (accounts that are not current assets or liabilities) should be explained by using an analyzing entry. This will provide you with a clearer picture of why the change took place. Sources of recently acquired funding and how it was used are also explained by this statement. It reviews the company's financial dealings and shows the working capital of the business.

It is not uncommon to find an analysis of the changes of working capital directly following the statement of changes in financial position. Using the balance sheet data from the beginning and end of a accounting period, the analysis of the working capital is performed.

CASH FLOW STATEMENTS

The cash flow statement of a business shows any increase or decrease of their cash. It will explain how the funds were utilized and how the capital was obtained. This kind of statement is commonly for the internal use by a company and permits the proper authorities to observe cash receipts and disbursements. Since the information needed is quite complex, cash flow is determined by adjusting the net income from an accrual basis to net income on a cash basis.

COMPARATIVE STATEMENTS

This kind of statement compares entries for two or more successive years. They are situated next to one another on one statement so that the comparison is easier. Both balance sheets or income statements can be compared in this manner.

Any entries that demonstrate a noteworthy difference are then reviewed for the reason(s) why the dissimilarity exists. When used to control a situation, the comparative income statement is commonly employed.

RATIOS, PERCENTAGES, AND TURNOVERS

In order to analyze a business's financial situation, you must use certain measuring devices. These implements, when properly used, assist the analyst in comparing two or more segments of information to one another.

Ratios are commonly used in the analysis and interpretation of financial statements. Ratios are used both for internal and external comparisons. Several of the common types of ratios are: liquidity, debt, profitability, and stock market. For example, suppose the debt ratio for the past two years is 2:1.

Percentages are often utilized to note increases or decreases in a business's financial statements. These index numbers are usually used when comparing information for several accounting periods (sometimes called trend percentages). For example, suppose the gross profits are up 15% over last year.

Turnover is another measurement that is deployed by analyst. The turnover ratio is calculated by the association of sales to assets of a given company. For example, suppose the goods turnover was 5.57 times.

CHAPTER 28

Insurance

One method of protecting a company's assets against fire, theft, and other calamities is through the purchase of insurance. In many businesses, the responsibility of insurance selection and recording falls upon the accounting department.

An *insurance policy* is a legal agreement between an insurer (insurance company) and the insured (purchaser of the policy). The *insurance premium* is the cost of the policy and can be usually paid monthly, quarterly, semi-annually, or yearly. The amount of coverage is different with each company, but a good rule of thumb is the replacement cost of the total assets minus depreciation.

PROPERTY INSURANCE

The purchase of property insurance is essential to both the individual's and company's overall insurance plan. A single accident or lawsuit can result in millions of dollars worth of losses; therefore, adequate coverage is imperative. Deductibles, replacement cost coverage, total insurance required, built-in inflation and other factors all must be considered. Riders for flood, fire, wind, and explosion insurance as well as other specialty addenda should also be deliberated. Others riders can include: business interruption insurance, replacement-cost insurance, fine-arts coverage, protection against boiler explosion, and damages by one's sprinkler system. In order to fully safeguard a company, the person responsible for the business's insurance must speak to many agents and companies before the final decision is reached.

Property insurance protects the building, furnishings, fixtures, equipment, and other contents (assets) utilized within the scope of one's business. Land and foundations are generally not insured because they will generally survive any disaster. Policies must be tailored to the individual company's needs.

CASUALTY-LIABILITY

This type of insurance is also called "third party" insurance. It protects you when a negligence action is brought against another person or company—the third party. Though many businesses carry a general liability package, one should check carefully to determine if all the important and pertinent aspects are included.

Product liability is a prerequisite for anyone manufacturing or selling a product while malpractice insurance is essential for physicians, lawyers, and other professionals. With the high settlements being awarded almost routinely, "umbrella insurance" policies are gaining popularity. This type of policy provides increased coverage beyond the normal policy. Slander, libel, punitive damages and invasion of privacy are often missing from the standard insurance contract and must be purchased if relevant to one's business.

LIFE

Life insurance provides the beneficiary of the policy an amount of money when the insured passes away. Life insurance is important to the business person for several reasons:

- It will provide funds to the family, enabling them to exist without the insured's income.
- When the insured is committed to a partnership, it will assist the surviving business partner(s) in buying out the heirs of the insured.
- It provides key employee insurance which can protect a company if a key person dies.

There are various kinds of life insurance, as described in the following sections.

Term Insurance

Term insurance provides protection with no investment. When the insured dies, the beneficiaries are paid the amount of the policy. Types of term insurance include: straight term, renewable term, decreasing term, and convertible term.

Whole Life

Whole life insurance provides protection as well as a cash value. There is little control over the policy. Can be ordinary life or limited payment.

Universal Life

Universal life insurance is nearly the same as whole life except that the cash is placed in short-term investments and the return in the accumulation fund is flexible. The insurance amount and premium can be altered easily.

Variable Life

Variable life insurance is similar to whole life except the insured can select the investment portfolio.

DISABILITY INSURANCE

If an accident or illness occurs and prevents an employee from working, disability insurance will provide income. The amount paid by the insured will depend on the following: amount of money to be received if disabled, time necessary to wait before actually receiving the benefits, and the duration of the benefits or payments. Insurance policies are available that will supplement a business while a proprietor or partner is unable to work.

HEALTH

With the rising costs of health services today, health insurance is essential. The number of companies offering health insurance and the plans can vary greatly. Most basic plans will provide coverage for hospital, surgery, and some medical expenses whereas extended policies cover a larger variety of services.

Many plans offer riders to cover additional areas. Some of these are: dental, maternity, private nursing, catastrophic illness or injury, nursing home care. Major medical insurance generally includes most sections of health care but many require that the insured pay a deductible and often a percentage of the bill below a certain level (80% below $2,000.00).

The federal government also provides health care for a variety of qualified persons. Medicare and Medicaid are two of the existing programs.

Another method of obtaining health insurance is through a health maintenance organization (HMO). For a set price, the HMO will care for all your medical requirements. In some cases, a copayment is required when seeing a physician.

Companies usually qualify for group rates (depending on size) and are able to be selective. An individual generally finds that health insurance is not only costly but sometimes difficult to obtain. Shop and compare not only cost but all the aspects of the policy carefully. A single illness can easily eliminate your assets.

FIDELITY AND SURETY INSURANCE BONDS

A fidelity bond is insurance against an employee embezzling or being dishonest with an employer. Generally, a blanket coverage is recommended to cover everyone working for a company.

A surety bond is a performance bond. It insures that work will be completed. An insurer will purchase a surety bond to guarantee that a contractor will satisfactorily complete a job. If a problem develops, the insurance company can hire another contractor to finish the task.

CO-INSURANCE

When the insurance company joins with the insured for a percentage of the risk, a co-insurance situation exists. Many health insurance policies require that the insured pay part of the bill above a deductible.

OTHER FORMS OF INSURANCE

There are many types of insurance policies available to the business person. Some of the more common are the following:

- *Workers' Compensation and employer's liability insurance*—Protects workers on the job and is required by all employers.
- *Ocean marine*—Protects ships and vessels (goods also).
- *Inland marine*—Covers goods damaged in transit (common carriers).
- *Automobile liability insurance*—Covers damage, death, and damages by the cars owned by the company. One should also consider automobile non-ownership liability insurance and be fully aware of the no-fault laws and insurance implications in the state in which they work or perform business.

INSURANCE RECORD MAINTENANCE

Since there are so many policies that are necessary in the operation of a business, an insurance register is frequently utilized to record any transactions concerning the subject of insurance. All policies should be stored in a safe place so that they are protected against damage and easily accessible whenever needed.

Insurance Register

CHAPTER 29

Managerial Accounting

The role of management requires a working knowledge of the basics of finance. This will enable the manager to transcribe both the previous and present financial activities as well as obtain capital for any future requirements. A Controller (comptroller) must be able to lead a financial staff and at the same time provide the remainder of the management team with financial advice and direction. The ability of an executive to comprehend basic accounting elements and procedures can lead to a more cohesive and smoothly running operation.

COST ANALYSIS

Careful, on-going cost analysis allows an executive to see how the costs of the operation will alter as the volume of business fluctuates. Companies must at least break even financially in order to survive.

Determining Unit Costs

When utilizing the process cost system, one must determine the unit processing costs in every section of the business. To ascertain the cost per unit the following must be performed:

1. Total the supplies, labor, and overhead costs for every section of the business for a selected time.
2. Total the units processed during that section of time (partly finished units are termed *equivalent finished units*).
3. Divide the costs by the units processed.
4. The final figure is the unit cost (partly finished unit costs are termed *equivalent finished unit costs*).

Unit costs assist management in many areas. Forecasting and determining inventory costs and the costs of the products sold are examples of segments wherein unit cost plays an important role.

Variable And Fixed Costs

A *fixed cost* is one that does not fluctuate during a established undertaking throughout a selected segment of time. Examples of fixed costs are rent and depreciation. Should expansion occur, the fixed rates may have to be altered accordingly.

A *variable cost* is one that digresses in relationship to any alterations of an established undertaking. An example of a variable cost is sales commission. Throughout this period, the cost per unit remains the same, though the cost may vary.

Break-Even Charts (Cost-Volume-Profit Analysis)

The cost-volume-profit analysis is used by management to help plan for the future. It utilizes different procedures that can elucidate the varying costs and amount of output. This analysis can help management to decide on the price of their products, assist in production selection, and also aid in capital investment matters. In essence, the analysis will attempt to determine how alterations in cost and volume will effect profits.

The break-even point is the level at which a company's expenses equal their revenues generated. There is neither a profit nor loss for that particular period and it is one of the concepts utilized in the cost-volume-profit analysis. The break-even point for a business can be obtained by either an equation, contribution margin, or a break-even chart.

Construction

When the cost-volume-profit analysis is displayed graphically, it is called a *break-even graph* or *chart*. In order to construct such a graph, the following must be performed:

- A horizontal line depicting fixed costs is drawn (it can provide essential data but is not necessary for the actual analysis).
- A sales line is drawn from the zero points (units and sales) to the maximum point of sales.
- The variable cost line is drawn (which starts at the fixed cost level).
- The variable cost line and the sales line cross at the break-even point.

Break Even Chart

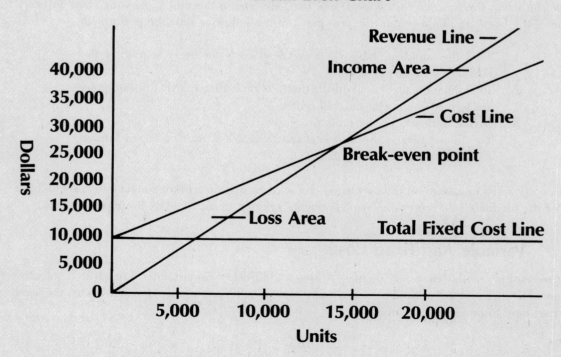

Use And Interpretation

By utilizing cost-volume-profit analysis, a manager can forecast and anticipate if and when deviations occur to revenues, products, and/or other cost components. Since this analysis predicts the future, one can only assume that the information utilized is correct and applicable to the actual future. Since some costs are variable, the results may only be estimates in nature.

The break-even analysis can assist management in determining the number of units required to sell in order for the company to break even financially. It can be used to ascertain how changes of fixed priced items will influence the break-even point. It can aid in establishing a company's net income as well as its pretax income.

BUDGETS

The process and plan in which management develops a course of future action (expressed in financial terms) is termed *budgeting*. The various supervisors or department heads formulate proposed expenses, revenues, and other financial aspects. Once all sections of the company have responded, the business's operating budget is developed (using accounting terms and principles) and often written as a projected financial statement.

In order for the budgeting process to work effectively, the company should utilize the following: control, exploration, research, and planning. It should be noted that the budget period usually synchronizes with the company's accounting periods. Either an executive, specific committee, or budget director (huge companies have individual budget departments) generally develops a budget for a company.

Kinds Of Budgets

The company's primary plan of financial operations is termed the *master budget*. It is assembled from the various smaller budgets developed by the individual department heads and/or other designated personnel. Some of the more common kinds of budgets are:

- *Sales budget*—Estimates items sold and revenue received.
- *Merchandising budget*—Estimates needed merchandise to be bought.
- *Production budget*—Estimates the number of items to be produced.
- *Materials budget*—Estimates the materials required to manufacture the final product.
- *Expense budget*—Estimates expenses such as labor costs and overhead expenditures.
- *Plant and Equipment budget*—Estimates new equipment needed and the removal of obsolete pieces.
- *Selling and Administrative budget*—Estimates the selling and administrative costs of running the operations.
- *Cash budget*—Estimates cash needs to operate effectively.

Factors Considered In Budget Preparation

The accounting department is ultimately responsible for developing the final budget. In order to do so, it must gather the data presented by the various sources of input and transcribe it into accounting terms.

Standard costs are useful in determining the final budget. They are expenditures that occur during "normal" working situations and each is used to establish a guideline to which other costs can be compared.

Several items that are frequently standardized are: materials, labor, and overhead costs. Extensive investigation and research is often carried out in order to standardize these costs (which must be updated on a regular basis). Regardless of how a company develops standard costs, a variation may occur during the actual production.

Standard Cost

Material (1 pound per unit at $20.00 per pound) $20.00
Labor (1 hour per unit at $10.00 per hour)   10.00
Overhead ($10 per standard direct labor hour)   10.00
Standard cost per unit $40.00

Budget Variation And Analysis

A *variance* occurs when the actual cost deviates from the standard cost. A *favorable variance* exists when the final cost is below the standard cost, whereas, an *unfavorable variance* is when the final or actual cost is above the standard cost.

Whenever a variation does manifest itself, it should be examined and attempts should be made to determine why it occurred. Any corrections should be corrected and appropriate steps taken to prevent it from happening again.

Material Variance And Analysis

Actual cost (5,200 tons at $3.00/ton) $15,600.00
Standard cost (5,000 tons at $2.50/ton) $12,500.00
Amount over standard cost $3,100.00

To locate the material variance, the following is performed:

Quantity variance:
Actual units at standard price (5200 tons @ $2.50) $13,000.00
Standard units at standard price (5000 tons @ $2.50)   12,500.00
Unfavorable variance 200 tons @ $2.50 $500.00

Price variance:
Actual units at actual price (5200 tons @ $3.00) $15,600.00
Actual units at standard price (5200 tons @ $2.50)   13,000.00
Unfavorable variance   2,600.00
Extra material cost $3,100.00

It is then the responsibility of management to analyze the data and to determine why 200 tons of extra material were utilized (this amount resulted in a cost of an extra $500.00). The $.50 difference in price also added another $2,600.00 to the final outcome and presented another aspect that had to be examined.

By utilizing similar principles, management can analyze labor variances. Overhead variances can be subdivided to volume and controllable variances which use similar accounting procedures to ascertain the reasons for any deviations.

FORECASTING

One of the methods available of financial analysis is the use of forecasting, the viewing or peering into the future. By applying the computer and advanced mathematical technology, one can perform econometric forecasting. Since in-house forecasting is quite expensive, it is not uncommon for a company to utilize an outside business or consultant to perform this task. Forecasting is an essential element in both the intermediate and long-term financial planning of most companies.

Kinds Of Forecasting

Several types of forecasting that are commonly performed are:

- *Cash-flow forecast*—Prediction of future cash receipts and cash disbursements.
- *Sales forecast*—Prediction of future expected sales. Important in scheduling and projecting production and expenses.
- *Collection and other cash receipts*—Prediction of collection and other cash receipts.
- *Cash disbursements forecast*—Prediction of cash disbursements.
- *Production costs forecast*—Prediction of the cost of manufacturing or production.
- *Additional disbursement forecast*—Prediction of other cash disbursements (taxes, dividends, and so on).

Factors Considered In Forecast Preparation

In order to forecast a company's financial status, one must analyze the flow of funds that exists. The funds statement is used to compare a business's net fund flow during two periods of time.

A source and use of working capital statement should also be completed. This kind of statement is often required by lending institutions and by a company's internal control procedures.

Once these statements are completed, one should receive a clear picture of the company's financial status. At that point, forecasting can be performed. Variations from a business's expected cash flow must also be considered.

Pro-Forma Statements

Many companies will desire not only a forecast of their flow of cash but also a *pro-forma* (projected) income statement and balance sheet. These will provide more detail and forecast the business's total assets, liabilities, and income statement components.

The pro-forma income statement projects income during a prospective time period. This statement can provide the following:

- Furnish more detailed analysis.
- Provide data for precise forecasts.

The pro-forma balance sheet can the following:

- Assist in forecasting assets.
- Aid in forecasting net worth and liabilities.

PART V

Office Administration and Communication

CHAPTER 30

Office Administration

EXECUTIVE TRAVEL

Before you engage in the time-consuming task of making travel arrangements, ascertain the following information:

- Is there a travel department within your organization?
- Is an outside travel agency used?
- Is a secretary designated to handle travel arrangements?
- How do the executives travel? First-class? Coach?
- How are payments for reservations handled?
- What procedures are used for cash advances?

When making travel arrangements, a travel agency is your best bet. Travel agencies earn commissions from the airlines, hotels, and so on; therefore, you do not incur any out-of-pocket fees. They have access to the most up-to-the-minute information and can offer great assistance in both domestic and international travel.

The names of accredited travel agencies are available from the American Society of Travel Agents (ASTA), 360 Lexington Avenue, New York, NY 10017. Many reputable travel agents are not members of ASTA; therefore, you may additionally want to check with the Better Business Bureau.

Sources of Reference

American Express Space Bank (worldwide hotel, motel and auto reservations), call 1-800-238-5000.

Hotel & Motel Red Book, a copy of which is available at all member hotels.

Hotel and Travel Index (lists rates, accommodations, and distance from airport), published by Robinson-Ingeldue Publications, division of Ziff-Davis Publishing Company, Hollywood Boulevard, Hollywood, CA 90028.

Leahy's Hotel-Motel Guide and Travel Atlas of the United States, Canada, Mexico and Puerto Rico, published by American Hotel Register Company, 226 Ontario Street, Chicago, IL 60610.

Mobil Travel Guides (series of seven regional guides listing motels, hotels, resorts, and local restaurants), published by Prentice Hall Press, One Gulf + Western Plaza, New York, NY 10023.

Official Airline Guides (North American and International Editions available), published by The Reuben H. Donnelley Corporation, P.O. Box 6710, Chicago, IL 60680.

The Official Guide of the Railways (U.S., Canada, Puerto Rico, Mexico, Cuba, and Central America), published by the National Railway Publishing Company, 424 West 33 Street, New York, NY 10001.

The Official Steamship Guide, International, published by Transportation Guides, 299 Madison Avenue, New York, NY 10017.

Russell's Official National Motor Coach Guide (U.S., Canada and Mexico), published by Russell's Guides, Inc., 817 Second Avenue SE, Cedar Rapids, IA 52403.

NOTE: Check with each resource for the current fee, if any.

Making the Arrangements

Making arrangements should include the following:

- Confirm destination(s).
- Confirm dates and times of departures and returns.
- Establish transportation preference (mode, carrier, and class).
- Establish preferred time of day for travel.
- Confirm hotel preference and accommodations (availability of conference rooms, in or near city, price and type of room(s), and so on).

Prior to the Trip

Don't tempt "Murphy's Law." Be certain to double-check the accuracy of the airline tickets and confirm hotel reservations in writing, if possible. If international travel is on the horizon, a passport and/or visa should be investigated. Does your employer have a valid passport? If so, when does it expire? Passport and visa information are available at your local passport office or by sending a nominal fee to the Superintendent of Documents, Government Printing Office, Washington, DC 20402.

How about immunization requirements? Contact your local health department, your nearest consulate office or the Foreign Quarantine Program, National Communicable Disease Center, Atlanta, GA 30333.

Preparing the Itinerary

An itinerary is the chronological, easy-to-read schedule of daily events, and it *must* be accurate. (Your employer should get the original, his or her superior may require a copy, you should retain a copy, and a copy should be prepared for your employer's family.) The itinerary should contain the following information:

1. Date, time, and place of departure.
2. Mode(s) of transportation throughout the trip (confirmed).
3. Dates, times, and places of arrival(s).
4. Lodging accommodations throughout the trip (confirmed).
5. Appointments and any information pertinent thereto (names, addresses, phone numbers).
6. Date, time, and place of return.

ITINERARY FOR SANDY ZUCKER

From May 1 to May 6

Monday
May 1

9:30 AM EST   Leave Newark Airport via TWA, Flight No. 205 (tickets in envelope)

10:30 PST   Arrive in Las Vegas—Reservations at MGM Grand Hotel (confirmation attached)

7:00   Dinner with Andrea Teisch—phone her prior to meeting at (702) 123-7654

Tuesday
May 2

9 AM   Convention at MGM Grand (program attached)

Evening   Free

Wednesday
May 3

10:30 AM   Leave Las Vegas Airport via TWA Airlines Flight No. 145 (tickets in envelope)

11:05 AM   Arrive San Francisco. Hotel reservations at Sheraton Inn (confirmation attached)

Thursday
May 4

12 noon   Address San Francisco Bar Association in Cypress Room of Hyatt-Regency (notes on 3 x 5 cards in briefcase)

Friday
May 5   No scheduled activities

Saturday
May 6

9 AM   Leave San Francisco Airport, TWA Flight No. 56 (tickets in envelope)

5 PM EST   Arrive Newark Airport. Limousine will be waiting.

Enjoy your trip!

The final planning steps are the following:

1. Personally hand your employer the airline tickets and hotel confirmations.
2. Place the papers needed for each appointment in a separate envelope and submit them in chronological order. Be certain that each envelope is properly identified.
3. Review the itinerary.

During the Trip

In your employer's absence, do the following:

1. Although you will know where your employer is at all times, you must be very discreet about disclosing this information. Adhere to the adage: "If in doubt, don't give it out!" You can always relay a message.
2. Arrange in advance where to forward selected correspondence, and be certain to use good judgment.
3. If there is a significant change in the itinerary, notify all persons possessing copies of same.

Preparing for your Employer's Return

The first day back will focus on exchanging news on the activities that transpired in the interim. Have the mail presorted in order of importance and telephone calls arranged in order of priority. You will undoubtedly be involved in preparing special reports and letters of appreciation and so on.

Preparing the Expense Report

The Internal Revenue Service is closely monitoring corporate travel; therefore, you must fill out the expense report properly and accurately. Use the form supplied by your organization and be certain to include receipts for all transportation, lodging, meals, entertainment, and miscellaneous expenditures, where applicable. Obtain the necessary signatures and retain a copy for your files.

OFFICE MANAGEMENT

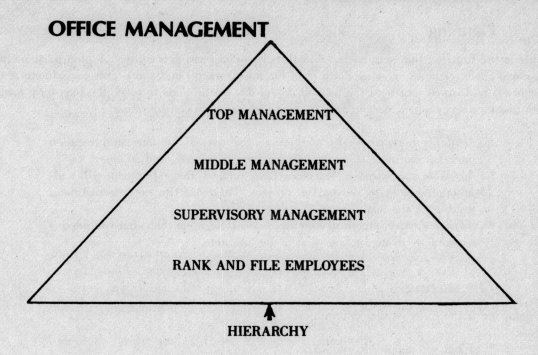

TOP MANAGEMENT

MIDDLE MANAGEMENT

SUPERVISORY MANAGEMENT

RANK AND FILE EMPLOYEES

HIERARCHY

Managing an office involves the circular concept of management functions which includes *planning, organizing, staffing, directing,* and *controlling*. It is a vicious cycle because the circular flow of functions must run continuously in order for a project to reach completion. As soon as the cycle is completed, it starts again.

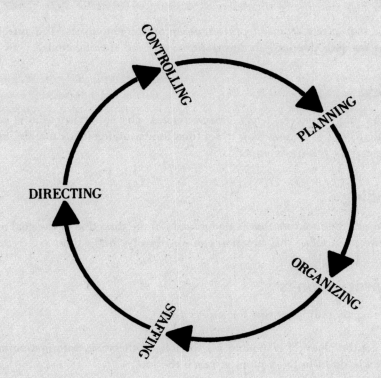

Planning

This is the function that sets goals, objectives, policies, and procedures. A plan must include long-range goals (generally coming down from top management) and short-term goals (done at the lower levels and which represent the tactical day-to-day battle plans to reach the long-term goals). When planning any project, certain factors must be taken into consideration:

- *Available manpower*—In addition to the normal holidays and vacation periods, you must allow for training time, absences, and so on.
- *Available equipment*—"Murphy's Law" dictates that equipment will malfunction before or during the project. Therefore, do not procrastinate, waiting for the last minute.
- *Available space, materials and supplies*—Determine that what you need is available—arrange to get what is not available.

Organizing

Organizing is the function that determines:

- What you should do yourself.
- What you should do but get others involved in.
- What you should do but others can effectively do if given the opportunity.
- What others should do—you can pitch in during a crunch.
- What others should completely do.

Staffing

This is the function that *selects, trains, appraises, and promotes* employees. You must determine the number of employees needed, develop job descriptions, and job specifications.

Directing

This is the function that *influences, leads, and motivates*. The supervisor who is effective knows how to "ask" rather than "order," knows how to set time limits, understands morale, and knows how to discipline employees in a positive manner.

Controlling

Controlling determines the progress that is being made in the direction of the goal and whether or not the objectives have been met. This function can also involve budgeting.

Supervisory Don'ts

The following lists some additional tips for supervisors.

- Don't let the chain of command get too long. Otherwise, information may not trickle down to the bottom or reach the top.

- Don't, if possible, have one person report to two bosses. This can create a real problem in deciding whose work is done first.
- Don't assign an assistant to do the same work as the boss. (This is self-explanatory!!)
- Don't leave fuzzy areas in job assignments. Be specific about each job to avoid inviting conflicts and duplication of efforts.
- Don't mix responsibilities within the same group. For example, do not expect the purchasing department to cope with issues that should be addressed by the human resources department.

WORK SIMPLIFICATION

In the 1930s, Allen Morgenson, an industrial engineer, had been working in factories. He found much resistance when he tried to implement a new idea or suggest any improvement. Rather than looking upon his changes as constructive, people took his suggestions as a form of criticism.

Morgenson thereafter established a school of work simplification in Lake Placid, New York, which is still in operation. He "graduates" executives from some of the most prominent and prestigious companies.

Basically, Morgenson defines work simplification as the *development of a questioning attitude* regarding the way things are done and the *provision of an organized approach* for suggesting and evaluating improvements. Once a questioning attitude has been developed, you can spot bottlenecks, high-cost operations, errors, or excessive movements or delays.

Many evaluative methods are suggested:

- The *flow chart* depicts the flow of work from one person to another, one department to another, process loops, etc. Some of the basic symbols used in flow charts are:

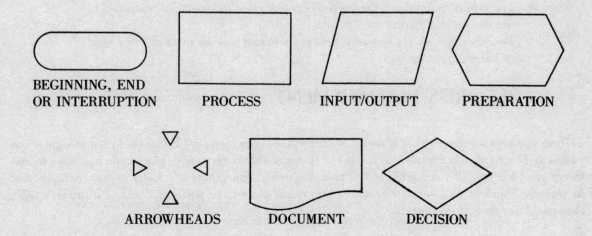

BEGINNING, END OR INTERRUPTION   PROCESS   INPUT/OUTPUT   PREPARATION

ARROWHEADS   DOCUMENT   DECISION

- The *daily log* (diary) records your ongoing tasks on an individual basis, indicating the amount of time you are absorbed in each one. This can be broken down into hourly, daily, or weekly segments.

Name *Janice Morton*	Department *Adv.*		
Date *4/17/XX*	Position *Exec. Secy.*		
Time	Word Processing	Telephone	Records Management
9⁰⁰	25	5	
9³⁰	15	5	10
10⁰⁰	5	10	15

- The *work station* or *office analysis* is a diagram of the environment in terms of placement of furniture and items. For example, are your files located conveniently or must you leave your desk each time you need access to one? Are reference materials within easy reach? Are air conditioning, heating, and lighting effective? If the answers to any of the aforementioned are "no," you are not utilizing your time and space to the maximum.

Time Management

Work can be greatly simplified by managing your time most efficiently. Consider the following:

- Prepare and stick to a daily "to-do" list on which tasks have been prioritized.
- Don't procrastinate; do tasks as they arise—especially the difficult ones. Once they are done, they are out of the way.
- Take advantage of support services when appropriate.
- Try to avoid work overloads by just saying no or by delegating requests you can't handle. Be certain to keep yourself informed of all work you have delegated. Remember, its successful completion is still your responsibility.
- Be aware of the time you are on "hold" for a phone call. Often it is better to call back.
- Try to find "quiet time" for the projects that need the most concentration or are the most difficult.
- Periodically evaluate how your time is spent and look for more efficient ways of handling things.

RECORDS MANAGEMENT

Have you ever wondered what it would be like to lose your memory? If you could not recognize the names and faces of your friends and relatives? If you could not remember places you had been to and things you had seen? If you could not find valuable items? Now, *think of a hospital that could not find its records. Think of an insurance company that could not find its policies. Think of a lawyer's office that could not find its documents.*

Records have been and will always be the memory of an office. Without these valuable records and the ability to locate them quickly, the office would be as lost as you would be without YOUR memory. In the sections that follow, analyzing records and record systems will also be considered.

Records Retention

Records management *is not just filing*. It includes the creation, control, use, and disposition of records. It involves classifying records in terms of importance to determine the length of time they should be retained. For example:

- Vital records (corporate papers, ownership papers, contracts, stock certificates, insurance policies) should *never* be destroyed and should perhaps be kept in a fireproof vault.
- Important records (tax statements, sales records, quotations, some correspondence) are replaceable at great cost. Some of these records can be transferred to inactive storage areas where they will not be destroyed (depending on the need for accessibility). Many companies keep duplicates of vital and important records in an off-site facility to afford themselves additional security.
- Useful records (bank statements, memos, general correspondence) can be of temporary importance and should be kept only as long as necessary.
- Nonessential records (announcements, routine mailings) may be destroyed after they have served their purposes.

Designing and Controlling Records (Forms)

Forms are the most widely used method of communication in that they provide the most expedient means of transferring essential information with the least amount of input. When evaluating the need for existing forms or revising new forms it is important to determine what information is essential.

A form (or portions thereof) should be eliminated or not included if: the information is no longer applicable, another source is available, or the cost of the form (including printing, filing, and so on) is greater than its value. It must be *easy to understand, easy to fill in, and easy to store.*

Types of Forms

Forms vary in size, color, paper stock, and serve a variety of functions.

- Single copy forms (telephone message pads).
- Multiple-copy forms (four-copy purchase orders).
- Specialty forms (continuous form registers).
- Unit-set forms (often used with charge cards).

Developing Forms

When developing forms, adhere to the following:

1. Keep the design simple.
2. Eliminate unnecessary and unlawful information such as age, religion, and so on.

3. Identify with name of form and/or form number.
4. If a check mark can be substituted for writing, use the check mark format.
5. Allow enough room for appropriate information to be included. (For handwritten fill-ins, figure approximately one-quarter-inch vertical spacing; for typewritten fill-ins, figure for double spacing or one-third inch.

Forms Management

Consider the following checklist for forms management.

- *Analyze* for actual need.
- *Design* for practicality.
- *Order, purchase, and print* for best quality at least cost.
- *Store and inventory* to keep supplies up-to-date and in adequate supply.
- *Distribute* to appropriate users.
- *Dispose* of those no longer in use.

Filing Procedures For Manual Systems

When setting up or maintaining a manual filing system you must evaluate your equipment and supplies and make sure they meet the needs of your organization.

- Is there a manual that describes the records management operation of your company? (It is important that all responsible personnel be able to find records when necessary!)
- Can the records be obtained promptly?
- Is the present system adequately serving your needs?
- Are the records protected against fire, theft, "improper eyes"?
- Are standard records management rules used? Is there adequate cross-referencing where applicable?
- Are file drawers bursting at the seams? If so, how can the system best be expanded?
- Do the file drawers display descriptive labels? Captions?
- Have adequate provisions been made for transferring and disposing of files?
- Are the forms currently used sturdy enough to withstand the stress of the records management cycle?
- Can the location of the files be changed so as to provide a more efficient flow of traffic?

Filing Equipment

A variety of filing cabinets is available for the storage of paper records in every conceivable size, price, color, and design. The choice will be on the basis of cost, available space, needed protection, and personnel. Sources of up-to-date information can be found in showrooms, magazines and catalogs, stationers, business equipment dealers, and office furniture stores.

- Centralized filing systems are housed in one location, generally under the supervision of a particular person or department.
- Decentralized filing systems are housed in various locations to accommodate the needs of particular persons or departments.

Vertical files—are conventional filing cabinets where files are stored in the drawers facing front to back. They generally consist of two to five drawers, depending on the amount of material to be stored. Hanging folders may be used that offer more expandability than regular folders.

Lateral files—have the same features and functions as vertical filing cabinets only the length of the cabinet is against the wall and the drawers extend only about a foot toward the operator when opened. Files are stored so that the front of the folders face the left side of the drawer and the sides face the operator.

Open-shelf files—resemble steel bookcases. The files are placed in the same manner as a book on a shelf. They are becoming very popular because a fifty-percent saving of space is offered. Shelving is adjustable and tracks allow movability. A major disadvantage is the lack of protection.

Rotary files—offer round, spinning file storage, much like a carousel. They are especially useful when files need to be accessible to many people simultaneously. They also lack protection.

Visible-card files—feature small drawers, generally two inches high and twelve inches wide. Records can lay flat and pull out and horizontally down. This is ideal for the storage of small maps, charts, and so on.

Power unit files—offer a wide variety of files that can be mechanically operated. The desired shelf can be accessed often by the push of a button. The file units are enclosed and are generally equipped with an electric eye for security.

Tickler files—are small filing boxes housing index cards that are generally used as reminders and follow ups. Guides can be divided by the day, week, month, and so on.

Whether you realize it or not, you already know many of the records management rules. If you have ever looked up a name in the white pages of a telephone directory, you have applied *alphabetic* filing rules. If you have ever looked up the name of a company in the yellow pages of a telephone directory, you have applied *subject* filing rules. The telephone book itself is an example of *geographic* filing. If you have a checking account, either you or the bank arranges your checks in *numeric* filing order.

Alphabetic Filing

The alphabetic filing system is one of the most commonly used of all—the one in which you file from A to Z. This is the same system used in white pages of telephone books, in dictionaries, and in encyclopedias. By learning a few rules, filing will be as easy as A, B, C.

Rule 1—Order of Units

Before you begin filing, reverse the names so that they appear in the following order: (I) last name (surname), (II) first name or first initial, (III) middle name or middle initial. This is known as indexing each unit.

	Unit I	Unit II	Unit III
D. Seth Dworkin	Dworkin	D.	Seth
David S. Dworkin	Dworkin	David	S.
David Seth Dworkin	Dworkin	David	Seth

Rule 2—Personal Names

Alphabetize names by comparing each letter in the last name (Unit I). *And*ers would come before *And*rews. When Unit I is identical, alphabetize according to the first name or first initial (Unit II). When Units I and II are identical, alphabetize according to the middle name or middle initial (Unit III). The golden rule of filing is:

Nothing comes before something. Adams would come before *Adams*on.

	Unit I	Unit II	Unit III
Joan A. Josephs	Josephs	Joan	A.
A. Mary Josephson	Josephson	A.	Mary
Gerald Sullivan	Sullivan	Gerald	
Gerald A. Sullivan	Sullivan	Gerald	A.

Rule 3—Prefixes

A prefix in front of a last name is considered part of the name and not a separate unit, e.g., Mc, Mac, d, de, Van, O', St. Therefore, you would treat the name O'Hara as if it were Ohara. When you are alphabetizing St. (a male saint) or Ste. (a female saint), always alphabetize it as if it were spelled out (Saint). When a person's last name is St. George, for example, it is treated as one unit as if it were spelled Saintgeorge.

	Unit I	Unit II	Unit III
Carla d'Angeli	d'Angeli	Carla	
Rita Sue Dangeli	Dangeli	Rita	Sue
William St. Andrews	St. Andrews	William	
Carlos B. Samuels	Samuels	Carlos	B.

Rule 4—Hyphenated Names

A personal name that has a hyphen is considered a single unit and should be treated as a single name.

	Unit I	Unit II	Unit III
Mary-Ann Addison	Addison	Mary-Ann	
Ann-Marie C. Jackson	Jackson	Ann-Marie	C.
Michael Johns-Allen	Johns-Allen	Michael	
A. Jane Spencer-Day	Spencer-Day	A.	Jane

Rule 5—Titles, Seniority

Professional titles and educational degrees (e.g., Ph.D., R.P.T., CPA, Esq.) are dropped from the end of the name for filing purposes. Seniority titles (Jr., Sr., II) are listed.

When a married woman's first name is known, use it. When her first name is unknown (Mrs. Ronald Sherwood), she should be listed with her husband's first name as Unit II instead of her first name, and "Mrs." as Unit III would indicate that you are not referring to the husband.

	Unit I	Unit II	Unit III
Bob Dumont, C.P.A.	Dumont	Bob	
Mark Gritt, Jr.	Gritt	Mark	Jr.
Mr. Morton Teisch	Teisch	Morton	
Mrs. Morton Teisch	Teisch	Morton	Mrs.

Rule 6—Abbreviated Names and Nicknames

Abbreviated names (e.g., Geo. for George, Rbt. for Robert, Jas. for James, Chas. for Charles) would be filed as if they were written out. Nicknames (e.g., Red, Patty, Butch, Joe) would be filed as they appear if the true name is not known. If the true name is known, file under the true name.

	Unit I	Unit II	Unit III
Patty Aster (Patricia)	Aster	Patricia	
Buddy Nicholas	Nicholas	Buddy	
Liz Scott-Wrey	Scott-Wrey	Liz	
Jas. Thomas Wilson	Wilson	James	Thomas

Rule 7—Company Names

Each word in a company name is treated as a separate unit. When the name of the company includes the name of a person, the name is filed in reverse order.

	Unit I	Unit II	Unit III
Ace Chemical Company	Ace	Chemical	Company
I. Branson Co.	Branson	I.	Co.
Reda Pharmacy, Inc.	Reda	Pharmacy	Inc.
Morton Teisch Associates	Teisch	Morton	Associates

Rule 8—Articles, Prepositions, and Conjunctions

Articles (the, a, an), prepositions (with, of, in, to, for), and conjunctions (and, &) are not included for filing purposes. The only time they are included is when they are foreign or Old English names (thy, ye, el, los, la, las).

	Unit I	Unit II	Unit III
The Apple Market	Apple	Market (The)	
Roberts & Sons	Roberts(&)	Sons	
La Pluma Cafe	La	Pluma	Cafe
Ye Olde Shoppe	Ye	Old	Shoppe

Rule 9—Single Letters

Single letters in a name are treated as separate units even if they are written together without spaces.

	Unit I	Unit II	Unit III	Unit IV
ABC Stationery	A	B	C	Stationery
B & B Brothers	B(&)	B	Brothers	
S. L. Cleaners, Inc.	S	L	Cleaners	Inc.
WPIX	W	P	I	X

Rule 10—Hyphenated Company Names

Hyphenated company names are treated as two units.

	Unit I	Unit II	Unit III	Unit IV
E-Z Shipping Co.	E-	Z	Shipping	Co.
Marshall-Dillon Department Store	Marshall-	Dillon	Department	Store
Sly-Fox Dress Shop	Sly-	Fox	Dress	Shop
Tom's Drive-In	Tom's	Drive	In	

Rule 11—One Word or Two?

Company names that can be written as either one word or two are treated as one unit.

	Unit I	Unit II	Unit III
Aero Space Foundation	Aero Space	Foundation	
Hill Crest Saloon	Hill Crest	Saloon	
Inter National Movers, Inc.	Inter National	Movers	Inc.
International Movers, Ltd.	International	Movers	Ltd.

Rule 12—Numbers

Numbers in company names are treated as if written in words as one unit. (Three and four digit numbers are read as hundreds and five or more digit numbers are read as thousands.)

	Unit I	Unit II	Unit III
A-1 Hospitality Center	A-One	Hospitality	Center
Fifth Avenue Shoppe	Fifth	Avenue	Shoppe
5th Street Market	Fifth	Street	Market
22nd Street Cafe	Twenty-Second	Street	Cafe

Numeric Filing

Many offices find a numeric filing system to be the most efficient means of identification and are resorting to the ubiquitous Social Security number to facilitiate this process. When a numeric system is enacted, a supplementary alphabetic card system must be maintained for obvious reasons.

Consecutive number filing—It's as easy as "A B C"; or we should say "1 2 3."
When using numbers with many digits, they are often grouped as units to avoid transpositions.

```
          √
     053 35 1321
     054 35 1321
```

Terminal number filing—This is a variation of the above in that you treat the final group of digits as the first filing unit.

```
          √
     054 35 1321
     053 35 1322
```

Middle number filing—This is yet another variation in that you treat the middle group at the first filing unit.

```
          √
     055 35 1322
     053 36 1321
```

Geographic Filing

Geographic filing is implemented when records need to be filed by location (sales organizations, utility companies, real estate agencies, postal services).

When sorting in this fashion, alphabetize by State as Unit 1, City as Unit II, Firm Name as Unit III. For example, Rockland Physical Therapy, 3 College Road, Monsey, New York would be filed as:

Unit I	Unit II	Unit III
New York	Monsey	Rockland Physical Therapy

Subject Filing

Subject filing, as previously mentioned, follows the convention of the yellow pages of a telephone directory. The captions generally represent items, objects, businesses.

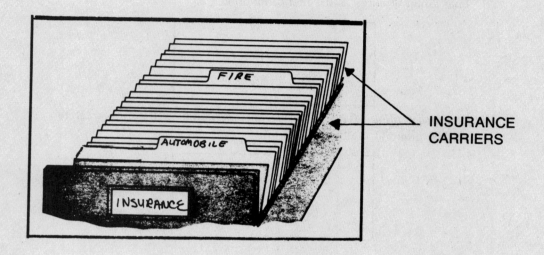

REFERENCE MATERIALS

The partial list of reference materials that follows should be available at your local library, local college or university, or on your company bookshelf. The limits of this are list in no way intended to indicate that other references are not equally useful.

Guides to Reference Books

- *Subject Guide to Books in Print* or *Books in Print* (found in your local library).
- *Guide to Reference Books* by Constance M. Winchell, published by the American Library Association.
- *Reference Books: A Brief Guide* by Mary N. Barton and Marion V. Bell, published by Enoch Pratt Free Library.
- *How and Where to Look It up—A Guide to Standard Sources of Information* by Robert W. Murphy, published by Mc-Graw Hill Book Company.

Dictionaries

- The abridged dictionary is desk-size and handy.
- The unabridged dictionary contains a wealth of information over and above the "dictionary" section. Depending on the publication, you can have access to biographical and geographical names, colleges and universities, signs and symbols, foreign words and phrases, punctuation, preparation of

footnotes, forms of address, styles of business correspondence, history of the English language, and so on.

- The crossword puzzle dictionary and thesaurus (storehouse of words) offer extensive sources of synonyms for word variety.

Financial Information

- *Dun & Bradstreet Reference Book* (credit and capital ratings).
- *Moody's Manual for Investment, American and Foreign* (financial statements, list of officers, history, and other pertinent information about major companies).
- *Poor's Register of Corporations, Directors and Executives* (referencing 34,000 corporations in the United States and Canada).

Biographical Information

- *Biography Index: A Cumulative Index to Biographical Material in Books and Magazines*, published quarterly by H.W. Wilson Company).
- *Who's Who in America* (and other "Who's Who . . ." covering various regions and professions).

Etiquette

- *Amy Vanderbilt's New Complete Book of Etiquette*, by Amy Vanderbilt, published by Doubleday & Company, Inc.
- *Business Etiquette Handbook*, published by Prentice Hall, Inc.
- *Manners in Business*, by Elizabeth G. MacGibbon, published by Macmillan Company.

Periodical Indexes

- *Reader's Guide to Periodical Literature* (housed by most libraries and universities).
- *Ulrich's International Periodicals Directory*, published by R.R. Bowker Company (arranged by subject).

U.S. Government Publications

- *Monthly Catalog of United States Government Publications* (available in most libraries).
- Write to Superintendent of Documents, U.S. Government Printing Office, Washington, DC 20402.

English Usage

Many, many valuable books are available offering fingertip reference to spelling, word division, punctuation, grammar, sentence structure, and so on.

CONFERENCES AND MEETINGS

meeting—an assembly for a common purpose
conference—a meeting with a larger scope
convention—large formal meetings focused in scope

The nature of a meeting can vary from small and informal to regular executive meeting to special executive meeting to stockholders' meeting to directors' meetings.

Responsibilities Before the Meeting

The following steps should be taken before a meeting.

- Acquire a meeting site and reserve a meeting room or rooms. (If possible, go with a *tried and tested* site; if not, be certain to inspect unfamiliar premises for layout, lighting, accommodations, and so on.) Additional provisions may be made for smokers and non-smokers; pitchers of water and glasses should be placed in strategic places; refreshments and/or meals should be prearranged; place cards should be prepared if meals are involved; and coat checking facilities may be needed.

  Lodging facilities may be needed for out-of-towners. As an added note, many executives may bring their spouses and in some cases special arrangements may be made for trips or social events.

- Materials needed for the conference (tables, reports, financial statements, advertisements, and so on) will need to be prepared, edited, printed, and assembled.
- Guest speakers may be needed. Be certain to acquire a vita or autobiographical information about the speaker(s) and send a follow-up letter verifying date, time, and place.
- Invitations and notices will be generated from mailing lists, which you should keep current. Registration material may be needed.
- Special arrangements may be made for acquiring: chalkboards, lecterns, projectors, easels, tape recorders, microphones, and so on.
- News releases should be prepared and press coverage should be arranged, if applicable.
- An itinerary and/or schedule will serve the purpose of informing everyone of the day's events and will help to keep the meeting *on track*.

SAMPLE

The Marric Corporation

(Date)
<u>Schedule</u>

8:00 A.M.	Registration	Front Desk
8:15 A.M.	Breakfast	Conference Room A
9:00 A.M.	General Workshop	Conference Room B
12:30 P.M.	Lunch	Main Dining Room
2:15 P.M.	Individual Workshops	(Select from Below)
5:00 P.M.	Cocktail Reception	Main Dining Room
6:00 P.M.	Departure	

<u>Workshop Agenda</u>

Title	Name of Speaker Title or Association	Room 101
Title	Name of Speaker Title or Association	Room 102
Title	Name of Speaker Title or Association	Room 103

Responsibilities the Day of the Meeting

On the day of the meeting, follow these steps.

- With a written checklist, examine the facilities to be certain all your requirements have been addressed.
- The registration desk needs to be supervised and conference folders and name tags will need to be distributed. Remember, a friendly greeting will set a very positive tone and will promote the good will of your firm!
- Minutes will be necessary; they can be taken in shorthand, by machine shorthand, or by tape recorder.
- Meet with media representatives and direct them to the proper people and locations.
- Arrange place cards for meals, if applicable.
- *Keep your eyes and ears open* and be helpful where needed.

Audio-Visual Aids

Varieties of audio-visual aids are used throughout business and industry to enhance sales presentations, market products, train employees, augment seminars, and so on. The most commonly used projectors are:

- *Overhead projectors*—The light that extends from the arm of the overhead projector is focused on the transparency and projects the image onto a screen or wall. Overhead transparencies (also called foils or acetates) afford you the ability to prepare your own text, diagrams, charts, overlays, and so on, with special permanent or nonpermanent colored markers that can be purchased at an art store. You can also replicate prepared text (provided you are not violating copyright laws) via an infrared copier or most photocopier machines. Overhead projectors are quite simple to operate and rather lightweight for carrying purposes.
- *Movie projectors*—Business and industry generally use 16-mm film. The newer projectors are self-loading and sound is built in.
- *Slide projectors*—You have the option of using prepared slides, making your own, or having them professionally prepared for you. Most slides are displayed in a carousel in which the slides can be dropped in. Some projectors have sound built in; others utilize an external cassette player. If you are having slides prepared for you in a studio, you may have the option of using an electronic pulse that will automatically advance the slides and sound simultaneously. Otherwise, the sound can be advanced manually.
- *Video cassette recorder (VCR)*—VCRs are widely used in business and industry. They are used as adjuncts to industrial training programs in which workbooks, leader's guides, and so on, accompany the tape as part of a larger training program. They are also used to videotape salespeople, management training personnel, and so on, in an effort to bring feedback to employees.

CHAPTER 31

Communications

EFFECTIVE WORD SELECTION

Successful communication is nothing more than effectively transmitting a message in a clear and concise manner. Do not pepper your communications with flowery words—simplicity and understandability are the key elements.

- **Use positive words** such as: of course, immediately, generous, qualified, satisfactory, convenient, honest, congratulations, gladly, etc. Be certain to tell the reader what you *can do* rather than what you *can't do.*
    Negative: We are sorry that your order cannot be delivered until March 1.
    Positive: We are glad to tell you that your order will be delivered on March 1.
- **Use a tone** that will reflect the "tone of voice" or attitude you want to project. ARE YOU ANGRY WITH THE READER? ARE YOU ENTHUSIASTIC ABOUT THE SUBJECT MATTER?
- **Use clear and concise language** and do not be verbose (wordy).
    No: We would be most appreciative if you would forward your check in the amount of $10.
    Yes: Please send us your check for $10.
        Also, avoid idioms, contractions, and outdated expressions.
- **Use concrete language** which conveys a clear picture.
    No: I WILL CALL YOU *soon* so that . . .
    Yes: I WILL CALL YOU *in two weeks* so that . . .
- **Use coherent sentences and paragraphs** that are logically consistent and flow smoothly from one point to another.
- **Use sex-fair language** and avoid the use of the male or female gender unless referring to specific people.
- **Use a good will approach** (when possible and appropriate) showing consideration, empathy, courtesy, sincerity, and respect for the reader.

EFFECTIVE SENTENCE AND PARAGRAPH CONSTRUCTION

Words alone cannot communicate; they must be joined together in sentences that are grammatically correct. A paragraph is basically a series of sentences used to develop an idea. In addition to breaking a paragraph to change an idea, you must paragraph for readability.

Short, underdeveloped paragraphs can give the impression of poor organization and detract from the message. Conversely, if the paragraph is too long, it can appear as a mass of uninviting words and can discourage the reader. The "average" letter generally contains three paragraphs—but do not manufacture a message to achieve this.

- **The opening paragraph** should get the reader's attention, set the tone, and offer a statement of purpose. Try to use the "you" approach and avoid mention of yourself or your company.
    No: WE RECEIVED YOUR LETTER DATED FEBRUARY 9 . . .
    Yes: YOUR LETTER OF FEBRUARY 9 . . .
- **The middle paragraph(s)** should develop the basic idea(s), be descriptive, and contain explanations and/or persuasive arguments. There should be a transition between paragraphs so that the reader knows an idea is being developed.
- **The final paragraph** should inspire action, strengthen your position, summarize, thank, and end on a positive note. Examples follow:
    Please take a few moments to . . .
    If you need additional information, please contact me at . . .
    Thank you for your cooperation.

BUSINESS LETTERS

There are several kinds of business letters and the following are examples.
- *Positive letters*—These are the easiest to write because they can be enthusiastic and gracious. Although the word "yes," is not necessary, 1) let the reader know at the outset that his or her request is being granted; 2) give the pertinent facts; 3) end with a good will statement.
- *Negative letters*—There are instances when requests and inquiries must be refused. In such cases: 1) begin with a positive or at least neutral statement; 2) give the pertinent facts; 3) focus on what you can do rather than on what you can't do; and 4) end on an optimistic note.
- *Persuasive letters*—These are for the purpose of getting attention, creating a desire, getting a conviction, making a request for action, etc. At the outset, let the reader know the benefit he or she will derive.
- *Form paragraphs and letters*—These are also known as boilerplate paragraphs and letters. You will often find yourself repeatedly using standard paragraphs and letters. With word processing equipment, these boilerplates can be stored and accessed whenever needed.

BUSINESS REPORTS AND INTEROFFICE MEMOS

The main purpose of the business report is to: request information, report progress, make recommendations, state facts, communicate decisions and findings. Because the writer of a report is interested in a factual presentation, personal opinions should be withheld.

Analytical reports can involve library research, questionnaires, surveys, observations, studies, and/or experiments. All facts and findings must be accurate and reliable. Remember, you are not reporting your opinion, just unbiased results, recommendations, and/or conclusions.

Reports can take the form of an outline, an interoffice memo, or a formal business report.

OUTLINES

The outline separates the data into divisions and subdivisions for easy identification. Notice the use of capitalization for the divisions and subdivisions in the example that follows.

SAMPLE OUTLINE

I. FIRST MAJOR DIVISION

    A. First Secondary Division
    B. Second Secondary Division
    C. Third Secondary Division

II. SECOND MAJOR DIVISION

    A. First Secondary Division
    B. Second Secondary Division
    C. Third Secondary Division

III. THIRD MAJOR DIVISION

    A. First Secondary Division
       1. First third division
       2. Second third division
       3. Third third division
          a. First fourth division
          b. Second fourth division

    B. Second Secondary Division
       1. First third division
       2. Second third division
          a. First fourth division
          b. Second fourth division

INTEROFFICE MEMOS

Many companies provide special printed memo forms if they frequently use them as a means of communication. If no printed forms are available, type the interoffice memo on a plain sheet of paper (not letterhead) using any of the following headings.

To: From: Date: Subject:	TO: FROM: DATE: SUBJECT:	Date: To: From: Subject:

The body of the message should be single-spaced, leaving a blank line between each paragraph. Paragraphs should not be indented.

FORMAL BUSINESS REPORTS

The formal business report is often more complex than the interoffice memo and differs in terms of general appearance and length.

The formal report usually has a title page containing the name of the report, the person preparing same, the place of origination, the date presented, and possibly to whom presented.

AN EXPERIMENTAL STUDY TO DETERMINE THE
EFFECT OF THE SPELLING TEST ON
THE ABILITY OF STUDENTS TO SPELL

Presented to
the Faculty of the
Department of Business Education
and Office Systems Administration
Montclair State College

by
Sheryl Lorenz
B.S., Saint Thomas Aquinas College

December 19XX

The table of contents lists subject headings and their respective pages.

TABLE OF CONTENTS

The first page is generally not numbered and starts on line 13 (2″ from the top). The side margins will be 1″ and the report should end 1″ from the bottom.

INTRODUCTION TO THE PROBLEM
Chapter 1

"Johnny can't read"; Johnny can't spell either. The researcher and colleagues have a consensus of opinion that students graduating from our high school systems are deficient in the area of spelling. This is evidenced by the lack of spelling ability in transcriptions, in sentences, in basic English drills, and in business subjects. At the postsecondary level of a private business school, the students have one year to hone their spelling skills prior to entering the world of business.

Many of today's students were educated when basics were forsaken, and the emphasis was on creativity. Educators, viewing this alarming deficiency in the area of language arts in general, are reaffirming the importance of a back-to-basics education. It is, therefore, the responsibility of each educator to seek ways to overcome this problem.

The researcher would like to determine whether the use of weekly spelling tests will increase the spelling ability of students in a private postsecondary business school.

This problem will determine whether is is worthwhile for teachers to administer weekly spelling tests in order to improve the spelling ability of students.

The bibliography is a listing of all sources of reference. The format is the reverse of a paragraph. Many bibliographies are now handled in the new style with a page entitled "Works Cited."

BIBLIOGRAPHY

Helphill, Phyllis David. *Business Communications With Writing Improvement Exercises*. Englewood Cliffs, NJ: Prentice-Hall, 1958.

Tuckman, Bruce W. *Conducting Educational Research*. 2d ed. New York: Harcourt Brace Jovanovich, 1978.

Warriner, John and Sheila Y. Laws. *English Grammar and Communication*. New York: Harcourt Brace Jovanovich, 1973.

PROOFREADING

This is the skill that refers to the systematic method of locating errors and noting them for subsequent correction.

Each document should be carefully proofread several times checking for:

- Formatting.
- Styling.
- English usage.
- Word repetition.
- Omissions.
- Spacing.
- Transpositions.
- Hyphenations.
- Names and addresses.
- Numbers.
- Spelling.
- General sense of the text.

Some factors to keep in mind when proofreading are:

1. Scan the overall text to make certain that the format and style are correct.
2. Accurately pinpoint any typographical errors, punctuation errors, and/or grammatical errors.
3. Double-check the spelling of all names, initials, and any statistical information.
4. Pay special attention to small words (as, in, an, and, it, if) that are often overlooked.
5. Pay special attention also to homonyms (their and there, its and it's). Many word-processing programs feature a spelling check; however, no spelling check can differentiate between homonyms.
6. Check the continuity of all numbered pages, paragraphs, and exercises.
7. Spelling can be double-checked by reading the text from bottom to top or right to left, concentrating on each individual word.
8. When revising text on a word processor, you need only to proofread the portion of the text that has been changed because (assuming you proofread accurately the first time) only the portion you changed has been altered.
9. If you are proofreading technical or statistical data, the "buddy system" is recommended when another person is available. Give a copy of your typewritten text to the other person and read from the original copy. Carefully pronounce all word endings (-s, -ed, -ing) and spell out any unusually spelled names.
10. If you are proofreading technical or statistical data and there is no one who can assist you, place the information side by side and follow line by line with a straightedge (ruler or envelope).

Proofreader's Marks

tr	transpose	to completely finish or about
∧ *like*	insert	we would to have your input
ℓ	delete	in our our judgment
⌒	close space	ear ache
ℒ	delete and close space	it is our conscern
#	leave space	stomachache
STET	retain deleted material	the President has asked
l.c.	lower-case (small letter)	their Accounting Department
C	upper-case (capital letter)	Star wars or Star Wars
SS	single space	We would like to have your SS opinion of what transpired
DS	double space	We would like to have your DS opinion of what transpired
TS	triple space	We would like to have your TS opinion of what transpired
⧣	remove underscore	a very well-known man
SP	spell out fully	Fed.
#⟍	indent (# of spaces)	Now is the time
¶	new paragraph	we have been. This would be
NO ¶	no new paragraph	This would have been
run in	center on page	> TOTALS <
BF	boldface type	WHO AND WHOM
↺	reverse order	pencils and paper staples and staplers
∨	apostrophe	men's department

:/	colon	the following ∧
,/	comma	If you will please ∧
;/	semicolon	New York, New York ∧ Trenton
⊙▫⊙▫⊙▫	ellipsis	Now is the . . . .
!/	exclamation point	Alas ∧
=/	hyphen	well ∧ trained staff
⊙	period	as well ∧
˅/˅	quotation marks	∧ The Good Life ∧
⊓	move up	The Trials of Time
⊔	move down	The Great Deception
⊏	move to the left	⊏ this is the one
⊐	move to the right	⊐ this is the one
//	align type	// We are in the midst of a very important
⑦	Verify information or add question mark	on May 6 ⑦ we were
italic	italicize	Safe at Any
___	underscore	Words

EDITING

This is the skill that refers to amending the text by modifying words, sentences, paragraphs, or the general structure of the text until the desired output has been achieved. You must edit for the following:

- *Word selection*—Is the communication appropriate for the level of the reader? Is there roundabout wording, etc? (For example, *"Thank you for . . ."* rather than *"We want to take this opportunity to thank you for . . ."*
- *Sentence and paragraph construction*—Is the communication complete and is there continuity of thought? Are sentences or paragraphs too long, too short, too wordy?

- *Omissions or extraneous wording*—Are there missing or extra words? (For example, *"As know, we are in the process . . ."* or *"As you you know, we are in the process . . ."*
- *Tone*—Is the communication "you" directed? Were tact and empathy communicated?
- *Completeness and accuracy*—Have you included sufficient information to demonstrate your point, make the sale, etc? Is your information accurate to the best of your knowledge?

ABSTRACTING COMMUNICATIONS

When abstracting materials from other sources, it is wise to use a highlighting pen to accentuate all the key points. In view of the fact that photostating copies of certain materials is in violation of the copyright laws, you may consider preparing a summary of the key points.

You will want to summarize all the key points, all major conclusions, accurately list all sources, and present same in an easy-to-read format. Some people find preparing an outline to be helpful in this regard.

BUSINESS LETTER FORMAT

Your letter should resemble a symmetrically framed picture with even margins forming a frame around the typewritten portion and should be one on which you would be proud to place your signature or reference initials.

Business letters reflect four basic styles that are illustrated as follows:

ATLAS FIVE AND TEN INC.
HILDE AND HELMUT FEILER

—

179 MAIN STREET
FORT LEE, N. J. 07024
(201) 947-2999

February 20, 19—

Mr. and Mrs. Benjamin Swartz
138 Tapia Drive
Paramus, NJ 07652

Dear Mr. and Mrs. Swartz:

Re: Account No. 94132

We are delighted to welcome you to our Atlas family
of charge customers. Your application for a charge
account has been approved, and our staff is waiting
to make your shopping a satisfying and pleasurable
experience.

On the tenth of each month you will receive a
statement of your purchases, and you will have until
the twenty—fifth of the month to make your payment.
From the outstanding credit reputation you have
earned, we are certain that your payments will be
made promptly, thus avoiding any service charges.

We are taking this opportunity to send you our latest
catalog so that you can take advantage of our easy
shop—at—home service.

Thank you for giving us the opportunity to show you
why Atlas has earned the fine reputation for
high—quality merchandise and superior service.
Remember: "If we don't have it; you don't need it."

Very truly yours,

ATLAS FIVE AND TEN INC.

Michael Feller, President

sll
Enclosure

Full block style—This modern letter style is becoming more and more popular. Everything begins at the left margin; nothing is indented.

Taylor
Business Institute

April 15, 19—

Mr. and Mrs. Harry Lorenz
36 Lincoln Road
Monroe, NY 10950

Dear Mr. and Mrs. Lorenz:

Re: Scholarship Awards

On behalf of the faculty and staff at
Taylor Business Institute, I wish to
congratulate your daughters, Jacqueline and
Nicole, for winning one-half tuition
scholarships for the accounting program.

You can be extremely proud of their
results as there were many other competitors
who took the exam in your area.

Our early registration will be held on
Saturday, May 3 from 9 AM to 2 PM, and we look
forward to welcoming Jacqueline and Nicole to
our Taylor family.

Sincerely,

Marilyn Sarch, Dean

sll

291 Buehler Place at Route 17, Paramus, New Jersey 07652

Semiblock style—This letter style is identical to the modified block style, except each paragraph is indented five to seven spaces from the left margin and the subject line is centered.

OFFICE
ORegon 5-2043

Max H. Lorenz
PUBLIC ACCOUNTANT
408 West 14th Street
New York, N. Y. 10014

ANSWERING SERVICE
BA 7-5816

November 14, 19--

Mr. Warren Bergstein
Business Club
103 Samuel Lane
Grasmere, NY 10305

Dear Mr. Bergstein:
Subject: New Tax Laws for 19--

It is with great pleasure that I accept
your invitation to speak to your
membership about "New Tax Laws for 19--"
at your January meeting.

I would appreciate your having available
an overhead projector, a chalkboard, and
a table in front of the room where I can
display literature and current tax forms
for distribution. Also, please let me
know approximately how many members will
be in attendance.

Immediately following my presentation, I
will gladly entertain any questions your
members may have, either of a general or
personal nature. I am certain that your
members will find the information both
useful and informative.

Thank you for giving me the opportunity
to address your organization.

Sincerely yours,

Max H. Lorenz

ML/el

Modified block style—This traditional letter style is the most commonly used. Everything begins at the left margin with the exception for the date line and complimentary closing. Both start at the center or slightly to the right of center.

Real World Counselling Service
P.O. Box 502
Nanuet, New York 10954

(914) 352-3240
(914) 352-9113

April 21, 19—

Mr. Brian Karen
35 Amy Court
Highland Falls, NY 10928

RE: MARVIN KAREN, FILE NO. 5857

I greatly value you as a client and would like
to be of service to you in the future should
the need arise.

Your son Marvin has successfully completed the
career counseling program designed,
especially for him; and, as a result, is now
gainfully and happily employed. Yet, you have
made no effort to pay any part of the $250
which has been due and owing since January.

As a business person, I know that you
appreciate those of your customers who meet
their obligations promptly.

Won't you, therefore, send me your check for
the full amount of $250 and retain the good
credit standing you have earned.

JANICE TEISCH, DIRECTOR

sll

Simplified style—This letter style is written in full block with the salutation and complimentary closing omitted. The subject line appears in all capital letters three lines below the inside address and three lines above the body. The writer's name appears four lines below the final paragraph, also in all capital letters.

This streamlined letter style has been recommended by the Administrative Management Society and is expected to be the trend of the future as it is less time consuming, thereby cutting costs.

PUNCTUATION STYLES

The two most important punctuation styles are as follows:

- *Open punctuation*—The salutation and complimentary closing are unpunctuated. (All other marks of punctuation remain the same.)
- *Mixed punctuation*—The salutation is punctuated with a colon, and the complimentary closing is punctuated with a comma.

ENVELOPE STYLES

The styles of envelope available are as follows:

- Conventional style envelopes are No. 10 (legal size), measuring 9-½ inches by 4-⅛ inches. They accommodate the standard 8-½ inch by 11-inch piece of stationery when said stationery is folded in thirds.
- Computer style envelopes come as continuous-form envelopes and can be fed (continuously) through the printer.
- Optical Character Readers (OCR) are now expediting the mail in most large cities. The post office is requesting that the two-letter state abbreviations be used (NY, MI, CA) and that vertical and horizontal bars be properly placed when envelopes are being prepared that bear same.

STATISTICAL DATA

Statistical data is often best presented as a graphic aid (table, chart, map, flowchart, or diagram). A graphic aid should be introduced by a statement and should be placed as close as possible to the sentence in which it is introduced. If the graphic aid is to be displayed several pages after it is introduced, the page should be mentioned in the introductory statement. If the aid is to be displayed in the appendix, make reference to the appropriate appendix and the page number. Because of the complexity of tables, let's discuss their presentation.

1. Headings should be obvious to the reader.
2. If several columns are used, vertical lines can help clarify the identity of the data within the columns.
3. A horizontal line under the table can be used to separate the table from the footnote or source of information.
4. Unless a table is very formal in nature, it is not necessary to box it (draw lines around all four sides).

MINUTES

The notes you take at a meeting must be accurate, but they do not have to be verbatim. If the meeting is to be very formal, your company might want a record of every word; they will probably allow a tape recorder to aid you, but you must obtain permission to use it.

If you are not accustomed to taking minutes, acquaint yourself with minutes of previous meetings so that you can apply the format.

If you are expected to conduct a meeting, review parliamentary procedure as clearly explained in *Robert's Rules of Order Newly Revised*, the bible for conducting business meetings.

Keep in mind the following:

1. Record the date, time, and place of the meeting, and all those who were present. Also note the time the meeting commenced and adjourned.
2. Sit near the presiding officer so that you hear everything clearly and accurately.
3. Remain constantly alert so that each time a new topic is introduced, you are prepared to record the name of the person who introduced it, seconded it, and the main points covered.
4. Use your judgment; never expect any member of the meeting to tell you what is important. If in doubt, include it.
5. Record the name of each person who proposes any action, opinion, or plan.
6. Take verbatim notes on resolutions, amendments, decisions, and conclusions.
7. Have paper clips handy (attached to your notebook) so that you can tag any items on which action is to be taken after the meeting. This will aid you in picking out these duties before transcribing your notes.
8. Make certain that you have heard everything clearly. If unsure, ask for the unclear portion to be repeated. Names, amounts of money, and dates are of extreme importance.

PRESS RELEASES

The pyramid convention prevails in the preparation of a press release. Start with the main idea, follow with the major details, and conclude with supplementary information. The five W's (who, what, when, where, and why) still prevail; however, equally important is the big "H" (how).

Key Points

Key points to remember when writing press releases are as follows:

1. Double space to facilitate editing.
2. Type the word *more* (centered or at the right) at the bottom of the first page if the release continues.

3. Ensuing pages are numbered and feature a brief caption reflecting the title. (Example: *Title-2)*
4. Type *#####* or *-end-* at the point of conclusion.

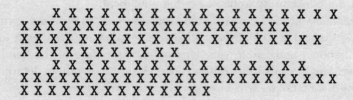

```
                    NEWS RELEASE

      For Immediate Release, September 16, 19XX


                   TITLE OF ARTICLE


          X X X X X X X X X X X X X X X X X X
        X X X X X X X X X X X X X X X X X X X
        X X X X X X X X X X X X X X X X X X X X X
        X X X X X X X X X X
            X X X X X X X X X X X X X X X
      X X X X X X X X X X X X X X X X X X X X X X X X
      X X X X X X X X X X X X X


                   # # # # #
```

SPEECHES

Try to imagine a mute world where people did not communicate. There would be no verbal exchanges, no news information, no entertainment, no buying and selling, no telephone calls (perhaps a blessing?). In any event, without this remarkable human skill, living would be quite awkward.

Franklin D. Roosevelt once said, "He who can phrase it, can lead it." *The ability to communicate can either be your stepping stone or your stumbling block to success.* If you are called upon to deliver a speech or an informal talk, think of what you want your talk to accomplish: You can inform, persuade, or strengthen relationships. You must know your audience and direct your talk toward how they will perceive your message.

There are several types of speeches:

- *The impromptu speech*—There is obviously no advance planning; however, the speaker is generally an expert in the area.
- *The manuscript speech*—This is completely written out or typed, usually double-spaced for easy reading. Even though the speech is written in advance, it is important that the speaker maintain eye contact to give the illusion of speaking—not reading.

- *The memorized speech*—This carefully prepared speech has the disadvantage of limiting feedback from the listening audience. No notes are used; therefore, the speaker tries to remain on track.
- *The extemporaneous speech*—The speaker has the opportunity to gather facts and place key phrases on note cards for quick reference.

Key Points

Key points for speeches are the following:

1. If you are preparing a speech, be certain that the manuscript or note cards are neat, and key points should be highlighted.
2. Practice in front of a mirror so that the "ever-important" eye contact can be maintained.
3. Taping your speech will give you insight into how you sound and will give you the opportunity to be somewhat analytical.
4. If handouts are to be distributed, you may want to consider giving them out at the end of your speech; otherwise people have a tendency to look at the handout and ignore you. Of course, the nature of the handout will determine the feasibility of the above. Also, be certain to determine how many listeners you will have, so you don't run short.
5. If you are using visual aids, be certain that you are facing your audience. Advance preparation and positioning of visual equipment will help accomplish this.

PART VI

Office Technology

CHAPTER 32

Ergonomics

Now that the "office of the future" is here, much emphasis has been placed on maximizing the physical and psychological well-being of today's office worker. Therefore, the science that adapts working conditions, the environment, and equipment has emerged under the umbrella of *ergonomics*.

OFFICE FURNITURE

Chairs and tables should be adjustable because many of us do not have "typical" body dimensions. If you have a tilting screen, a detachable keyboard, and furniture that can be adjusted to suit you, you will be much happier and much more productive.

LIGHTING

Proper lighting can avoid both physical psychological effects (eyestrain, muscular tension, lower productivity, and a higher rate of errors). Fluorescent lighting is recommended in a word processing environment because it produces less glare and generates less heat. Also, compared to incandescent lighting, it adds less to the electric bill.

COLOR

Color has been proven to influence morale, health, and efficiency. Warm colors (reds, yellows, oranges) are considered friendly and tend to keep you more alert. Cool colors (greens and blues) tend to be more relaxing.

SOUND

Soft music is used in many environments and has been attributed to increased productivity. To offset the noise of the equipment, walls can be covered with acoustical surfaces and draperies can be hung three to four inches from the wall or window.

Carpeting will also absorb sound whereas tiled or wooden floors will not. If you are purchasing carpeting, you might want to ask if the carpeting has passed the shuffle test of the Carpeting & Rug Institute. Some carpets produce an electrostatic charge which can "blip" your text.

TEMPERATURE

High temperatures and high humidity can have an adverse effect on your equipment, causing accelerated deterioration. Low temperatures, on the other hand, can allow static electricity to build up, causing errors in the central processing unit of your computer or word processor. An ideal temperature range would be between 67 and 75°F (18 and 24°C), and an ideal humidity range would be 40 to 60 percent.

Office layout and office landscaping are also challenges of ergonomists. This refers to the layout of desks, files, screens, clusters of furniture, and so on. A key word today is "flexibility;" therefore, many companies are making use of modular furniture and movable partitions to afford them the flexibility that may be necessary.

In addition to convenience and comfort, the overall layout must promote the most efficient flow of paperwork from one department to another and from one work area to another.

CHAPTER 33

Word Processing

- **When the Egyptians first inscribed their hieroglyphs on the walls of tombs, they were processing words.**
- **When our country's founders wrote the Declaration of Independence with quill pens, they were processing words.**

WHAT IS A WORD PROCESSOR?

At the turn of the century when women began "manning" the office, anyone who performed typing tasks was known as a *typewriter*. Thus, the word *typewriter* became synonomous with both the person and the equipment. *Word processor* seems to bear the same connotation in that it is both a piece of equipment that processes words and/or the person who performs the task.

When word processing (WP) first became the high-tech buzzword, educators and businesspeople tried to capture a uniform definition. None were able to do so. WP is merely the fastest and most expedient method of transferring information and ideas into the printed word. People have been doing that for many years so there is no great mystique to the concept. Now, however, we have highly sophisticated equipment to make us more efficient.

Know your Terminology

Administrative secretary—One who performs all clerical nontyping tasks.

Alphanumeric—A combination of alphabetic and numerical characters.

Automatic equipment—Equipment that performs many tasks such as carriage return, line spacing, and centering either automatically or by key-stroke command.

Basic document cycle—Creation, storage, use, transfer, and disposal of a record.

Batch—A collection of similar work that can be produced in a single operation.

Bit—The smallest unit of information.

237

Byte—A sequence of bits, usually shorter than a word.

Career path—Opportunities available for advancement.

Cassette—A plastic or metal cartridge used in recording information.

Character—A letter, number, or symbol.

Cluster—A work group or unit of employees and/or equipment.

COM—Computer output microfilm.

Command—Instruction of the WP machine to perform a certain function.

Communicating typewriter—Equipment that can send and receive information with another communicating typewriter via telephone hookups.

Correspondence secretary—One who performs all typing tasks.

CPS—Characters per second.

CPU—Central processing unit.

Crash—Disk down (inoperable).

CRT—Cathode ray tube, a TV-like screen for the display of characters.

Cursor—A movable indicator on a CRT which indicates the place for editing a document.

Daisy print wheel—A printing element, resembling a flattened daisy, that has a character at the end of each petal.

Data base—Files of information used by an organization.

Delete—Instruction to remove a character, a word, a line, or more from a document.

Discrete media—Belts, disks, cartridges, and cassettes that are removable for storage.

Disk (or diskette or disc)—WP machine equipment used for recording, transcribing, and storing data.

Down—Equipment inoperable.

Edit—To revise a text.

Element—A removable, replaceable printer.

Endless loop—A sealed, continuous loop inside a tank that allows for simultaneous dictating and transcribing.

Ergonomics—The science of adapting working conditions, the working environment, and the worker.

Facsimile (FAX)—The transmission and reception of textual copy through telephone lines.

Flowchart—A system of diagrams and symbols sequencing the progression of work from origin to completion.

Floppy disk—A pliable type of disk.

Font—An assortment of characters in one type size and style.

Hard copy—Typed or printed texts.

Hardware—Word processing equipment.

Hot zone—The area in which editing equipment will determine where the right-hand margin should be.

Ink jet printer—A printing device that electronically squirts ink onto paper in character form.

Input—Information entered into a system for processing.

I/O—Input/output device.

IWP—International Word Processing Association, an association that deals with systems and methods of word processing.

Job description—A written description of each worker's duties and responsibilities.

Keyboarding—Typewriting.

Logging—A method of recording incoming and outgoing work in order to monitor its flow.

Menu—Selection of tasks.

OCR—Optical character recognition.

Off-line—Equipment not connected to or dependent on peripheral equipment.

On-line—Equipment connected to and dependent on peripheral equipment.

Output—The final results produced.

PBX—Private branch exchange (telephone system).

Peripheral equipment—Equipment that works with the central unit, such as keyboards and printers.

Pitch—The number of characters per horizontal inch (10 on a pica and 12 on an elite).

Principal—The originator of a document who requires secretarial support.

Procedures manual—A manual that gives the step-by-step process for completing a certain task.

Reprographics—Reproduction of a document.

Search—A command given to locate automatically previously recorded information.

Shared logic—A system that allows two or more units to utilize the memory of a single CPU.

Software—Programs and routines needed to use hardware.

Stand-alone unit—A self-contained, independent unit.

Station—The work location for a WP operator.

Store—To place in memory information not subject to change.

Terminal—A device that can send and receive information.

Text-editing equipment—A WP typewriter capable of revising texts.

Time-sharing—The simultaneous use of the CPU.

Traditional secretary—An all-purpose secretary responsible for typing and nontyping tasks.

Turnaround time—The time that elapses from the beginning to the completion of a task.

Variable—A segment of a document subject to change.

VOR—Voice operated relay, a device that activates a recorder when it senses that a voice is coming over the line.

WP system—The combination of people, procedures, and equipment that constitutes a total support system.

KNOW YOUR EQUIPMENT

A vast array of word processors and computers have flooded the market, ranging from simple to complex. Regardless of the complexity, however, all hardware (equipment) bears the same components: keyboard, central processing unit (CPU), disk drive, display, and printer.

NOTE: Configurations will vary; components will be peripheral and/or attached.

Keyboard

The placement of alphabetic and numeric keys are *standard* and conform to any typewriter keyboard. Additional function keys (varying from one machine to another) enable you to communicate instructions to the CPU. Once you have learned the electronic keyboard, transferring from one machine to another will not be difficult because the similarities far outweigh the differences. Many keyboards have an additional ten key-pad (similar to a calculator) for faster numeric entry.

Central Processing Unit

The central processing unit, also known as the terminal or computer, is the "brains" of the unit that receives commands from the keyboard. It serves as the central location for the storage and distribution of data.

You will be hearing (possibly strange) numbers such as 64K, 128K, and so on. "K" refers to the per thousand internal memory capabilities that can be stored in the memory of the computer. The greater the number, the more the memory.

Disk Drive

The disk drive functions in much the same way as a tape recorder with "read" and "write" heads. A floppy disk/diskette (described on page 242) is inserted into the drive for recording text and communicating instructions to the CPU.

A *hard drive* is used by many larger companies who have the need to store and retrieve a large number of documents. This negates the need, in many cases, for floppy disks.

Display

The display, also known as monitor, cathode ray tube (CRT) or video display terminal (VDT), is basically a TV-like screen that displays the text. It enables you to view a document for editing, thereby producing error-free final copy. Displays are available in full color or in monochrome combinations of green on black, white on black, white on green, or amber on black.

Printer

Computer printers can be one of several types.

- *Daisy wheel* (or letter quality) printers produce the typewriter-quality lettering that is needed for business letters, legal documents, and so on. The name *daisy wheel* is derived from the shape of the circular wheel with the print characters on the "petals."
- *Dot matrix printers* produce small dots that form characters and/or shapes. This is used for drafts, graphics, and data where "letter quality" is not essential (e.g.,).
- *Laser printers* offer the ultimate in speed and quality but are exceptionally costly. They utilize a laser beam that burns characters onto light-sensitive paper.

Modem

We cannot conclude the section on hardware without including reference to the modem. (The term *modem* is an acronym for *mo*dulating and *dem*odulating.) The modem gives you the ability to communicate with other terminals. It also gives you the ability to subscribe to and access databases, affording you on-line reference materials, stock quotations, electronic mail and games, and so on.

The modem converts the digital signals from the computer into the analog signals of the telephone line. It serves, somewhat, as an interpreter between two people speaking different languages.

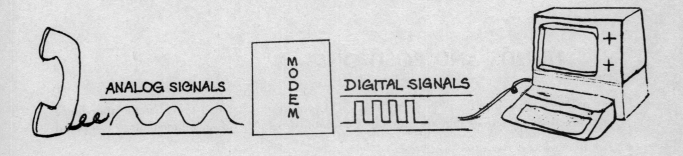

Software

So far we have dealt with hardware—the equipment. Let's briefly discuss software. Software is the preprogrammed set of instructions that tells your computer what you want it to do. A software package consists of (generally) a floppy disk together with documentation—known in English as "user guide." Your data will be stored on a blank disk that you will format (prepare to receive information as per instructions).

You do not need to be a computer programmer or a computer genius to use any software. The user manuals will often take you through the basics of the programs and many are self-prompting.

Although the following list is merely the "tip of the iceberg," it gives a basic idea of the wide array of software programs that are available.

- Word processing.
- Accounting/financial planning.
- Graphics.
- Games.
- Tutorials.
- Spelling/thesaurus.
- Forms generation.
- SAT and standardized test preparation.
- Telecommunications.
- Linguistics.
- Architecture.
- Legal.
- Real estate.
- Estimating.
- Travel.
- Cooking/recipe files.

TRENDS AND POSITIONS

You only need to review the "Classified" section of your local newspaper to realize the abundance of word processing positions that are available for qualified people. Advanced technology has paved the way for entry-level personnel to advance to management personnel.

Traditionally, WP specialists have been divided into two categories: *correspondence* positions and *administrative* positions. Employees in correspondence positions must possess outstanding oral and written communication skills, human relations skills, organizational skills, and mastery of equipment operations, and are responsible for paperwork. Employees in administrative positions assume a wide range of responsibilities ranging from filing, telephone communications, records management, and paraprofessional support.

Each offers its own career path to those employees who are highly motivated and see their jobs as stepping stones. Vertical career paths lead upward to managerial positions within a defined category, and lateral career paths cross from administrative positions to correspondence positions (and vice versa) at the same level. The following chart represents a simplification of these career paths.

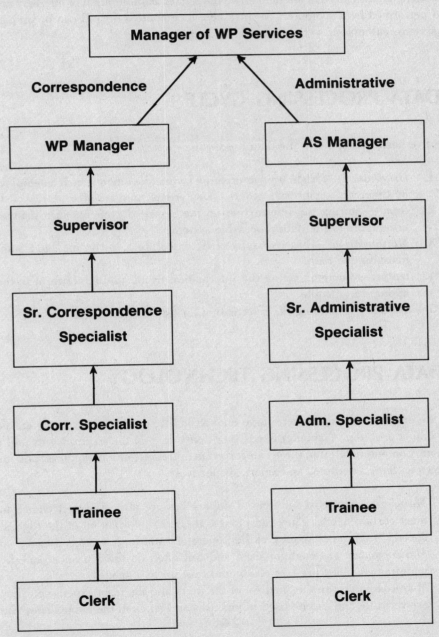

CHAPTER 34

Data Processing

Data processing is basically the mathematical and logical manipulation of numbers and/or symbols fed into and performed by a computer. For instance, a company's payroll can be prepared by a data processing system, calculating variable hours, and so on.

DATA PROCESSING CYCLE

There are five basic functions in the data processing cycle:

1. *Origination*—Originating or creating source documents such as employee time cards, purchase orders, sales orders, and so on.
2. *Input*—Storing the information on the source documents in a manner acceptable to the data processing system.
3. *Manipulation*—Classifying, sorting, calculating, recording, and summarizing the data.
4. *Output*—Communicating the information in an intelligible form to the appropriate people.
5. *Storage*—Retaining the information for future reference.

DATA PROCESSING TECHNOLOGY

Although the original computers were large enough to fill several rooms, many are now compact enough to fit onto a desk top. Computer needs vary depending on the requirements and resources of an organization. Computers fall into three categories: mainframes, minicomputers, and microcomputers, also known as large, medium, and small, respectively.

- *Mainframes* can cost millions of dollars but are often the best choice to meet certain needs. They can process the most information at the highest speed. Mainframes require skilled operators and large storage areas.
- *Minicomputers* are medium-sized and can often do the job once done by mainframes. They are less costly and take up less space.
- *Microcomputers* are the smallest of the units and the least expensive. They are versatile and can be used in business as well as in the home. They can

244

process information quickly and efficiently and often rival the performance of a minicomputer. Microcomputers can additionally be used with central processing units (CPUs) in shared logic systems and can supplement larger systems.

INPUT/OUTPUT DEVICES (I/O)

Input/output devices can be one of several types.

- The *card reader* is a basic input device through which data is entered into the computer. It causes the computer to recognize one character at a time.
- The *punch card* is an output device that transfers data onto punched cards (e.g., telephone bills). The cards are relatively inexpensive and can be read by humans—not just machines. They cannot, however, be erased or reused and have a limited amount of space.
- The *printer* is an output device that affords the greatest flexibility. It can accommodate continuous paper or cut forms, offer different font styles, operate at high speeds, produce graphic illustrations, and a wide variety of additional features.

SOFTWARE FOR DATA PROCESSING SYSTEMS

Software for data processing systems include the following:
- *System software* runs the hardware (computer) somewhat as an architecture program. (The **d**isk **o**perating **s**ystem known as DOS, for example.)
- *Application software* is designed for you, the end user, to offer word processing, spreadsheets, graphics, and the software to meet your individual needs.

TYPES OF PROGRAMMING LANGUAGES

Computer languages range from low level to high level. Although there are many, some of the most common are the following:

- *BASIC (Beginners' All-Purpose Symbolic Instruction Code)*—A high-level programming language designed for interactive use.
- *COBOL (COmmon Business Oriented Language)*—A high-level language used to meet the data processing needs of business.
- *FORTRAN (FORmula TRANslator)*—A high-level programming language used in science and engineering for numerical computations.
- *RPG (Report Program Generator)*—A high-level, problem-oriented programming language used to produce business-oriented business reports.

The proper language for your organization would be determined by the purpose of the program, the time and money allocated for the design, the availability of the language, and your equipment.

Machine language was developed during computer infancy and remains tedious, time-consuming, and costly. It is a series of binary codes (zeroes and ones) requiring the programmer to write an instruction for each operation to be performed. It is used infrequently today because of the sophistication that has evolved in other languages.

Assembler language was aided by software called an assembler program. It uses symbolic names (mnemonics), thus relieving the programmer of many clerical chores that would be required for machine language. It further organizes all the instructions into one unit called a source program.

Compiler language (or generator language) is a high-level language that is replacing assembler language. It enables the programmer to bypass the step of writing program statements and enables this programmer to write what is needed in more general terms.

NOTE: Knowledge of programming is not necessary to operate a computer. Software is readily available to meet most of your day-to-day needs.

CONCEPTS AND APPLICATIONS

A large utilization of data processing is in an area called *batch processing* which is the "grouping" of data at specified intervals. For example, a bank may process millions of checks and thousands of loan applications; utility companies may process thousands of bills; insurance companies may process thousands of policy applications. Processing can take place at designated intervals and the files can constantly be updated.

Real time is the actual time during which a process takes place.

Office systems are becoming integrated, utilizing what is referred to as the *systems approach* or *networking*. Rather than a company treating word processing, data processing, typesetting, mail distribution, etc. as separate entities, they are all integrated as part of an overall information processing system. Basically, the systems approach ties together various functions so that the equipment can offer a wide array of functions, thereby maximizing the use of the equipment and the information it is processing.

CHAPTER 35

Communication Technology

TELEPHONE COMMUNICATIONS

Dialing Information

The following summarizes dialing information.

1. There is a slight charge for operator-assisted information calls within your calling area. Therefore, use the telephone directory provided by the telephone company. When it is necessary to contact the operator to obtain a local number, dial either 411 or 555-1212.

2. There is no charge for operator-assisted information calls outside your calling area. When such a number is needed, dial 1 + area code + 555-1212. (In some areas, the 1 is not necessary.)

3. Many organizations, in an effort to promote business, have adopted toll-free 800 numbers so that the caller will not have to pay to initiate the call. Before placing a long-distance call, always check to see if an 800 number is available. Dial 1 + 800 + 555-1212. (Again, in some areas, the 1 is not necessary.) If you call toll-free numbers frequently, you should call or write for information about the directory available for a small charge from *The Toll-Free Digest Company*, Claverack, NY 12513.

Types of Services and Equipment

Before placing a call outside your calling area, be certain that you have the correct area code. Also, when placing long-distance calls, be sure to calculate the difference in time zones.

Station-to-station—(direct distance dialing) calls save time and money. Place this type of call when you are willing to speak to anyone who answers. Merely dial the area code plus the number. This type of call bears the lowest rates, and charges start when the called party answers the phone.

Person-to-person—calls require operator assistance and are used when you are not certain that the called party will be available. Rates are higher than for the station-to-station calls, but there is no charge if the person you are calling is not available. Charges begin only when the called party (or

247

extension) is connected. You dial 0 + area code + the number, and the operator comes on the line. Tell the operator that you are placing a person-to-person call and the name of the person to whom you wish to speak.

Collect—calls also require operator assistance and are used when the person being called is expected to accept the charges. You dial 0 + area code + the number, and the operator comes on the line. Tell the operator you are placing a collect call. A collect call can be placed either to the number or to a particular person.

Wide-Area Telephone Service (WATS)—is used by firms that make regular long-distance calls to designated areas. Access lines can be national, regional, or statewide; and rates are based on geographic area, not each call.

Mobile—calls can be made to mobile units in cars, trucks, airplanes, buses, trains, and news services by contacting the mobile-service operator or by direct dialing.

Ship-to-shore—calls can be made to a person at sea by giving the long-distance operator the name of the ship, the person being called, and the number.

Conference—calls can be accomplished with or without Dimension PBX equipment. You can contact the conference operator by dialing 0 and giving the operator the required numbers, names, and the time the call is to be put through. The charge for a conference call is equivalent to that of a person-to-person call for each party involved. This service can very often save the cost of travel for face-to-face meetings.

Telex or TWX—services are provided by Western Union and the Bell Telephone System. Teletypewriters provide the promptness of a telephone call and the documentation of a letter. These electromagnetic waves can be transmitted twenty-four hours a day, seven days a week to both domestic and international networks.

Records of times and charges are often required for accounting purposes. Many companies keep complete and accurate records of all toll calls so that the calls can be charged to the clients. Toll charges can be obtained by dialing the operator prior to placing the call and asking the operator to notify you of the toll charges after the call has been completed.

Teleconferencing

Although the facilities for teleconferencing existed in the early 1960s, it took the high cost of travel to get it off the ground as a viable means of communicating. During the 1970s, expanded and more efficient telephone systems were being introduced and laid the foundation for the expanded teleconferencing techniques we have today.

This was assisted through the use of advances in microelectronic circuitry and computer systems. Thousands of transatlantic and intercontinental meetings, conferences, and conventions are held via this medium.

Teleconferencing is being used in business to enable people from distant locations to "meet" without being physically together. This is expedited by video cameras, microphones, television monitors, and FAX equipment. It has the distinct advantage of enabling people to engage in personal contact without necessitating the time and expense of travel.

- *Audio conferencing* (voice only) between two people in remote locations is aided by the use of extension phones. Additional sites can be included by means of an electronic device called a bridge. Telephones can be purchased with built-in bridges. The bridges help to equalize volume on each telephone and participants can dial into a conference in any location.
- *Video conferencing* (visual transmission) utilizes cameras, monitors, and projection equipment. Still pictures allow transmission of anything the camera is aimed at, while full-motion video requires the same kind of high-capacity transmission lines used by commercial television networks.
- *Computer conferencing* allows participants with computer terminals to call up from computer memory documents, graphics, and so on, and transmit them from one terminal to another. In order for terminals to communicate, a modem (explained earlier in this chapter) and communications software are required.

TELECOMMUNICATIONS

(The prefix *tele* means across, and *communications*—well, you wouldn't have gotten this far without knowing that.)

The ability to economically disseminate large amounts of information door-to-door, coast-to-coast, or around the world is vital to the profit of any organization. Advanced technology has made possible the communication of combined forms of digital, voice, and image transmission. The political climate is such that deregulation will undoubtedly increase the competition in the telecommunications industry. New technologies have included:

- *Special communications services* such as FAX, telex, text-editing machines, and teleconferencing that now provide for the quick, expedient transmission of information.
- *Satellites* (relay stations in space) operate around the clock sending messages that are beamed via microwave and/or radio frequency to satellites on earth.
- *Protocol conversion and switching techniques* known as value-added service, speed the flow of information.
- *Voice/data terminals and intelligent copier/printers* further speed the flow of information.

Telecommunications has enabled industry to tap labor pools that were at one time considered unreachable. Consider the handicapped person who is unable to commute to an office or a person at home because of a young child, and so on. With a computer and some basic communicating equipment, home-based people can join and enhance the work force. This has created what is commonly referred to as a "cottage industry."

Voice Transmission

Extensive research is currently underway into voice transmission or voice recognition. Advantages are: 1) data can be input at a speed much faster than can be accomplished by keyboarding; 2) documents can be dictated directly into the equipment making them easily accessible to non-typists; and 3) hands are freed to compile information, turn pages, and so on.

Voice recognition is used on a very limited scale because technology is not sophisticated enough (yet) to combat certain inherent problems such as: differentiating between homonyms *(there, their, they're)*, compensating for accents, speech patterns, voice differences, and so on.

Teleconferencing

We have all witnessed a form of teleconferencing when we view a newscaster conversing with and viewing a person at another geographic location.

Teleconferencing is being used in business to enable people from distant locations to "meet" without being physically together. This is facilitated by video cameras, microphones, television monitors, and FAX equipment. Teleconferencing has the distinct advantage of enabling people to engage in personal interaction without the time and expense of travel.

ELECTRONIC MAIL (E-Mail)

E-Mail is emerging as the most expedient way to transmit information at high speeds via communications lines. The main advantages are: 1) the high speeds at which large quantities of information can be transmitted from one place to another; 2) the information can be stored as electronic signals until it is accessed by the receiving party; and 3) the need for paper to move from one location to another can be eliminated. Some departmental uses for E-mail are:

- Marketing can send simultaneous messages to the national sales forces.
- Speedy notification of production changes can enhance quality control.
- Order entry departments can coordinate delivery schedules between warehouses, and so on.

Equipment and Services

The following are common forms of equipment:

- *Telex* and *TWX* are also known as teletypewriters. These systems can communicate with each other and can be accessed through many word processors and computer terminals, provided the company subscribes to the system.
- *Mailgram*® messages (a product of Western Union) incorporate the services of the telephone, the telegraph, and the United States Postal System. You merely contact your nearest Western Union office, dictate the message, and

the message is electronically transmitted to the post office nearest the recipient. Mailgram messages are delivered by the post office on the next business day.

- *Communicating word processors* enable the user to transmit data electronically from one workstation to another. Not all word processors can communicate; you must have the proper equipment (a word processor, a modem, a telephone line).
- *Computer-based message systems* will prioritize messages and will display a blinking light to let the recipient know a message is waiting.
- *Facsimile (FAX) equipment* can be used to transmit documents, photographs, drawings, charts, and so on, from one FAX machine to another. Portable FAX units are available and can fit into an attache case.
- *Electronic computer originated mail (E-COM)* is a system designed to expedite the delivery of batch mailings. For example, utility companies can use E-COM to expedite monthly bills. In conjunction with a service called Serving Post Offices (SPO) the bills are printed, automatically inserted into envelopes, and sent through the mail stream.

CHAPTER 36

Records Management Technology

AUTOMATED RECORDS SYSTEMS

An automated system refers to one that uses an electronic computer to process and store information. There is a great emphasis in today's office to minimize the proliferation of paperwork via computerization and the electronic storage of records. We have often heard the "modern office" referred to as the *paperless office*. However unlikely that may really be, there are many types of computer storage files that are helping to move us in the direction of the *paperless office*. Examples include the following:

- *Magnetic tape*—Film-like rolls of tape storing records in binary code. The cost is very low and little storage space is needed, but you cannot read an isolated file without first reading all preceding files.

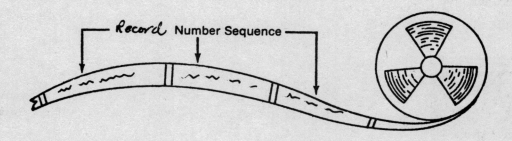

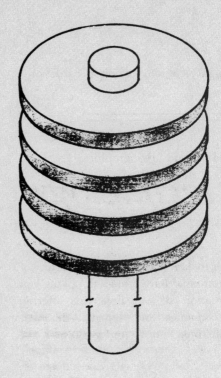

- *Magnetic disk*—Cylinder-like in appearance storing records on circular tracks much like a jukebox arrangement of phonograph records. As opposed to magnetic tape, you can access a file directly without going through all preceding files, but storage costs are higher.

MICROGRAPHICS

A variety of micrographics is also available in response to the wide variety of applications and needs of today's office. Micrographics must be stored in an environment free of dust, moisture, and extreme temperature changes.

Microfilm

Microfilm is similar to movie film, storing a series of pictures.

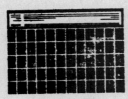

Microfiche

Microfiche (or fiche) is a sheet of film containing microimages. Although the size can vary, four by six inches is the most common.

Ultrafiche

Ultrafiche is similar to microfiche but it can store thousands of images.

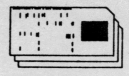

Aperture Cards

Aperture cards are standard eighty-column punched cards prepared on a keypunch machine.

NOTE: Special equipment is needed to prepare micrographics and to read micrographics.

COMPUTER DATA BANKS

A collection of data bases (sources of information) offers the user instant access to a wide variety of information. In order to access a data base (for a fee, of course) you must have a modem, giving you the ability to communicate. You can have a library of information at your fingertips offering information on banking, biographies, computers, dissertations, economics, encyclopedias, finance, government, inventions, law, medicine, newspapers, patents, publishing, sports, transportation, and so on.

CHAPTER 37

Reprographics Technology

The daily barrage of paperwork that infiltrates today's offices is estimated to be in the range of fifteen trillion pieces of paper and upward. This barrage is rapidly growing due to the technological advances in reprographics.

Magazines, books, bills, forms, newsletters, form letters, announcements—these are items you see daily and are all examples of reprographics. This rather complex term merely indicates the methods and types of equipment used to reproduce written materials.

EQUIPMENT

Reprographic equipment includes the following:

- *Carbon paper* (the long-time staple in office supplies) has lost ground in the high-tech office. Although inexpensive, it is messy and errors are difficult to correct. Office technology has paved the way for more sophisticated reprographic methods.
- *Duplicating equipment* requires the preparation of a master. Spirit and stencil duplicators are not very popular in the business environment but are popular in school systems due to their low cost. They are messy to use and produce poor-quality copies.
- *Repetitive printing* became popular with the advent of word processing inasmuch as the printer will produce as many copies as directed. For large volume, however, photocopy equipment or other means may still be more expedient.
- *Photocopying* is the most popular form of reprographics. Photocopiers are available in a wide variety of models, and very few instructions are needed to master their use. There are models that can reproduce color; enlarge and/or reduce; automatically feed, sort and staple, and so on. The per cost copy is higher than with other duplicating processes. Photocopiers are moving closer to becoming part of the fully integrated office information system. Many experts see the next logical step as integrating the photocopier with the printer, thus creating a device producing copy similar to that of a laser printer.
- *Carbon packs* are commercially preassembled copysets that contain sheets of carbon paper and (generally) colored sheets for distribution.

- *Facsimile (FAX)* means an exact reproduction. Facsimiles of pictures, maps, diagrams, and so on, are sent electronically via telephone lines or other electronic means and will reach the recipient within two to six minutes. (Both sender and receiver must have FAX equipment.)
- *Offset duplicating (lithography)* requires the preparation of a master and a special offset machine. Copies are generally clear with each copy looking like an original. Two-sided copies can be produced as well as color copies. The equipment is relatively expensive and trained personnel are required.
- *Phototypesetting* or *photocomposition* is used to produce books, catalogs, directories, newspapers, books, and other printed matter. "Typeset" pages contain more copy than typewritten pages and are economical for certain publications. Superior professional quality is generally produced at very high speeds.

WHICH IS BEST?

The selection of a reprographic process is, of course, dependent on quality, quantity, and budgetary limitations. When dealing without constraints, however, keep in mind the following:

- *Appearance of the desired copy*—If the material is to be distributed in-house, you may opt for a lower quality. If the material is being mailed to those outside your organization, a more superior quality may be required.
- *Necessary quantity*—Your decision may be determined by the number of copies that are needed. Remember, large quantities reduce the per copy cost.
- *Budgetary considerations*—The rule of thumb is: The higher the quality, the higher the cost. If high quality is a priority, you will undoubtedly be able to justify the additional expenses.
- *Time constraints*—If copies are needed instantly, your choices will be somewhat limited.
- *Additional factors*—Special needs (unusual size, special copy design, and so on) may further limit your options.

APPENDIX A

Sample Application

APPLICATION TO TAKE THE certified professional Secretary EXAMINATION

institute for certifying Secretaries ®

TESTING OFFICE • PO BOX 11246 • LEXINGTON KY 40574

Complying with the Applying and Qualifying regulations, application is being submitted as (check):

☐ **SECRETARY**
Experience
Completed

☐ **SECRETARY**
Employed Full-Time
Experience
to be Completed

☐ **BUSINESS EDUCATOR**
Secretarial
Experience
Completed

☐ **STUDENT**
Now Enrolled
Experience
to be Completed

FOR THE EXAMINATION TO BE ADMINISTERED
(Check preference)

☐ **First Thursday and Friday**
of NOVEMBER
Application postmarked by September 15*

☐ **First Friday and Saturday**
of MAY
Application postmarked by March 15*

*Applicants outside continental U.S. should apply by September 1 or March 1.
Late applications will be processed for the next examination.

ID: PSI Member Only
Nonmember OMIT   FSA Member ☐   Social
                                             Security
                                             Number

(1) Last Name   First Name
                                            and Middle Initial

(2) Street

Street

1
USA   CITY   ST   ZIP

2
CANADA CITY   PR   PC

3
FOREIGN COUNTRY   UPU/PUAS

(3) Telephone
(include area code) Bus.   Res.

(4) Which option do you choose with regard to use of your name and address by ICS?   Official business only ☐   Professionally related material ☐   Unrestricted ☐

(5) Have you ever previously filed an application for the CPS Examination?   NO ☐ YES ☐   If yes, Month   Year

(6) Name, if you have previously filed an application under a name other than given above.

Name
     First, Middle, Last

(7) Present Employer
                    Organization Name

Address
        Number and Street

City   ST PR   ZIP PC

FOREIGN COUNTRY   UPU PUAS

Date
Started   Number
                     Years   Number
                                        Months   Hours
                                                        Per Week

COMPLETE REVERSE

CPS⁴ Capstone 7 87-3

Previous Secretarial Employment Only (Begin with most recent; exclude present)

Organization Name	City State	Month/Year Started	Month Year Ended	Number Years Months	Hours Per Week
Organization Name	City State	Month/Year Started	Month Year Ended	Number Years Months	Hours Per Week
Organization Name	City State	Month Year Started	Month Year Ended	Number Years Months	Hours Per Week

Highest Educational Level ☐ Official transcript or copy of degree enclosed, if used to reduce experience requirement

Some High School	High School Graduate ☐	Some College ☐	Associate Degree ☐	Bachelor's Degree ☐	Master's Degree ☐	Doctoral Degree	Other

(10) **STUDENT APPLICANT** If still in college, certification must be completed by staff member of college/university.

This is to certify that _____
Name of Student Applicant

is a candidate for _____
Degree

and is scheduled to complete requirements of the program by _____
Date

CERTIFICATION
Must be signed and school seal affixed.

(11) **BUSINESS EDUCATOR APPLICANT** Certification must be completed by staff member of college/university.

This is to certify that _____
Name of Business Educator Applicant

is an instructor of _____
course(s)

(12) Signature _____ Date _____

Title _____

Educational Institution _____

Address _____

ALL APPLICANTS I certify that I have read and understand the Applying and Qualifying regulations, that the information supplied is correct and in accordance with the instructions, and that I am responsible for submitting information to keep my file current. I further certify that my secretarial experience as submitted conforms to the PSI definition of a secretary as stated in the regulations and that the Institute for Certifying Secretaries reserves the right to obtain verification of information provided in this application. I understand and agree that all examination materials, answers, and scores are the exclusive property of Professional Secretaries International. I also agree to accept the scores as final as reported by the Institute for Certifying Secretaries. I agree that PSI may at its discretion release information contained in this application; my examination results; and my test scores to researchers selected by PSI to study testing issues for the CPS examination program under appropriate conditions of confidentiality established by PSI. I understand that my individual examination results and test scores, aside from such research purposes, will be considered by PSI to be confidential unless authorized by me and will not be released to others except pursuant to legal process.

Signature of Applicant _____ Date _____

Fees must accompany application and are payable in U.S. Funds by check, money order, or credit card charge authorization. Do not send cash or postdated check.

PROCESSING FEE (nonrefundable) — Check appropriate box and enter $ amounts.

☐ Member of Professional Secretaries International ($10) _____
☐ Member of Collegiate Secretaries International ($10) _____
☐ Member of Future Secretaries Association ($10) _____
☐ Nonmember ($35) _____

EXAMINATION FEES

☐ All Six Parts or ☐ Five Parts (specified below). When taking all six parts or five parts at one sitting, total fee is ($90) _____

When registering for six or five parts at $90, those parts must be taken in the same administration. If parts are transferred to another administration, $20 per part applies.

When taking from one to four parts, total fees are $20 per part. Check appropriate boxes, specifying parts to be taken, and enter $ amounts.

☐ Part I Behavioral Science in Business ($20) _____
☐ Part II Business Law ($20) _____
☐ Part III Economics and Management ($20) _____
☐ Part IV Accounting ($20) _____
☐ Part V Office Administration and Communication ($20) _____
☐ Part VI Office Technology ($20) _____

Total amount enclosed $ _____

CHECK APPROPRIATE VERSION

☐ American   ☐ Canadian   ☐ Jamaican

EXAMINATION CENTER CHOICES
(Select 1st, 2nd, and 3rd from page 7)

| | | | | | | | | | | | |

CHARGE CARD INFORMATION

Charge my ☐ VISA ☐ MASTERCARD

Account Number

| | | | | | | | | | | | | | | | |

Cardholder's Name   Expiration Date

Signature (Mandatory on all charge orders)

MAIL APPLICATION WITH FEES AND ENCLOSURES REQUIRED FOR APPLYING AND QUALIFYING TO INSTITUTE FOR CERTIFYING SECRETARIES TESTING OFFICE • PO BOX 11246 • LEXINGTON KY 40574

When You Qualify as a CPS Candidate

You will be notified as quickly as possible if you qualify as a candidate for the Certified Professional Secretary Examination.

Capstone 7/87-4

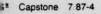
*Reprinted by permission of Professional Secretaries International®

APPENDIX B

Sample Examination Questions

Sample Certified Professional Secretary® Examination Questions

PART I—BEHAVIORAL SCIENCE IN BUSINESS

1. The leader who attempts to help a group organize themselves into a productive unit is using
   A authoritarian leadership
   B bureaucratic leadership
   C free-rein leadership
   D participative leadership

2. You have been working for two months in the purchasing department of a large company. The supervising secretary gives you a new assignment to do, and she tells you that she hopes you will do "this" job accurately. You should
   A ask her what she means by her remark since no one has complained about your work
   B ignore the remark
   C say nothing but make sure everything is completed perfectly
   D suggest that she have someone else do the job if she does not like your work

3. Brooks' position is satisfying, and there is opportunity for advancement; but Brooks has been offered a position with another company with a substantial increase in salary. What type of conflict will be involved in Brooks' decision?
   A Approach-approach
   B Approach-avoidance
   C Avoidance-avoidance
   D Double approach-avoidance

4. The process of copying the behavior of a person highly regarded in a group or organization in order to enhance his or her chances of acceptance is called
   A cognitive dissonance
   B conformity
   C identification
   D reaction formation

5. When Rosen joined a new firm, Rosen wanted to feel a part of the group. This is called
   A   physiological drive
   B   security drive
   C   self-esteem
   D   social drive

6. Pat is seeking certification as a CPS and has accepted most of the professional values and beliefs communicated by the CPS members of her local PSI Chapter. These CPS members provide Pat with what is commonly known as a
   A   control group
   B   formal group
   C   informal group
   D   reference group

7. Roosevelt gives Floyd a high rating as a secretary because Floyd is pleasant, cooperative, a fast typist, willing to learn, and always punctual. Floyd's typing accuracy is poor to fair. The high rating is an example of
   A   harmonizing
   B   the halo effect
   C   the Hawthorne effect
   D   Theory Z

8. The tendency to evaluate an individual as high or low in many traits because the evaluator already knows or believes the individual to be high or low in one trait is known as
   A   "halo" effect
   B   first impression
   C   mind-set
   D   mistaken identity

9. The most common response to the fear stimulus is
   A   aggressive behavior
   B   flight or fight
   C   high blood pressure
   D   internal reactions

10. You are the newly employed secretary to the manager of a small, but rapidly growing, insurance company, with the responsibility of supervising a clerical staff of twelve. You have been given a free hand to make any changes in procedures and routines that you see fit. You have been proceeding cautiously but have observed that you might have some opposition from five clerical workers who are very friendly—they go together and socialize after hours. In order to avoid some of these possible difficulties, you should
    A   do all of the following
    B   determine the personal goals of individual members and work with them
    C   listen carefully to suggestions from members of the informal group
    D   try to find out how members of this informal group feel about certain changes you want to introduce

11. The office manager who stresses the importance of getting along, whose staff production is on a plateau, who closely follows outdated policies, and who discourages new ideas is characterized by
    A   conflict
    B   conformity
    C   creativity
    D   flexibility

12. Translating an idea into a message is called
    A   communicating
    B   decoding
    C   encoding
    D   feedback loop

13. Fear of change can be disturbing as change itself because
    A   all changes are not resisted
    B   all types of change are normal in employment
    C   it produces identical symptoms
    D   people will not secure themselves from disturbance of that balance

14. After Hall explains a new procedure to Taylor, a new employee, she realizes from some nonverbal cues that Taylor does not understand completely what she has said. Hall should say:
    A   "Ask me if you have any questions when you do it."
    B   "I'll repeat what I just said so I'm certain you understand."
    C   "Let's go over it again. This time you describe the procedure to me."
    D   "You don't understand, do you? I guess I didn't explain it very well."

15. A committee formed to organize a career conference is best described as a (an)
    A   ad hoc
    B   project group
    C   standing
    D   task group

PART II—BUSINESS LAW

1. A contract which has full legal effect as to one of the parties, but is not enforceable against the other party against his will is
   A valid
   B void
   C voidable
   D unenforceable

2. Subject to certain exceptions, the contracts entered into by minors are
   A nonvoidable
   B valid
   C void
   D voidable

3. While Ginger was visiting Margie, Margie offered to sell her a figurine for $50.00. Ginger said she would like to have the figurine for $40.00. When Margie refused to take $40.00, Ginger agreed to pay the $50.00. Must Margie part with the figurine for $50.00?
   A No. By making a qualified acceptance, Ginger rejected the original offer.
   B No. An offer lapses if it is not accepted within the specified time or within a reasonable time if no time is stated.
   C Yes. The tardiness of Ginger in making up her mind to pay the $50.00 should not preclude her from purchasing the figurine.
   D Yes. There is a valid offer and acceptance.

4. The Statute of Limitations provides that
   A after a certain number of years have passed a contract in claim is barred
   B the number of parties to a contract is limited in accordance with the Statute
   C the terms of a contract are limited in accordance with the Statute
   D the time a contract may run is limited in accordance with the Statute

5. In order to establish title to real property by adverse possession, the party so claiming must, among other things
   A be acting in good faith
   B have had a continuous possession for the period prescribed by the statute of limitations
   C have originally been on the land with the consent of the owner
   D record the claim

6. If Bill owed Barbara a debt that became due and payable June 1, 1982 (assuming a six-year statute of limitations), the claim would be outlawed June 1, 1988. However, Bill made a payment on account on May 1, 1988, and the claim thus would be outlawed
   A June 1, 1988
   B June 1, 1994
   C May 1, 1988
   D May 1, 1994

7. The Statue of Frauds provides that contracts must be in writing unless performance can be completed within
   A   three months
   B   six months
   C   one year
   D   two years

8. A professional agent such as a lawyer or broker
   A   can be either a general or a special agent
   B   is under his principal's control as to the business acts he performs for himself
   C   may not serve in that same capacity for a number of persons
   D   must have a signed contract of agency

9. When the endorser merely signs the paper, the endorsement is
   A   blank
   B   qualified
   C   restrictive
   D   special

10. Carmichael, as agent of Superior Construction Company, was authorized to purchase various quantities of different types of building materials. He made a contract to purchase such materials from Benderson Concrete Corporation, but did not disclose that he was acting as agent for the construction company. Under these circumstances, which of the following statements is *true?*
    A   The construction company is not liable for the contract made by Carmichael, unless it ratifies the contract.
    B   The concrete corporation may hold the construction company liable when it discovers the identity of the principal.
    C   The concrete corporation may not hold the construction company liable since the contract was not made in its name.
    D   Since Carmichael entered into the contract with the concrete corporation in his own name, he alone is responsible for the contract.

11. All employees of the XYZ Corporation are required to sign an agreement stating that any inventions they design while employed there are the property of the corporation. Bill Smith, an employee, designed a camera smaller than the one marketed by the XYZ Corporation. He did the work on his own time but used the corporation's equipment to build the model. Bill Smith then left the XYZ Corporation to market this camera. The XYZ Corporation brought suit against Bill Smith. Under these circumstances
    A   Bill Smith should be awarded judgment. He designed the camera on his own time and was not compensated for his efforts by the corporation.
    B   Bill Smith should be awarded judgment. Since he is no longer an employee of the XYZ Corporation, he can no longer be held to the agreement.
    C   the XYZ Corporation should be awarded judgment. The employment agreement is valid.
    D   the XYZ Corporation should be awarded judgment. Their equipment was used in designing the model so it has a claim on the invention.

12. Blair was negotiating to purchase an oil painting owned by Whitney's estate. Blair insured the painting against fire, windstorm, and theft. Could Blair recover the loss if any of these perils damaged the painting?
A Yes—Blair paid for the insurance and could recover the loss.
B Yes—Blair was negotiating to purchase the painting and therefore had proved intent to purchase.
C No—Blair did not have an insurable interest in the painting.
D No—once the painting was destroyed or stolen, Blair lost any insurable interest.

13. A buyer who, after accepting goods, discovers defects that could not have been found earlier by a reasonable inspection
A may make repairs and bill the seller
B may revoke acceptance
C must keep the goods that have been already accepted
D must return the goods immediately

14. George bought an expensive watch from Joe who claimed that it was an inheritance and that his grandfather's initials were engraved on the back. A short time later, Phillip saw the watch and claimed that Joe had stolen it from him. Phillip proved ownership of the watch and forced George to return the watch because
A Joe did not have title to the watch
B Joe's actions were not covered by the Uniform Sales Act
C Joe could be prosecuted under the Statute of Frauds
D George can sue for recovery of the purchase price plus damages

15. To enable a creditor to receive any distribution from the assets of a bankrupt debtor's estate, he or she must
A appear in court to prove the claim
B file in court a suit against the debtor
C file with the court a sworn statement of the claim and the basis thereof
D write a demand letter to the debtor

PART III—ECONOMICS AND MANAGEMENT

1. The setting of objectives, utilization of these objectives in the management process, and measurement process, and measurement of individual and organizational performance against these objectives is known as
    A   the Law of Diminishing Returns
    B   management by exception
    C   management by objectives
    D   the management process cycle

2. Which of the following schools of management relates specifically to an analysis of the experience of successful managers?
    A   Decision theory
    B   Empirical
    C   Mathematical
    D   Social systems

3. The first step in achieving effective delegation is to
    A   assign duties necessary to complete the task
    B   determine objectives
    C   establish necessary controls
    D   select best candidate based on job requirements

4. One of the major drawbacks of the division of work principle is that
    A   it leads to boredom and cuts down on productivity
    B   no consideration is given to interpersonal relations
    C   no consideration is given to the working environment
    D   the focus is upon a single segment of a company

5. One of the primary advantages of individual proprietorship is the
    A   availability of unlimited resources
    B   control over issuance of stock
    C   decision-making flexibility afforded the owner
    D   limited liability of the owner for any debts incurred

6. Management is defined as
    A   money, materials and human resources
    B   setting goals and objectives for the benefit of an organization
    C   setting goals and measuring results
    D   the coordination of all resources

7. Discrimination against women in employment is prohibited by the
    A   Civil Rights Act of 1964
    B   Equal Rights Amendments
    C   Fair Labor Standards Act of 1938
    D   Nineteenth Amendment

8. A serious problem facing business today, in attempting to comply with pollution controls, involves
   A all of the following
   B complying with the requirements of the Occupational Safety and Health Administration
   C maintaining good standing with the Organization of Petroleum Exporting Countries
   D providing convenience products while maintaining environmental quality

9. Which of the following is *not* considered a progressive tax?
   A Corporate income
   B Excise
   C Inheritance
   D Personal income

10. When prices go down consumers will buy more. How much more is determined by the
    A elasticity of demand
    B income elasticity
    C price elasticity
    D unitary elasticity

11. The rate of interest paid to the Federal Reserve Banks by member banks is called the
    A discount rate
    B federal reserve rate
    C prime loan rates
    D reserve rate

12. If national income falls, unchanged tax rates on personal and corporation income will
    A not change tax receipts to the government
    B result in higher tax receipts for the government
    C results in lower tax receipts for the government
    D tend to be flexible

13. Who or what has ultimate control over what will be done with the nation's resources?
    A Consumers
    B Special interest groups
    C The economy
    D The rise and fall of the GNP

14. When producers decide how much they will produce without giving thought to the effect each one may have on price, what is taking place?
    A An increase in supply
    B Equilibrium
    C Monopolistic competition
    D Pure competition

15. Rising wages of American workers are made possible by
    A aggregate demand
    B the growing supply of labor
    C a higher standard of living
    D increased productivity

PART IV—ACCOUNTING

1. The check register is a simplified version of the
   A   Capital account
   B   Cash Payments journal
   C   General journal
   D   Petty Cash journal

2. To minimize the possibility of inefficiency, errors, and fraud, assignments of a sequence of related operations should be the responsibility of
   A   one department within the company
   B   one individual
   C   the owner of the company
   D   two or more persons

3. Tight Corporation has established the policy that advantage be taken of all available cash discounts on purchases, even though it may be necessary to borrow the money with which to make the payment. An invoice for $1,000.00 with terms of 2 10 n 30, is to be paid within the discount period with funds borrowed for the remaining 20 days of the credit period at an annual interest rate of 6 percent. The net savings to the purchaser is
   A $3.27
   B $10.20
   C $16.73
   D $20.00

4. When a voucher system is used, the voucher register replaces which one of the following journals?
   A   Cash receipts
   B   General
   C   Purchases
   D   Sales

Questions 5 and 6 are based on the following information:
January 1: Inventory 200 units at $9; March 10: Purchase 300 units at $10; September 21: Purchase 400 units at $11; November 18. Purchase 100 units at $12. The physical count on December 31 indicates that 300 units of the commodity are on hand.

5. Based on the last in—first out method of inventory, what is the value of the December 31 inventory?
   A $2,800
   B $3,120
   C $3,400
   D $3,500

6. Based on the weighted-average method of inventory, what is the value of the December 31 inventory?
   A $2,800
   B $3,120
   C $3,400
   D $3,500

7. A trial balance indicates
   A complete proof of the accuracy of the ledger
   B net profit or loss
   C postings to the ledger are accurate
   D the debits and credits are equal

8. The journal entry to record the issuance of a check to replenish the imprest petty cash fund is a debit to
   A Cash and a credit to Petty Cash
   B Petty Cash and credit to Cash
   C the appropriate expense account and a credit to Cash
   D the appropriate expense account and a credit to Petty Cash

9. After closing entries are posted, the temporary accounts are ruled to indicate
   A that all temporary accounts have been totaled
   B that the books are in balance
   C that the totals have been verified
   D the end of one period and the beginning of another

10. A trade discount is a (an)
    A allowance for trade-in
    B credit for defective material
    C deduction from list or catalog prices
    D discount for prompt payment

11. The ledger balance in the Petty Cash account changes when
    A a balance sheet is made
    B a check is written to increase the petty cash fund
    C a check is written to reimburse for items paid from the petty cash fund
    D the books are closed

12. Which of the following entries should be made to record the expiration of prepaid insurance at the end of the fiscal year?
    A Debit Cash, credit Prepaid Insurance
    B Debit Insurance Expense, credit Prepaid Insurance
    C Debit Prepaid Insurance, credit Cash
    D Debit Prepaid Insurance, credit Insurance Expense

13. If a company gives a note payable for $4,000, which one of the following describes the effect of the transaction upon the accounting period?
   A   Assets increase by $4,000; owner's equity decreases by $4,000.
   B   Both assets and liabilities increase by $4,000
   C   Both assets and owner's equity increase by $4,000.
   D   There would be no change in the equation.

14. The entry to record the cash payment for the store building rental would be
   A   debit Cash, credit Prepaid Rent
   B   debit Prepaid Rent; credit Accounts Payable
   C   debit Prepaid Rent; credit Cash
   D   debit Rent Expense, credit Prepaid Rent

15. If union dues have been deducted from employees' earnings, the company must consider this deduction until the amounts are paid to the union as a (an)
   A   current asset
   B   current liability
   C   expense
   D   fixed liability

PART V—OFFICE ADMINISTRATION AND COMMUNICATION

1. In organizing a report there must be
   A   a common denominator
   B   a conclusion
   C   a recommendation
   D   subject coverage

2. The basic requirement of a form sales letter would be to
   A   ensure a positive response
   B   gain attention
   C   introduce the product
   D   outline sales strategy

3. Coherence in a letter is *best* achieved by
   A   arranging data in a logical order
   B   repetitious use of the same words
   C   the use of transitional words to tie in with the following sentence
   D   using action words

4. Deciding the caption by which an item is to be filed is called
   A   coding
   B   indexing
   C   screening
   D   sorting

5. A convenient memory aid where pending work is noted by due date is called a
   A   daily work plan
   B   schedule
   C   tickler file
   D   work flow chart

6. In reprographics, the term "duplexing" is used when referring to
   A   copying on both sides of a sheet of paper
   B   dual finishing
   C   dual imaging
   D   two drums on a copier

7. Which one of the following answers correctly completes this statement: A passport
   A   has no expiration date
   B   includes a photograph
   C   is issued at no charge
   D   may include more than one member of a family

8. A broken bar chart is used to show that
   A   components are from two different time periods
   B   different factors contribute to a total figure
   C   quantities are so large some parts have been left out
   D   the zero is placed at midpoint on the scale instead of on the vertical axis

9. The "you" attitude in letter writing is *best* expressed by which one of the following statements?
    A Avoid too frequent use of the pronoun "I"
    B Repeat the reader's name frequently in the letter
    C Use the pronoun "you" frequently
    D Write from the reader's point of view

10. When typing a report for the next board meeting, Sharon had to use various levels of headings (or captions). Which one of the following statements is *correct?*
    A Subheadings may be flush with left margin or indented, depending on degree.
    B Subheadings will be all capital letters, without underlining.
    C Superior headings may be flush with left margin or indented five spaces.
    D Superior headings will be flush with left margin and underlined.

11. Which one of the following statements would be the *best* indication of the respect a writer has for the reader?
    A Although you did not make your payment on time, we will still credit your account.
    B Since we are the largest dealer in this product, we can afford to give you a good deal.
    C Since we value your opinion, please complete the enclosed reply card concerning your recent order.
    D The only way to ensure prompt delivery is to mail your order early.

12. An ultimate goal of business communications is to create
    A a good corporate image
    B diversification
    C good will
    D less paperwork

13. When organizing a report, you should build the outline around
    A new items
    B predetermined problem factors
    C the objective of the report
    D the table of contents

14. Which one of the following sentences illustrates *correct* capitalization?
    A A familiar New Orleans landmark is the French Quarter area.
    B A 1984 Porsche emerged from the Holland Tunnel.
    C Correct Capitalization helps to clarify ideas and also emphasize words.
    D The White House is located in Washington in the District Of Columbia.

15. Air fares and services vary substantially. Which one of the following statements regarding air fares and services is *correct?*
    A Coach fares are the least expensive of all air fares.
    B Excursion fares are higher because of special arrangements available.
    C First class service provides more "frills."
    D Night flights provide more specialized services because of fewer travelers.

PART VI—OFFICE TECHNOLOGY

1. The office management concept of integrating key information functions into one computer-based system is called a (an)
   A automated office
   B satellite office
   C systems office
   D technology office

2. Copies that appear to have been professionally printed most likely come from
   A copysets
   B phototypesetting
   C spirit duplicating
   D xerography

3. If your firm does not have a computerized mailing list system to handle a large monthly mail-out, it likely uses a (an)
   A addresser-printer
   B copier-duplicator
   C electronic typewriter
   D typing pool

4. A centralized purchasing process that is established for the procurement of office furniture equipment
   A allows flexibility to adjust to individual needs
   B may have functions assigned to each option
   C provides improved planning and control
   D requires agreements to match individual department budgets

5. Which one of the following is *not* a magnetic medium?
   A Card
   B Disk
   C Record
   D Tape

6. The most efficient method of producing catalogs, brochures, and reports, wherein varied type styles, sizes, and colors are desired, is the
   A azograph process
   B diazo process
   C duplicator
   D offset composer

7. The majority of word processing feasibility studies focus on the work performed by
   A managers and principals
   B managers and secretaries
   C principals
   D secretaries

8. A traditional letter-sized cabinet in a central filing system requires
   A   3 to 5 square feet
   B   5 to 7 square feet
   C   8 to 10 square feet
   D   10 to 12 square feet

9. The Jones Company has decided to restructure its office system to use automated preparation of typewritten and printed documents prepared by specialized office personnel. This function is known as
   A   administrative support
   B   computation support system
   C   records management
   D   word processing

10. Jordan has a microcomputer at home. To communicate with the computer system at the office, which of the following equipment will be required at his residence?
    A   Modem
    B   Linking cable
    C   Electronic typewriter
    D   Cathode ray tube

11. Which one of the following devices processes data transferred to it by an input device and, in turn, transfers the results to an output device?
    A   Central processing unit
    B   Control unit
    C   Batch processor
    D   Report program operator

12. The reprographic process which combines capabilities of a computer and phototypesetter is the
    A   electronic copier
    B   fiber optic copier
    C   intelligent copier
    D   photocopier

13. To integrate word processing with other office functions, a linkage can be used to facilitate communications within the office or company. This electronic linking is
    A   central processing unit
    B   local area network
    C   shared resource system
    D   word processing module

14. The process of relaying messages from one place to another without paper is called
    A   telecommunications
    B   distribution
    C   laser printing
    D   OCR

15. The primary objective of both data and word processing is
    A   to complete the work in less time
    B   to produce more information
    C   create fewer jobs
    D   to have one piece of equipment to perform both functions

CPS Sample Examination
ANSWER KEY

PART I	PART II	PART III	PART IV	PART V	PART VI
1. D	1. C	1. C	1. B	1. A	1. A
2. A	2. D	2. B	2. D	2. B	2. B
3. A	3. A	3. B	3. C	3. A	3. A
4. C	4. A	4. A	4. C	4. B	4. C
5. D	5. B	5. C	5. A	5. C	5. C
6. D	6. D	6. D	6. B	6. A	6. D
7. B	7. C	7. A	7. D	7. B	7. D
8. A	8. A	8. D	8. C	8. C	8. B
9. B	9. A	9. B	9. D	9. D	9. D
10. A	10. B	10. A	10. C	10. A	10. A
11. B	11. C	11. A	11. B	11. C	11. A
12. C	12. C	12. C	12. B	12. C	12. C
13. C	13. B	13. A	13. B	13. C	13. B
14. C	14. A	14. D	14. C	14. B	14. A
15. A	15. C	15. D	15. B	15. C	15. B

APPENDIX C

Bibliography

*CPS Examination Bibliography**

Titles that are preceded by an asterisk are suggested reading for students preparing for the Canadian test.

PART I—BEHAVIORAL SCIENCE IN BUSINESS

Davis, Keith. *Human Behavior at Work: Organizing Behavior.* New York: McGraw-Hill Book Co., 1981.

Hersey, Blancard. *Management of Organizational Behavior: Utilizing Human Resources.* Fourth Edition. Englewood Cliffs: Prentice-Hall, 1982.

Ivancevich, Donnelly, and Gibson. *Managing for Performance.* Plano: Business Publications, Inc., 1983.

Strauss and Sayles. *Personnel: The Human Problems of Management.* Fourth Edition. Englewood Cliffs: Prentice-Hall, Inc., 1980.

PART II—BUSINESS LAW

Anderson, Ronald A. *Business Law, UCC Comprehensive Volume.* Eleventh Edition. Cincinnati: South-Western Publishing Co., 1980.

Ashcroft, John D., and Ashcroft, Janet E. *College Law for Business.* Ninth Edition. Cincinnati: South-Western Publishing Co., 1981.

Clarkson, Kenneth, *et al. West's Business Law.* St. Paul: West Publishing Co., 1980.

Goodwin, John. *Business Law: Principles, Documents & Cases.* Third Edition. Homewood: Richard D. Irwin, Inc., 1980.

Howell, Rate A., *et al. Study Guides to Accompany Business Law: Tests & Cases.* Second Edition. Hinsdale: Dryden Press (division of Holt, Rinehart and Winston, Inc.), 1981.

*Jennings and Zuber. *Canadian Law.* Fourth Edition. Toronto: McGraw-Hill Ryerson Ltd., 1985.

Lusk, Harold F., *et al. Business Law and the Regulatory Environment: Concepts & Cases.* Fifth UCC Edition. Homewood: Richard D. Irwin, Inc., 1982.

*Reprinted by permission of Professional Secretaries International®

Special References

Equal Employment Opportunity Commission (EEOC). *Affirmative Action Guidelines*. U.S. Government Printing Office.

U.S. Government Manual, 1980–81. Office of the Federal Register. National Archives and Records Service. General Services Administration.

Your Social Security. U.S. Government Manual. Current Edition. U.S. Government Printing Office.

PART III—ECONOMICS AND MANAGEMENT

Economics

Amacher, Ryan C., *et al. Principles of Microeconomics, Principles of Macroeconomics*. Cincinnati: South-Western Publishing Co., 1980.

Bach, George. *Economics: An Introduction to Analysis and Policy*. Tenth Edition. Englewood Cliffs: Prentice-Hall, Inc., 1980.

Bowden, Elbert V. *Principles of Economics: Theory, Problems and Policies*. Third Edition. Cincinnati: South-Western Publishing Co., 1980.

Hailstones, Thomas J. *Basic Economics*. Sixth Edition. Cincinnati: South-Western Publishing Co., 1980.

McConnell, Campbell R. *Economics*. Eighth Edition. New York: McGraw-Hill Book Co., 1981.

Peterson, Willis L. *Principles of Economics: Macro*. Fifth Edition. Homewood: Richard D. Irwin, Inc., 1983.

Peterson, Willis L. *Principles of Economics: Micro*. Fifth Edition. Homewood: Richard D. Irwin, Inc., 1983.

Samuelson, Paul A. *Economics*. Eleventh Edition. New York: McGraw-Hill Book Co., 1980.

Management

Beach, Dale S. *Personnel, The Management of People at Work*. New York: Macmillan Publishing Co., Inc., 1980.

Burke, Ronald S. *Administrative Skills for the Manager*. Homewood: Dow Jones-Irwin, 1983.

Cutlip, Scott M. and Center, Allen H. *Effective Public Relations*. Fifth Edition. Englewood Cliffs: Prentice-Hall, Inc., 1982.

Daly, James M. *Interpersonal Skills for the Manager*. Homewood: Dow Jones-Irwin, 1983.

Fulmer, Robert M. *The New Management*. New York: Macmillan Publishing Co., Inc., 1980.

Glos, Raymond E., *et al. Business: Its Nature and Environment*. Ninth Edition. Cincinnati: South-Western Publishing Co., 1980.

Heneman, Herbert C., *et al. Personnel/Human Resource Management*. Revised Edition. Homewood: Richard D. Irwin, Inc., 1983.

Koontz, Harold and Fulmer, Robert M. *A Practical Introduction to Business*. Third Edition. Homewood: Richard D. Irwin, Inc., 1981.

Koontz, Harold, Cyril O'Donnell and Heinz Weihrich. *Essentials of Management*. Third Edition. New York: McGraw-Hill Book Co., 1982.

Kotler, Philip. *Marketing Management, Analysis, Planning and Control.* Fourth Edition. Englewood Cliffs: Prentice-Hall, Inc., 1980.

Perlick, Walter. *Introduction to Business.* Third Edition. Homewood: Learning Systems Co., 1981.

Robbins, Stephen P. *The Administrative Process.* Second Edition. Englewood Cliffs: Prentice-Hall, Inc., 1980.

Rue, Leslie W. and Byars, Lloyd L. *Management: Theory and Application.* Third Edition. Homewood: Richard D. Irwin, Inc., 1983.

Ryan, William. *Principles of Marketing.* Third Edition. Homewood: Learning Systems Co., 1980.

Stoner, James. *Management.* Second Edition. Englewood Cliffs: Prentice-Hall, Inc., 1982.

Terry, George R., *et al. Principles of Management.* Eighth Edition. Homewood: Richard D. Irwin, Inc., 1982.

Terry, George R. and Rue, Leslie W. *Principles of Management.* Fourth Edition. Homewood: Dow Jones-Irwin, 1982.

Werther, Jr., William B. and Davis, Keith. *Personnel Management and Human Resources.* New York: McGraw-Hill Book Co., 1981.

PART IV—ACCOUNTING

Carlson, Arthur E., *et al. Secretarial Accounting.* Eleventh Edition, Parts 1 and 2. Cincinnati: South-Western Publishing Co., 1982.

Carlson, Heintz, and Carson. *College Accounting.* Eleventh Edition. Cincinnati: South-Western Publishing Co., 1982.

Edwards, James D. and Bergold, Lynn. *Career Accounting.* Homewood: Richard D. Irwin, Inc., 1981.

Edwards, James D., *et al. Financial Accounting, A Programmed Text.* Fourth Edition. Homewood: Richard D. Irwin, Inc., 1978.

Fess and Warren. *Accounting Principles.* Fourteenth Edition. Cincinnati: South-Western Publishing Co., 1984.

Helmkamp, Imdieke, and Smith. *Principles of Accounting.* New York: John Wiley & Sons, Inc., 1983.

Internal Revenue Service. *1040 Federal Income Tax Forms and Instructions.* U.S. Government Printing Office.

Meigs, Walter B. and Meigs, Robert F. *Accounting: The Basis for Business Decisions.* Sixth Edition. New York: McGraw-Hill Book Co., 1984.

Needles, Anderson, and Caldwell. *Principles of Accounting.* Second Edition. Boston: Houghton Mifflin Company, 1984.

Pyle, William W., *et al. Fundamental Accounting Principles.* Tenth Edition. Homewood: Richard D. Irwin, Inc., 1984.

Reynolds, Sanders, and Hillman. *Principles of Accounting.* Third Edition. New York: CBS College Publishing Company, 1984.

Roueche, Nelda W. *Business Mathematics: A Collegiate Approach.* Fourth Edition. Englewood Cliffs: Prentice-Hall, Inc., 1983.

Skousen, Langenderfer, and Albrecht. *Principles of Accounting.* Second Edition. New York: Worth Publishers, Inc., 1983.

Tuttle, Michael D. and Walls, Elizabeth. *Accounting: A Basic Approach* Dubuque: William C. Brown Co., Publishers, 1981.

Walgenback, Paul H., *et al. Principles of Accounting*. Third Edition. New York: Harcourt Brace Jovanovich, 1984.

Williams, Stanga, and Holder. *Intermediate Accounting*. New York: Harcourt Brace Jovanovich, 1984.

PART V—OFFICE ADMINISTRATION AND COMMUNICATION

Office Administration and Office Management (Emphasis on Technological Application)

Branchaw, Bernadine, Joel Bowman, Alice Nuttall, and Michael Payne. *Office Procedures for the Professional Secretary*. Chicago: Science Research Associates, Inc., 1984.

Hanna, J. Marshall, Estelle L. Popham, and Rita S. Tilton. *Secretarial Procedures and Administration*. Eighth Edition. Cincinnati: South-Western Publishing Co., 1983.

Jennings, Lucy Mae. *Secretarial and Administrative Procedures*. Englewood Cliffs: Prentice-Hall, Inc., 1983.

Keeling, B. Lewis and Norman F. Kallaus. *Administrative Office Management*. Eighth Edition. Cincinnati: South-Western Publishing Co., 1983.

Littlefield, C. L., Frank M. Rachel, Donald L. Caruth, and Robert E. Holmes. *Management of Office Operations*. Englewood Cliffs: Prentice-Hall, Inc., 1978.

Smith, Harold T. and William H. Baker. *The Administrative Manager*. Chicago: Science Research Associates, Inc., 1978.

Stallard, John J. and George R. Terry. *Office Systems Management*. Ninth Edition. Homewood: Richard D. Irwin, Inc., 1984.

Records Management (Emphasis on Technological Application)

Johnson, Mina M. and Norman F. Kallaus. *Records Management*. Third Edition. Cincinnati: South-Western Publishing Co., 1982.

Maedke, Wilmer, Mary Robek, and Gerald Brown. *Information and Records Management*. Second Edition. Encino: Glencoe Publishing Co., 1981.

Place, Irene and David Hyslop. *Records Management: Controlling Business Information*. Reston: Reston Publishing Co., 1982.

Composing Communications

Hatch, Richard. *Business Communication: Theory and Technique*. Chicago: Science Research Associates Inc., 1983.

Himstreet, William C. and Wayne M. Baty. *Business Communication*. Revised Edition. Homewood: Richard D. Irwin, Inc., 1982.

Krevolin, Nathan. *Communication Systems and Procedures for the Modern Office*. Englewood Cliffs: Prentice-Hall, Inc., 1983.

Lesikar, Raymond V. *Basic Business Communication.* Revised Edition. Homewood: Richard D. Irwin, Inc., 1985.

Sorrels, Bobbye D. *Business Communication Fundamentals.* Columbus: Charles E. Merrill Publishing Company, 1984.

Treece, Malra. *Communication for Business and the Professions.* Second Edition. Boston: Allyn and Bacon, Inc., 1983.

Wilkinson, C. W. *et al. Communicating Through Letters and Reports.* Eighth Edition. Homewood: Richard D. Irwin, Inc., 1983.

Editing Communications

Clark, James L. and Lyn R. Clark. *How 3—A Handbook for Office Workers.* Third Edition. Boston: Kent Publishing Co., 1983.

House, Clifford R. and Kathie Sigler. *Reference Manual for Office Personnel.* Sixth Edition. Cincinnati: South-Western Publishing Co., 1981.

Format

Lloyd, Alan, *et al. Gregg Typing for Colleges, Complete Course.* New York: McGraw-Hill Book Co., 1979.

Mitchell, William M., James E. LaBarre, and K. A. Mach. *College Typewriting: A Mastery Approach Comprehensive.* Chicago: Science Research Associates, 1982.

PART VI—OFFICE TECHNOLOGY

General Office Automation and Office Management (including Ergonomics, Reprographics, and Communications Technology)

Fulton, Patsy J. and Joanna D. Hanks. *Procedures for the Professional Secretary.* Cincinnati: South-Western Publishing Co., 1985.

Kneeling, B. Lewis and Norman F. Kallaus. *Administrative Office Management.* Eighth Edition, Abridged. Cincinnati: South-Western Publishing Co., 1983.

Popham, Estelle L., Rita S. Tilton, and J. Marshall Hanna. *Secretarial Procedures and Administration.* Eighth Edition. Cincinnati: South-Western Publishing Co., 1983.

Tedesco, Eleanor Hollis and Mitchell, Robert B. *Administrative Office Management.* The Electronic Office First Edition. New York: John Wiley & Sons, Inc., 1984.

Wagoner, Kathleen P. and Mary Ruprecht. *Office Automation: A Management Approach.* New York: John Wiley & Sons, Inc., 1984.

Word Processing and The Automated Office

Bergerud, Marly and Jean Gonzalez. *Word/Information Processing Concepts of Office Automation.* Second Edition. New York: John Wiley & Sons, Inc., 1984.

Bergerud, Marly and Jean Gonzalez. *Word Processing: Concepts and Careers, a Step Toward Office Automation*. New York: John Wiley & Sons, Inc., 1984.

Casady, Mona. *Word/Information Processing Concepts*. Cincinnati: South-Western Publishing Co., 1984.

Cecil, Paula B. *Office Automation Concepts and Applications*. Menlo Park: The Benjamin Cummings Publishing Co., 1984.

Dolecheck, Carolyn C. and Danny M. Murphy. *Applied Word Processing: An Introduction to Text Editing with Keyboard Applications*. Cincinnati: South-Western Publishing Co., 1983.

Kleinschrod, Walter, Leonard Kruk, and Hilda Turner. *Word/Information Processing: Administration and Office Automation*. Indianapolis: The Bobbs-Merrill Co., 1983.

Data Processing and Communication Technology

Adams, David R., Wagner, Gerald E., and Terence J. Boyer. *Computer Information Systems: An Introduction*. Cincinnati: South-Western Publishing Co., 1983.

Clark, James F. and Lambrecht, Judith J. *Information Processing*. Cincinnati: South-Western Publishing Co., 1985.

Rademacher, Robert and Harry Gibson. *An Introduction to Computers and Information Systems*. Cincinnati: South-Western Publishing Co., 1983.

Robichaud, Beryl, Eugene Muscat, and Alix-Marie Hall. *Introduction to Data Processing*. Third Edition. New York: McGraw-Hill Book Co., 1983.

Shelly, Gary B. and Thomas J. Cashman. *Introduction to Computers and Data Processing*. Fullerton: Anaheim Publishing Co., 1984.

Verzello, Robert J. and John Reutter, III. *Data Processing Systems and Concepts*. New York: McGraw-Hill Book Co., 1982.

Records Management

Johnson, Mina M. and Norman F. Kallaus. *Records Management*. Third Edition. Cincinnati: South-Western Publishing Co., 1982.

Meadke, Wilmer, Mary Robek, and Gerald Brown. *Information and Records Management*. Second Edition. Encino: Glencoe Publishing Co., 1981.

Place, Irene and David Hyslop. *Records Management: Controlling Business Information*. Reston: Reston Publishing Co., 1982.

Ricks, Dr. Betty R. and Dr. Kay F. Gow. *Information Resource Management*. Cincinnati: South-Western Publishing Co., 1984.